T0316419

Climate Change and Global Equity

ANTHEM ENVIRONMENT AND SUSTAINABILITY

General Editor
Lawrence Susskind – Massachusetts Institute of Technology (MIT), USA

Our new **Anthem Environment and Sustainability** book publishing programme seeks to push the frontiers of scholarship while simultaneously offering prescriptive and programmatic advice to policymakers and practitioners around the world. In this programme, we publish research monographs, professional and major reference works, upper-level textbooks and general interest titles.

Another related project to the Anthem Environment and Sustainability programme is Anthem EnviroExperts Review. Through this online micro-reviews site, Anthem Press seeks to build a community of practice involving scientists, policy analysts and activists that is committed to creating a clearer and deeper understanding of how ecological systems – at every level – operate, and how they have been damaged by unsustainable development. On this site we publish short reviews of important books or reports in the environmental field, broadly defined.

ANTHEM FRONTIERS OF GLOBAL POLITICAL ECONOMY

Series Editors
Kevin Gallagher – Boston University, USA
Jayati Ghosh – Jawaharlal Nehru University, India

Editorial Board
Stephanie Blankenburg – School of Oriental and African Studies (SOAS), UK
Ha-Joon Chang – University of Cambridge, UK
Wan-Wen Chu – RCHSS, Academia Sinica, Taiwan
Léonce Ndikumana – University of Massachusetts-Amherst, USA
Alica Puyana Mutis – Facultad Latinoamericana de Ciencias Sociales
(FLASCO-México), Mexico
Matías Vernengo – Banco Central de la República Argentina, Argentina
Robert Wade – London School of Economics and Political Science (LSE), UK
Yu Yongding – Chinese Academy of Social Sciences (CASS), China

The **Anthem Frontiers of Global Political Economy** series seeks to trigger and attract new thinking in global political economy, with particular reference to the prospects of emerging markets and developing countries. Written by renowned scholars from different parts of the world, books in this series provide historical, analytical and empirical perspectives on national economic strategies and processes, the implications of global and regional economic integration, the changing nature of the development project, and the diverse global-to-local forces that drive change. Scholars featured in the series extend earlier economic insights to provide fresh interpretations that allow new understandings of contemporary economic processes.

Climate Change and
Global Equity

Frank Ackerman and Elizabeth A. Stanton

ANTHEM PRESS
LONDON · NEW YORK · DELHI

Anthem Press
An imprint of Wimbledon Publishing Company
www.anthempress.com

This edition first published in UK and USA 2014
by ANTHEM PRESS
75–76 Blackfriars Road, London SE1 8HA, UK
or PO Box 9779, London SW19 7ZG, UK
and
244 Madison Ave #116, New York, NY 10016, USA

British Library Cataloguing-in-Publication Data
A catalogue record for this book is available from the British Library.

Library of Congress Cataloging-in-Publication Data
Ackerman, Frank, author.
Climate change and global equity / Frank Ackerman and
Elizabeth A. Stanton.
pages cm. – (Anthem environment and sustainability)
(Anthem frontiers of global political economy)
Includes bibliographical references.
ISBN 978-1-78308-020-5 (hardcover : alk. paper) – ISBN 1-78308-020-5
(hardcover : alk. paper)
1. Climatic changes–Economic aspects. 2. Climatic changes–Political aspects.
I. Stanton, Elizabeth A., author. II. Title.
QC903.A144 2014
363.738'74–dc23
2014011576

ISBN-13: 978 1 78308 020 5 (Hbk)
ISBN-10: 1 78308 020 5 (Hbk)

Cover photo: "Houses and Factories"
c. 1941, courtesy of the US Library of Congress, Farm Security
Administration/Office of War Information collection

This title is also available as an ebook.

TABLE OF CONTENTS

INTRODUCTION

Technical solutions to the threat of climate change are not difficult to imagine. Existing technologies could eliminate most or all greenhouse gas emissions from electricity generation, transportation, and other carbon-intensive activities. Progress in this direction would undoubtedly spur the development of even better and cheaper techniques for reducing emissions in the future.

Yet ambitious measures to reduce carbon emissions are all too rare in reality. The obstacles to climate protection are primarily economic and political, rather than technological. Powerful interests strongly prefer the status quo to massive investment in emission reductions. Debates over equitable sharing of the costs of climate protection, both internationally and intranationally, have stymied many efforts to move forward on this urgent issue.

This book presents our research related to these themes, addressing the joint problems of climate and global equity. The articles included here, almost all from peer-reviewed journals, argue that the impacts of inaction on climate change will be far worse than the costs of ambitious climate policies, and that progress toward global equity is indispensable to the attempt to stabilize the climate.

The book is divided into four sections. The first presents our general economic perspectives on climate and equity. "Climate Economics in Four Easy Pieces" is a short summary of a framework for analysis, incorporating four fundamental principles that should shape the field: the importance of future generations, the central role of the risks of catastrophic outcomes, the impossibility of monetization of all important impacts (and hence the impossibility of traditional cost–benefit analysis), and the reasons why damage costs are worse than protection costs. "Carbon Markets Are Not Enough" argues that, especially for developing countries, carbon prices must be combined with extensive nonprice policies in order to create equitable, development-oriented climate policies. "Modeling Pessimism" suggests that many climate scenarios assume slow growth for low-income countries, a cynical assumption which has the effect of reducing projected global emissions. It outlines the policy adjustments that would be needed for emission reduction in an equitable world, where many developing countries achieve high rates of growth. "The Tragedy of Maldistribution" proposes a new approach to the question of equity, treating it as a public good that is an important component of sustainability.

In our recent review of the state of climate economics (Ackerman and Stanton 2012a), we identified the measurement of climate damages as one of the greatest weaknesses in current economic analyses of climate change. The second section of this book includes three articles addressing questions regarding climate damages. "Climate Impacts on Agriculture" examines an area where recent research challenges more complacent earlier conclusions and implies that there will be greater and more abrupt decreases in crop yields as the world warms and precipitation patterns change. "Did the Stern Review Underestimate US and Global Climate Damages?" coauthored by Chris Hope, the economic modeler for the Stern Review, reexamines the model runs and assumptions used by Nicholas Stern in his path-breaking analysis, finding good reasons to believe that climate damages will be even worse than implied by the Stern Review. "Can Climate Change Save Lives?" is a short critique of a published analysis by other economists, in which they suggest that the first stages of global warming could save vast numbers of lives; as we explain, that conclusion rests on a series of errors.

The third and fourth sections of the book turn to integrated assessment models (IAMs), which have become central to climate economics. IAMs model the interacting processes of long-run economic growth and climate change, aiming to capture the complex feedbacks between these processes. The third section examines the framework and theory of IAMs. "Inside the Integrated Assessment Models" is a review article assessing key aspects of 30 different IAMs found in recent literature, identifying wide differences in assumptions and results. "Limitations of Integrated Assessment Models of Climate Change" examines the economic theory underlying IAMs, finding that they rely on questionable approaches, minimize catastrophic risks and impacts on future generations, and do not provide reasonable policy guidance. "Negishi Welfare Weights in Integrated Assessment Models" highlights a technical procedure, used in solving many IAMs, that has the effect of freezing the current global distribution of income, ensuring that the models' solutions do not include significant movements toward international equity.

The fourth section of the book includes five articles on IAMs in practice, four based on well-known IAMs and a final one on our own efforts to create a better IAM. While there are numerous IAMs in economics literature, policy debate has often focused more narrowly on a handful of the best-known and simplest models. Both the periodic reviews of economic literature by the Intergovernmental Panel on Climate Change (IPCC) and the US government's calculation of a "social cost of carbon" (i.e., the value of the incremental damages caused by an additional unit of greenhouse gas emissions) for use in policy assessment have relied on IAMs that appear to have been chosen for familiarity or ease of use. In particular, the DICE model, developed and publicly released by William Nordhaus, has become a de facto open-access standard for research purposes. Like many other researchers, we have experimented with modifications to DICE; the bare-bones simplicity of the model, representing the entire global processes of economic growth and climate change in a system of only 19 equations, essentially guarantees that important features have been omitted.

"Climate Risks and Carbon Prices" develops sensitivity analyses of the US government's 2010 estimate of the social cost of carbon – the marginal damage caused by an additional ton of carbon dioxide emissions. Their estimate was a precise and small numerical value of $21 per ton. Using the DICE model, we demonstrate that important uncertainties about future damages, the discount rate, and the expected pace of climate change make this estimate highly questionable, with risks of values more than an order of magnitude higher. (The 2013 update to the US estimate raised the value somewhat, but did not change the methodology of calculation, and did not approach the higher values discussed in our article.)

"Epstein–Zin Utility in DICE" introduces an important theoretical innovation from finance literature, allowing separate treatment of time preference and risk aversion; conventional approaches in both climate economics and finance conflate these two distinct factors, with paradoxical results. With this innovation, DICE recommends much faster abatement of emissions, but remains all but unable to model the effects of risk aversion. "Fat Tails, Exponents, Extreme Uncertainty" is an attempt to provide an explicit treatment of catastrophic risks in DICE; modifications to both the climate sensitivity parameter (governing the pace of climate change) and the shape of the damage function are required to make DICE predict catastrophic outcomes. "Climate Damages in the FUND Model" addresses another one of the most-discussed IAMs. A complex model with many more "moving parts" than DICE, FUND often estimates lower climate damages and social cost of carbon values than other models. This article explores the calculation of damages in FUND, identifying serious problems of data and logic in its treatment of agriculture.

Finally, "Climate Policy and Development" reports on our own IAM, the Climate and Regional Economics of Development (CRED) model. CRED was designed to model substantial transfers of resources between world regions, simultaneously pursuing the goals of global equity and climate protection; each scenario reports both climate and equity outcomes. Under some, but not all, scenarios, development policy (modeled as the generosity of inter-regional resource transfers) makes the difference between success and failure in long-term climate stabilization.

We wrote these articles while working together on climate economics at the Stockholm Environment Institute's US Center, located at Tufts University. The third long-term member of our research team, Ramón Bueno, appears as a coauthor of several articles here, but his role was much bigger than that. A skilled software analyst and computer modeler whose knowledge and hard work made possible the more ambitious results in this book, Ramón is a wonderful colleague and friend, who we thoroughly enjoyed working with.

Thanks are also due to the other coauthors of articles in this book, and to our hard-working research assistants. The Stockholm Environment Institute, the E3 Network (Economists for Equity and Environment), and other funders provided the support that allowed us to carry out this research agenda. Thanks to Anthem Press for its enthusiastic support of our work and to Becca Keane for smoothly turning this scattered collection of articles into a more book-like manuscript.

We are now continuing work on related issues, with a more specific and applied focus on the US electricity system, at Synapse Energy Economics. Interested readers can follow our more recent work at http://www.synapse-energy.com. Frank Ackerman's publications are also available at http://frankackerman.com.

Frank Ackerman and Elizabeth A. Stanton, July 2013.

PUBLICATION HISTORY

This book is a compilation of articles authored and coauthored by Frank Ackerman and Elizabeth A. Stanton, all of which were previously published in various journals or as working papers.

Chapter 1, "Climate Economics in Four Easy Pieces," by Frank Ackerman, originally published in *Development* 51 (2008).

Chapter 2, "Carbon Markets Are Not Enough," by Frank Ackerman, originally published in the United Nations Conference on Trade and Development *Trade and Environment Review* (2009/2010).

Chapter 3, "Modeling Pessimism: Does Climate Stabilization Require a Failure of Development?" by Elizabeth A. Stanton, originally published in *Environment and Development* 3 (2012).

Chapter 4, "The Tragedy of Maldistribution: Climate, Sustainability and Equity," by Elizabeth A. Stanton, originally published in *Sustainability* 4, no. 3 (2012).

Chapter 5, "Climate Impacts on Agriculture: A Challenge to Complacency?" by Frank Ackerman and Elizabeth A. Stanton, originally published as working paper 13-01, Tufts University's Global Development and Environment Institute (2013).

Chapter 6, "Did the Stern Review Underestimate US and Global Climate Damages?" by Frank Ackerman, Elizabeth A. Stanton, Chris Hope and Stephane Alberth, originally published in *Energy Policy* 37, no. 7 (2009).

Chapter 7, "Can Climate Change Save Lives? A Comment on 'Economy-Wide Estimates of the Implications of Climate Change: Human Health,'" by

Frank Ackerman and Elizabeth A. Stanton, originally published in *Ecological Economics* 66, no. 1 (2008).

Chapter 8, "Inside the Integrated Assessment Models: Four Issues in Climate Economics," by Elizabeth A. Stanton, Frank Ackerman and Sivan Kartha, originally published in *Climate and Development* 1 (2009).

Chapter 9, "Limitations of Integrated Assessment Models of Climate Change," by Frank Ackerman, Stephen J. DeCanio, Richard B. Howarth and Kristen Sheeran, originally published in *Climatic Change* 95 (2009).

Chapter 10, "Negishi Welfare Weights in Integrated Assessment Models: The Mathematics of Global Inequality," by Elizabeth A. Stanton, originally published in *Climatic Change* 107, no. 3 (2010).

Chapter 11, "Climate Risks and Carbon Prices: Revising the Social Cost of Carbon," by Frank Ackerman and Elizabeth A. Stanton, originally published in *Economics E-Journal* 6 (2012).

Chapter 12, "Epstein–Zin Utility in DICE: Is Risk Aversion Irrelevant to Climate Policy?" by Frank Ackerman, Elizabeth A. Stanton and Ramón Bueno, originally published in *Environmental and Resource Economics* (March 2013).

Chapter 13, "Fat Tails, Exponents, Extreme Uncertainty: Simulating Catastrophe in DICE" by Frank Ackerman, Elizabeth A. Stanton and Ramón Bueno, originally published in *Ecological Economics* 69, no. 9 (2012).

Chapter 14, "Climate Damages in the FUND Model: A Disaggregated Analysis," by Frank Ackerman and Charles Munitz,[1] originally published in *Ecological Economics* 77 (2012).

Chapter 15, "Climate Policy and Development: An Economic Analysis," by Frank Ackerman, Elizabeth A. Stanton and Ramón Bueno, originally published as an E3 Network Working Paper (2012).

Thank you to our coauthors and to the publishers of these articles for granting permission to reprint them here.

Part I

PERSPECTIVES ON CLIMATE AND EQUITY

Chapter 1

CLIMATE ECONOMICS IN FOUR EASY PIECES

Frank Ackerman

Conventional economic analysis is rapidly replacing the arguments of the climate skeptics as the principal justification for inaction on climate change. It is important to create an alternative economics that is consistent with the urgency expressed by the latest climate science. This chapter presents four broad principles that are fundamental to a better analysis of climate economics. First, your grandchildren's lives are important: a low discount rate is needed to validate concern about far-future outcomes. Second, we need to buy insurance for the planet: prevention of catastrophic worst-case risks, not response to average, expected outcomes, should be the motivation for climate policy. Third, climate damages are too valuable to have prices: the impossibility of putting meaningful prices on human life, endangered species and ecosystems defeats attempts at cost–benefit analysis of climate policy. Fourth, some costs are better than others: the "costs" of active climate policies will create jobs, incomes and new technologies, while avoiding the physical destruction of the much worse costs of an increasingly extreme climate.

Introduction

Once upon a time, debates about climate policy were primarily about the science. Initially, at least in the United States, an inordinate amount of attention was focused on the handful of "climate skeptics" who challenged the scientific understanding of climate change. The influence of the skeptics, however, is rapidly fading; few people were swayed by their arguments, and doubt about the major results of climate science is no longer important in shaping public policy.

As the climate science debate is reaching closure, the climate economics debate is heating up. The controversial issue now is the fear that overly ambitious climate initiatives could hurt the economy. Economists emphasizing that fear have, in effect, replaced the climate skeptics as the intellectual enablers of inaction. For example, William Nordhaus, the US economist best known for his work on climate change, pays lip service to scientists' calls for decisive action. He finds, however, that the "optimal" policy is a very small carbon tax that would reduce greenhouse gas emissions only 25 percent below "business-as-usual" levels by 2050 – in other words, allowing emissions to rise well above current levels by mid-century.[1] Richard Tol, a European economist who has written widely on climate change, favors an even smaller carbon tax of just $2 per ton of carbon dioxide (Lomborg 2007). That would amount to all of $0.02 per gallon of gasoline, a microscopic "incentive" for change that consumers would simply ignore.

There are other voices in the climate economics debate; in particular, the Stern Review offers a different perspective (Stern 2006). Stern's analysis is much less wrong than the traditional Nordhaus–Tol approach, but even Stern has not challenged conventional wisdom enough. It is important to understand, challenge and replace the conventional fear of a damaged economy, because economists' doubts and conclusions about climate change echo throughout public debate; economic analysis has a major impact on the decisions that politicians and governments are willing to take. There is much more than an academic theory at stake.

What will it take to build a better economics of climate change? The problem is not in the technicalities; economists of all stripes are generally quite good at working out the technical implications of their underlying assumptions. The question is: what underlying assumptions are required to create a climate economics that is consistent with the urgency expressed by the latest climate science? The assumptions that matter are big, nontechnical principles, capable of being expressed in bumper sticker format. Here are the four bumper stickers for a better climate economics:

- Your grandchildren's lives are important
- We need to buy insurance for the planet
- Climate damages are too valuable to have prices
- Some costs are better than others

Each of these is elaborated below.

Your Grandchildren's Lives Are Important

The most widely debated challenge of climate economics is the valuation of the very long run. The time spans involved are well beyond those encountered in most areas of economics. For ordinary loans and investments, both the costs today and the resulting future benefits typically occur within a single lifetime. In such cases, it makes sense to think in terms of the same person experiencing and comparing the costs and the benefits.

In the case of climate change, the most important consequences of today's choices will be felt by generations to come, long after all of us making those choices have passed away. As a result, the costs of reducing emissions today, and the benefits in the far future, will not be experienced by the same people. The economics of climate change is centrally concerned with our relationship to our descendants whom we will never meet. As a bridge to that unknowable future, consider your grandchildren – the last generation that most of us will ever know.

Economists routinely deal with future costs and benefits by "discounting" them, or converting them to "present values" – a process that is simply compound interest in reverse. Suppose that you want your grandchildren to receive $100 (in today's dollars, corrected for inflation) 60 years from now. How much would you have to put in a bank account today to ensure that the $100 will be there 60 years from now? The answer is $55 at 1 percent interest, $17 at 3 percent, or just over $5 at 5 percent. In the standard jargon, the present value of $100, to be received 60 years from now, is $55 at a 1 percent discount rate, $17 at a 3 percent discount rate or about $5 at a 5 percent discount rate. As this example shows, a higher discount rate implies a smaller present value.

The central problem of climate economics, in a cost–benefit framework, is deciding how much to spend today on preventing future harms. Applying the same logic as in the previous example, what should we spend to prevent $100 of climate damages 60 years from now? The standard answer is no more than the present value of that future loss: $55 at a discount rate of 1 percent, $17 at 3 percent and $5 at 5 percent. Thus the higher the discount rate, the less it is "worth" spending today on protecting our grandchildren.

The effect becomes much more pronounced as the time period lengthens; at a 5 percent discount rate, damages of $1 million occurring 200 years from now have a present value of only about $60. At a 1 percent discount rate, on the other hand, the present value of $1 million of damages 200 years from now is more than $130,000. The choice of the discount rate is all-important to our stance toward the far future: should we spend as much as $130,000, or just $60, to avoid $1 million of climate damages in the early 23rd century?

For financial transactions within a single lifetime, it makes sense to use market interest rates as the discount rate. Climate change, however, involves public policy decisions with impacts spanning centuries; there is no market in which public resources are traded from one century to the next. The choice of an intergenerational discount rate is a matter of ethics and policy, not a market-determined result.

Using a framework that originated with Frank Ramsey (1928), it has become common to identify two separate aspects of long-term discounting, each contributing to the discount rate. One component of the discount rate is based on the expected upward trend in income and wealth. If future generations will be much richer than we are, they will need less help from us, and they will get less benefit from an additional dollar of income than we do. So we can discount benefits that will flow to our wealthy descendants at a rate based on the expected growth of per capita incomes. Among economists, the income-related motive for discounting may be the least controversial part of the picture.

The other component of the discount rate is the rate that would apply if all generations had the same per capita income, or the rate of "pure time preference." This is the subject of longstanding ethical, philosophical and economic debate. On the one hand, there are reasons to think that pure time preference is greater than zero: both psychological experiments and common sense suggest that people are impatient and prefer money now to money later. On the other hand, pure time preference of zero expresses the equal worth of people of all generations and the equal importance of reducing climate impacts and other burdens on them (assuming that all generations have equal incomes).

Chapter 2 of the Stern Review provides an excellent discussion of the debate, and motivates Stern's choice of a rate of pure time preference close to zero and an overall discount rate of 1.4 percent. This discount rate alone is sufficient to explain Stern's support for a substantial program of climate protection. At the higher discount rates used in more traditional analyses, the Stern program would look "inefficient," since the costs would outweigh the present value of the benefits.

We Need to Buy Insurance for the Planet

Does climate science predict that things are certain to get worse? Or does it tell us that we are uncertain about what will happen next? Unfortunately, the answer seems to be yes to both questions. For example, the most likely level of sea level rise in this century, according to the latest IPCC reports, is no more than 1m or so – a real threat to low lying coastal areas and islands that will face increasing storm damages, but survivable, with some adaptation efforts, for most of the world. On the other hand, there is a worst-case risk of an abrupt loss of the Greenland ice sheet, or perhaps of a large portion of the West Antarctic ice sheet. Either one could cause an eventual 7m of sea level rise – a catastrophic impact on coastal communities, economic activity and infrastructure everywhere; well beyond the range of plausible adaptation efforts in most places.

The evaluation of climate damages thus depends on whether we focus on the most likely outcomes or the credible worst-case risks; the latter, of course, are much larger. Cost–benefit analysis conventionally rests on average or expected outcomes. But this is not the only way that people make decisions. Faced with uncertain, potentially large risks, people do not normally act on the basis of average outcomes; instead, they typically focus on protection against worst-case scenarios. When you go to the airport, do you leave just enough time for the average amount of traffic delays (so that you would catch your plane, on average, half of the time)? Or do you allow time for some estimate of worst-case traffic jams? Once you get there, of course, you will experience additional delays due to security, which is all about worst cases: your average fellow passenger is not a threat to anyone's safety.

The annual number of residential fires in the United States is about 0.4 percent of the number of housing units.[2] This means that a fire occurs, on average, about once every 250 years in each home, not even close to once per lifetime. By far the most likely number of fires a homeowner will experience next year, or even in a lifetime, is zero. Why don't these statistics inspire you to cancel your fire insurance? Unless you are extremely wealthy, the loss of your home in a fire would be a devastating financial blow; despite the low probability, you cannot afford to take any chances on it.

What are the chances of the ultimate loss? In the United States, the probability that you will die next year is under 0.1 percent if you are in your 20s, under 0.2 percent in your 30s and under 0.4 percent in your 40s.[3] It is not until age 61 that you have as much as a 1 percent chance of death within the coming year. Yet most US families with dependent children buy life insurance.[4] Without it, the risk to the children of losing the parents' income would be too great – even though the parents are, on average, extraordinarily likely to survive.

The very existence of the insurance industry is evidence of the desire to avoid or control worst-case scenarios. It is impossible for an insurance company to pay out in claims as much as its customers pay in premiums; if it did, there would be no money left to pay the costs of running the company, or the profits received by its owners. People who buy insurance are therefore guaranteed to get back less than they, on average, have paid; they (we) are paying for the security that insurance provides, if the worst should happen. This way of thinking does not apply to every decision: in casino games, people make bets based on averages and probabilities, and no one has any insurance against losing the next round. But life is not a casino, and public policy should not be a gamble.

Should climate policy be based on the most likely outcomes, or on the worst-case risks? Should we be investing in climate protection as if we expect sea level rise of 1m, or as if we are buying insurance to be sure of preventing 7m?

In fact, the worst-case climate risks are even more unknown than the individual risks of fire and death that motivate insurance purchases. You do not know whether or not you will have a fire next year or die before the year is over, but you have very good information about the likelihood of these tragic events. So does the insurance industry, which is why they are willing to insure you. In contrast, there is no body of statistical information about the probability of Greenland-sized ice sheets collapsing at various temperatures; it is not an experiment that anyone can perform over and over again.

A recent analysis by Martin Weitzman argues that the probabilities of the worst outcomes are inescapably unknowable, and this deep uncertainty is more important than anything we do know in motivating concern about climate change (Weitzman 2009). There is a technical sense in which the expected value of future climate damages could be infinite, because we know so little about the probability of the worst, most damaging possibilities. Informally, if we had fewer than 100 empirical observations bearing on how fast the climate will worsen, we would have essentially no information about the 99th percentile risk. Yet US insurance statistics make it clear that people care a great deal about risks that are worse than the 99th percentile. The practical implication of infinite expected damages is that the most likely outcome is irrelevant; the only thing that matters is buying insurance for the planet – that is, understanding and controlling the worst-case risks.

Climate Damages Are Too Valuable to Have Prices

To decide whether climate protection is worthwhile, in cost–benefit terms, we would need to know the monetary value of everything important that is being protected. There are, however, no meaningful prices for many of the benefits of health and environmental protection. What is the dollar value of a human life saved? How much is it worth to save an endangered species from extinction, or to preserve a unique location or ecosystem? Economists have made up price tags for such priceless values, but the results do not always pass the laugh test. I have written at length about this elsewhere, and will offer only a brief summary here (Ackerman and Heinzerling 2004; Ackerman 2008b).

Is a human life worth $6.1 million, as estimated by the Clinton administration, based on small differences in the wages paid for more and less risky jobs? Or is it worth $3.7 million, as the (second) Bush administration concluded on the basis of questionnaires about willingness to pay for reducing small, hypothetical risks? Are lives of people in rich countries worth much more than those in poor countries, as some economists infamously argued in the IPCC's 1995 report? Can the value of an endangered species be determined by survey research on how much people would pay to protect it? Are large mammals and birds worth much more than other species, as such surveys suggest? If, as one study found, the US population as a whole would pay $18 billion to protect the existence of humpback whales, would it be acceptable for someone to pay $36 billion for the right to hunt and kill the entire species?

The only sensible response to such nonsensical questions is that there are many crucially important values that do not have meaningful prices. This is not a new idea: as Immanuel Kant put it, some things have a price, or relative worth, while other things have a dignity, or inner worth (Kant 2005 [1785]). No price tag does justice to the dignity of human life or the natural world. Since some of the most important benefits of climate protection are priceless, any monetary value for total benefits will necessarily be incomplete. The corollary is that it can be important to take action, even in the absence of a complete monetary measure of the benefits of doing so.

Some Costs Are Better than Others

The language of cost–benefit analysis embodies a clear normative slant: benefits are good and costs are bad. The goal is always to have larger benefits and smaller costs. Measurement and monetary valuation is easier for costs than for benefits; the costs of environmental protection often involve changes in such areas as manufacturing, construction, and fuel use, all of which have well-defined prices. Yet conventional economic theory distorts the interpretation of costs, in ways that exaggerate the burdens of environmental policy and hide the positive features of some of the costs.

The distortion and exaggeration of costs occurs across a range of time scales. In the short run, bottom-up studies of energy use and carbon emissions repeatedly find significant opportunities for emissions reduction at zero or negative net cost – the so-called "no-regrets" options.[5] Costless energy savings are, according to a longstanding tradition in economic theory, impossible. In the textbook theory of competitive markets, every resource is productively employed in its most valuable use, and every no-regrets option has already been taken. As the saying goes, there are no free lunches; there are no $20 bills on the sidewalk, because someone would have picked them up already. Traditional models of climate costs, based on economic theory, do not include free lunches. In these models, all emission reductions have positive costs. This leads to greater estimates of climate policy costs than the bottom-up studies with their extensive opportunities for costless savings.

In the medium term, we will need to move beyond the no-regrets options; how much will it cost to finish the job of climate protection? Again, there are rival interpretations of the costs based on rival assumptions about the economy. The same economic theory that proclaimed the absence of $20 bills on the sidewalk is responsible for the idea that all costs are bad. Since the free market lets everyone spend their money in whatever way they choose, any new cost must represent a loss: it leaves people with less to spend on whatever purchases they had previously selected to maximize their satisfaction in life. Climate damages are one source of loss, and spending on climate protection is another; both reduce the resources available for the desirable things in life.

Are the two kinds of costs really comparable? Are we indifferent between spending $1 billion on bigger and better levees, or not building the levees and losing $1 billion to storm damages? In the imperfect, real world economy, money spent on building levees creates jobs and incomes. The construction workers buy groceries, clothing and so on, indirectly creating other jobs. With more people working, tax revenues increase while unemployment compensation payments decrease.

None of this happens if the levees are not built, and the storm damages are allowed to occur. The costs of prevention are good costs, with numerous indirect benefits; the costs of climate damages are bad costs, representing pure physical destruction. One worthwhile goal is to keep total costs as low as possible; another is to have as many good costs as possible, rather than bad costs. Think of it as the cholesterol theory of climate costs. In the long run, the deep reductions in carbon emissions needed for climate stabilization will require new technologies that have not yet been invented, or at best exist only in small, expensive prototypes. How much will it cost to invent, develop, and implement the low-carbon technologies of the future?

Lacking a rigorous theory of innovation, economists modeling climate change have often assumed that new technologies simply appear, making the economy inexorably more efficient over time. A more realistic view observes that costs of producing a new product typically decline as industry gains more experience with it, in a pattern called "learning by doing," or the "learning curve" effect. Wind power is now relatively cheap and competitive in suitable locations; this is a direct result of decades of public investment in the United States and Europe, starting when wind turbines were still quite expensive. The costs of climate policy, in the long run, will include doing the same for other promising new technologies, investing public resources in jump-starting a set of slightly different industries than we might have chosen in the absence of climate change. If this is a cost, many communities would be better off with more of it.

Conclusions

A widely publicized, conventional economic analysis recommends inaction on climate change, claiming that the costs currently outweigh the benefits for anything more than the smallest steps toward reducing carbon emissions.

There are four big things wrong with this theory, four bumper stickers for a better economics of climate change.

First, your grandchildren's lives are important. Climate policy involves costs incurred now with their greatest benefits far in the future; the discount rate determines how large those benefits appear to be. As the Stern Review demonstrates, a low discount rate is required to validate the belief that your grandchildren, and other generations to come, matter to us today.

Second, we need to buy insurance for the planet. The predictable damages from climate change are large enough; the credible worst cases are disastrously greater. In private life, people routinely buy insurance against events that are worse than 99th percentile bad outcomes. Thus the average, expected climate damages are virtually irrelevant; all that matters is preventing the worst cases from occurring.

Third, climate damages are too valuable to have prices. Climate policy is aimed at saving human lives, protecting species and ecosystems and ensuring the survival of a natural world that is essential to our existence. Cost–benefit analysis utterly fails to comprehend these priceless values; the benefits of climate policy include many things that have a dignity rather than a price.

Finally, some costs are better than others. In the short run, there are no-regrets options that can save emissions at no net cost; in the medium term, there are job and income creation benefits of spending on climate protection; in the long run, public investment is needed to create and launch the new technologies of a low-carbon future. These costs are constructive, unlike the physical destruction caused by an increasingly extreme climate.

Put these four pieces together, and we have the outline of an economics that complements the science of climate change and endorses active, large-scale climate protection.

Chapter 2

CARBON MARKETS ARE NOT ENOUGH

Frank Ackerman

The good news is that all major voices in the climate policy debate are now taking the problem seriously. Skepticism about the science is no longer an option: the world's scientists have never been so unanimous, and so ominous, in their projections of future perils. The bad news is that too many participants in the debate consider climate policy to primarily consist of manipulating markets and prices. If the only tool available were market liberalization, then the solution to every problem would seem to be a matter of getting the prices right. But setting a price for carbon emissions is only the beginning of climate policy – not the end. To address the threat of climate change, it is not only necessary to charge a price for carbon emissions; governments have to do much more, through actions to support innovation and diffusion of new, low-carbon technologies.

Introduction: The State of the Debate

For market-oriented institutions, the path is clear. The International Monetary Fund (IMF) simply assumes that climate policy consists of adjusting the price of carbon, when it states: "An effective mitigation policy must be based on setting a price path for the greenhouse gas (GHG) emissions that drive climate change" (IMF 2008). Although it gives an occasional nod to the importance of developments such as hybrid vehicles, energy efficiency and new infrastructure spending, the IMF's approach to climate policy focuses almost entirely on market instruments. Moreover, it apparently does not consider the problem to be so serious. In the IMF's view, the world can afford to move at a comfortably slow pace: "Carbon-pricing policies [...] must establish a time horizon for steadily rising carbon prices that people and businesses consider believable. Increases in world carbon prices need not be large – say a $0.01 initial increase in the price of a gallon of gasoline that rises by $0.02 every three years" (IMF 2008).

However, changes in carbon prices of this magnitude have been dwarfed by recent swings in the price of oil. While it may be possible to achieve climate stabilization at a moderate total cost, considerable ingenuity and new policy directions will be required; by themselves, price changes of a few cents per gallon of gasoline are not enough to achieve anything of importance.

Other voices in the international debate have recognized the greater urgency of the problem, and have been willing to consider a broader range of policy instruments. In its Human Development Report, the United Nations Development Programme (UNDP 2007) states: "Carbon markets are a necessary condition for the transition to a low-carbon economy. They are not a sufficient condition. Governments have a critical role to play in setting regulatory standards and in supporting low-carbon research, development and deployment." The report calls for carbon markets to be accompanied by government incentives for renewable energy production, tightened standards for vehicle fuel efficiency, expanded research on carbon capture and storage technology and increased technology transfer to developing countries.

One of the most detailed recent proposals is Nicholas Stern's "global deal on climate change" (Stern 2008). Stern argues that climate stabilization requires cutting global emissions to half of their 1990 level by 2050, with continuing declines thereafter. Stern calls for binding national reduction targets to be adopted soon by developed countries and the fastest growing middle-income countries, and by all other countries by 2020. He envisions a carbon market in the form of a global cap-and-trade system that would allow developing countries to sell emission rights, combined with arrangements for technology transfer and large-scale government support for the development of new technologies. He states: "The world should aim for a liquid international carbon market in order to allow for the most effective, efficient and equitable emissions reductions. In addition, nonprice interventions are required to expand the global market for low-carbon technologies, support common standards, and promote cost-effective reduced deforestation" (Stern 2008, 3).

In short, all major proposals for climate policy include a substantial role for carbon markets and prices, either in the form of taxes or cap-and-trade systems. While some give greater emphasis to the manipulation of prices and financing in carbon markets, others see carbon markets as only one part of a complex ensemble of policies.

What Would Carbon Prices Accomplish?

Carbon prices will change energy costs, energy consumption and carbon emissions. They will also change the distribution of income available for nonenergy purchases. If carbon prices were increased by a tax or trading system, what would be the extent of the (intended) effect on emissions and the (unintended) effect on income distribution?

Increased energy costs to consumers fall disproportionately on low-income groups, since the poor spend a higher proportion of their income on energy. As incomes rise, total spending on energy usually rises, but more slowly; thus the fraction of income spent on energy decreases.[1] As a result, policies that raise the price of fossil fuels either reduce the use of those fuels (thereby reducing greenhouse gas emissions), or increase the economic burden on low-income consumers – or both. Thus, there is a trade-off between the effects of fuel prices on the environment and on the distribution of income. The relative importance of the two effects depends on the price elasticity of demand for energy.[2] A larger elasticity means that a price increase has a greater effect on emissions and a lower effect on income distribution; a smaller elasticity means that the same price increase does less to reduce emissions but more to increase inequality.[3] Since price elasticities are small for energy in general, and extraordinarily small for petroleum products in the short run, price incentives are a blunt and painful instrument for achieving lower emissions.

Consider the effects of a 20 percent increase in the price of energy. At an elasticity of −1, the 20 percent increase in price causes a 20 percent drop in demand. Consumers purchase 80 percent as much energy as before at 120 percent of the former price per unit, so that the total cost to consumers amounts to 96 percent of the former total. At this elasticity, most of the effect is seen in the change in the quantity of energy used (and therefore emissions), while total consumer spending is little affected. In contrast, at an elasticity of −0.05, a 20 percent price increase causes only a 1 percent change in quantity. Consumers buy 99 percent as much energy as before at 120 percent of the former price per unit for a total expenditure of 119 percent of the earlier cost. At this elasticity, there is almost no effect on the quantity of energy used, or on emissions, but a large effect on the total cost to consumers. Therefore, judged as a strategy to reduce energy consumption and emissions with minimal burdens on consumers, energy price increases seem quite effective at an elasticity of −1, but decidedly inferior at an elasticity of −0.05. Intermediate values naturally have results falling between these two extremes.

What elasticity values are applicable in reality? The largest elasticities are found in industry. Studies of 15 countries by three research groups found the price elasticity for industrial energy demand to be between −0.77 and −0.88. Estimated elasticities for Brazil and India were not significantly different from those for developed countries (Roy et al. 2006). Industrial energy use, in other words, provides fertile ground for the application of price incentives for emission reductions. Indeed, industry lowered its energy use much farther and faster than any other sector in response to the oil price shocks of the 1970s.

Household demand for electricity, on the other hand, is much less elastic than industrial energy use. Recent estimates for the United States found a short-run price elasticity of –0.20, and a long-run price elasticity of –0.32, broadly consistent with earlier research (Bernstein and Griffin 2006).[4] This finding of a small elasticity for electricity does not appear to be unique to the United States; for instance, the estimated long-run elasticity for Taiwan Province of China was estimated to be –0.16 (Holtedahl and Joutz 2004).

In both industrial energy use and electricity generation, there are alternative fuels that yield the same result with differing carbon emissions. An increased carbon price would cause a noticeable reduction in industrial energy demand (but less so in household electricity demand), and also a shift towards the use of lower carbon fuels, such as replacing coal with natural gas.

The picture is different in the transportation sector – the principal market for oil – where there is essentially no widely available alternative to the use of petroleum fuels. On a global basis, the available supply of biofuels is too small to make a noticeable dent in the demand for petroleum. In the wake of the oil crises of the 1970s, most countries and industries cut back on oil use wherever possible. Oil-fired electricity generation, for example, has become much less common, except among members of the Organization of the Petroleum Exporting Countries (OPEC). Today the largest proportion of crude oil is used for transportation, and a portion of the remainder is dedicated to nonfuel uses, such as petrochemicals for which there are no close substitutes. The connection between petroleum and transportation is projected to grow even tighter: an estimated two-thirds of the growth in oil demand through 2030 will be for transportation.[5] Thus the oil and transport market is almost disconnected from the market for other fuels and end uses.

The lack of alternatives to oil means that in the short run, price elasticity is close to zero for many consumers. Households in automobile-dependent environments – including the great majority in the United States, a large proportion in many Organization for Economic Co-operation and Development (OECD) countries and increasing numbers in fast-growing, middle-income countries – have little control over the amount of driving required to go to work, school, stores and other essential services. Thus, in the short run, purchases of gasoline will be quite insensitive to price, and higher prices will simply be a burden on consumers. However, in the long run, as old cars require to be replaced, high oil prices will stimulate purchases of smaller, more fuel-efficient vehicles, as was the case in 2007–2008. Over time this will affect oil consumption, as the fleet of cars on the road slowly becomes more fuel efficient, implying that the price elasticity is greater in the long run than in the short run.

A comparative international analysis estimated oil price elasticities for many countries for the period 1979–2000 (Cooper 2003). For the United States, it found a short-run elasticity of -0.06 and a long-run elasticity of –0.46,[6] and for the G-7 group of industrialized countries, it found a short-run elasticity ranging from –0.024 to –0.071 and a long-run elasticity from –0.18 to –0.57.

Short-run price elasticities for gasoline and other transport fuels are close to zero, which is why the 2007–2008 surge in the price of oil did not cause an immediate collapse in demand. Many months later, a global economic downturn depressed incomes and fuel use. As highlighted in this chapter, that downturn was not solely, or even primarily, caused by the high price of oil. Any feasible carbon policy would, in the near term, raise fossil fuel prices by less than the oil price increases of 2007–2008. While such a policy could cause a noticeable change in industrial energy use, it would have less effect on transportation than the recent surge in oil prices. Therefore, something more needs to be done to reduce emissions on the necessary scale and timetable.

Where Do New Technologies Come From?

Price signals lead to efficient choices among existing alternatives. This is the great success of the market economy. However, while it is an important step in climate change mitigation efforts, it is not enough. New technologies are necessary to solve the climate crisis and will not be created by high carbon prices alone. Where will the new technologies come from?

Conventional economic models have often finessed this question with the ad hoc assumption of a predictable rate of technical change, unrelated to investment choices or policy decisions. That assumption creates a bias toward passively waiting for new technologies to emerge: abatement, so the argument goes, will always be cheaper if it is done later, after better technologies have made their appearance. However, in reality, important innovations do not fall from the sky. New technologies are created by conscious effort. They typically start out expensive and become cheaper over time, a process that is often described in terms of "learning curves" or "experience curves." As a result, early investment in start-up costs can determine which technologies will become cost-effective in the future. Technological change is path-dependent: the current set of available choices depends on past policies and actions, just as the available technological options in the future will depend on our policies and actions today.

The learning curve phenomenon is particularly important when there is a benefit from standardization. In such cases, an early market leader can become "locked in," whether or not it represents the ideal technology, as occurred with the Windows operating system for computers, for example.[7] The current style of industrialization has been described as "carbon lock-in," meaning that carbon-intensive technologies gained an early lead at a time when fossil fuels were cheap and concern about global warming was not yet on the horizon (Unruh and Carrillo-Hermosilla 2006). Today, the economic benefits of standardization and the low costs of imitating and replicating existing technologies keep the world locked into that same undesirable path.

New energy technologies often display strong learning curve effects. Research on wind power, for example, has found reductions in unit costs as great as 20 percent from a doubling of production (Junginger et al. 2005), which made it competitive in the marketplace under many conditions. This success was made possible by decades of European and United States governments' investments in R&D. Brazilian ethanol production, another alternative energy industry launched by government policy, experienced a 29 percent reduction in costs when production doubled (Goldemberg et al. 2004).

With technological progress at these rates, often private enterprises only find it profitable to buy a new product after others have been buying it for a number of years, thereby bringing down the price. Hence the need for public sector involvement: governments can and must choose to support the new technologies, especially when – as with climate policy – there is a clear need for change. A plausible model of energy development projects finds that solar photovoltaics, which are at present one of the most expensive ways to generate electricity, could become one of the cheapest options by 2100 as a result of learning curve effects (Rao et al. 2006).

This is not a unique characteristic of new energy technologies; rather, it is the norm in technological change. Microelectronics, a major success story of the private sector today, was the outcome of United States government spending during the Cold War years. According to Morton (1999), "The U.S. military initially purchased nearly the total production of transistors in the early 1950s, using them to make the new generation of communications, radar and improved avionics systems, command and control systems, as well as for missiles and jet fighters [...] The U.S. government acted as the major market for integrated circuits in the early years [...] In 1962 [...] the U.S. government, with extensive research interests in space, defense, and other areas, purchased virtually 100 percent of all integrated circuits manufactured in the United States." As with wind power, a few decades of generous public support were sufficient to launch the microelectronics industry as a success in the marketplace. If the world had waited for automatic technical change, or relied on getting the prices right, microelectronics might never have happened.

Carbon Markets and Developing Countries

It has become commonplace to insist on the need for a globally harmonized price of carbon. Price harmonization is thought to ensure efficiency in worldwide abatement efforts: with appropriate market institutions, investment in emissions reductions will flow to the countries where the marginal abatement costs are lowest. Fears about the effects of unharmonized carbon charges have slowed climate policy initiatives in some high-income countries and prompted an unproductive and potentially protectionist discussion of border tariff adjustments. This notion is mistaken, both in fact and theory. Empirically, only a handful of industries are so carbon intensive that a difference in carbon charges could lead them to move from one country to another – and large segments of these industries have already moved to middle- and low-income countries.

In theory, remarkably enough, marginal abatement costs do not have to be equal in every country in order to achieve economic efficiency. Theorists who conclude that equal marginal costs are needed generally rely on the unexamined assumption that world income distribution is equitable, or, equivalently, that increases in per capita consumption are equally urgent everywhere (Sheeran 2006; Chichilnisky and Heal 1994). In the absence of that assumption, it is more efficient to carry out abatement efforts in richer countries, even though that might entail higher costs. That is, in an inequitable world, efficiency can be improved by imposing higher carbon prices in richer countries. This is not to suggest that the problem of climate change can be solved in high-income countries alone. Rather, it means that it is equitable for richer countries to invest in more costly measures, higher up on their marginal abatement curves.

It seems unlikely, however, that the movement towards a uniform worldwide carbon price will be blocked for long. Eventually, developing countries are likely to face a global carbon price, while their local prices for labor, land and other inputs remain far below the levels of higher income countries. The dissonance between expensive carbon and cheaper local inputs will create both an obstacle and an opportunity. The obstacle is that development may be distorted in the direction of activities of little or no value, simply because they yield marketable carbon reductions. Safeguards will be needed to prevent "carbon-allowance-seeking" investments. That is, in any global carbon market it will be essential to verify that emissions are not newly created in order to profit by reducing them. Unfortunately, the temptation to seek bogus allowances is a natural consequence of a global carbon price in a low-cost local economy.

The positive side of the same effect is that much deeper reductions in carbon emissions will be economical in developing countries. In the simplest terms, the fixed price of saving a ton of carbon in those countries is "worth" more hours of labor at a lower wage rate. Thus there will be a category of carbon-saving investments and technologies that are profitable only in developing countries, where the trade-off between carbon and other inputs is more favorable to emissions reductions. With appropriate public initiatives and financing for these technologies, developing countries could "leapfrog" beyond the patterns of energy use in higher income countries, thereby establishing a new frontier for carbon reduction. The potential for leapfrogging beyond the current technology frontier has been much discussed, but is difficult to achieve. The classic example is in telephones, where developing countries have been able to skip the expensive development of universal land lines and go directly to the use of cell phones. This, however, became possible only after cell phones were invented and commercialized in developed countries (Unruh and Carillo-Hermosilla 2006).

To realize the opportunity created by a global carbon price in low-cost economies, there will be a need for R&D in appropriate, cutting-edge technologies for carbon reduction. As with many of the new energy technologies that will be needed around the world, decades of public investment may be required before the developing country technologies are successful in the marketplace. This is one more reason why carbon prices are necessary, but not sufficient, for an equitable solution to the climate crisis.

Conclusions

Setting a price for carbon emissions is a valuable beginning, but not the end, of climate policy. Much more needs to be done to complement the new markets in carbon emissions and ensure an effective policy response to the threat of climate change.

Reliance on carbon price increases alone would be both ineffective and inequitable. For end uses with small price elasticities, such as residential electricity and, above all, transportation, a higher fuel price leads primarily to a less equal distribution of resources – not to a reduction in carbon emissions. Other policies are needed to offset the equity impacts of higher fuel costs, and to launch the development of new, low-carbon energy technologies of the future. Because technology choice is path dependent, with strong learning curve effects, public sector initiatives, such as investment in promising new energy technologies, are essential to ensure that the global economy follows a climate-friendly path.

Developing countries must play a leading role in key aspects of climate policy. If international agreements move towards a globally harmonized carbon price, it will become profitable for those countries to "leapfrog" beyond the technologies which are cost-effective in higher income countries.

Chapter 3

MODELING PESSIMISM: DOES CLIMATE STABILIZATION REQUIRE A FAILURE OF DEVELOPMENT?

Elizabeth A. Stanton

Climate economics models often assume that middle-income countries' per capita incomes will catch up with those of today's high-income countries, while low-income countries will lag behind. This choice underrates the least developed countries' chance to escape poverty. The consequences in terms of the resulting policy advice are stark: assumed slow growth for the poorest countries means lower projected business-as-usual emissions and, as a consequence, much weaker emissions reduction goals. But what if low-income countries grow more quickly, as China and India have? In the absence of emission reduction policies, fast economic development would mean higher business-as-usual emissions in the future, and would therefore require more ambitious global emissions reductions policies today. This chapter reviews current practices in modeling income growth in integrated assessment models of climate and economy; provides an empirical illustration of the impact that more optimistic economic development expectations would have on emissions mitigation targets; discusses the kinds of policies necessary to adequately reduce emissions per dollar of economic output in a scenario of robust economic development for the poorest countries; and concludes with recommendations for integrated assessment modelers.

Introduction

How big is the climate problem? That depends, in part, on one's assumptions about the inescapably uncertain scale of future economic growth and consequent emissions. If policy makers believe that economic growth will be slow, they should expect future emissions and the climatic changes that result from them to be relatively small. If instead policy makers believe that the global economy will expand rapidly, they should expect higher emissions, and therefore should plan for more stringent mitigation policies.

High versus low economic growth may seem, at first, like a bland parameter adjustment, made solely with the goal of more accurate emissions projections and policy goals. In actuality, the choice of growth scenarios is normative and politically laden. When climate economics models assume that middle-income countries' per capita incomes will catch up with those of today's high-income countries, while low-income countries will lag behind, a choice is made to underrate the least developed countries' chance to escape poverty. The consequences in terms of the resulting policy advice are stark: assumed slow growth for the poorest countries means lower projected business-as-usual emissions and, as a consequence, weaker emissions reduction goals.

But what if low-income countries grow more quickly, as China and India have? In the absence of emission reduction policies, fast economic development eclipses income-driven reductions to emissions intensity (where emissions per dollar shrink solely as a result of factors associated with increasing prosperity, and not policy initiatives). The result is higher business-as-usual emissions in the future that require more ambitious global emissions reductions policies today.

This chapter begins by briefly reviewing current practices in modeling income growth in integrated assessment models of climate and economy, demonstrating that these models assume rates of growth in low-income countries that are not consistent with goals for economic development (a more detailed description of common modeling assumptions is provided in the Appendix). The chapter then provides an empirical illustration of the impact that more optimistic economic development expectations would have on emissions mitigation targets. Next, I discuss the kinds of policies necessary to adequately reduce emissions per dollar of economic output in a scenario of robust economic development for the poorest countries. A final section brings together recommendations to integrated assessment modelers based on these findings.

A Review of Current Practices

Integrated assessment models combine climate and economy projections to arrive at recommendations of the optimal pace of greenhouse gas emissions reductions.[1] In these types of analyses, future emissions are typically modeled as the product of projected gross domestic product (GDP) and emission intensities per dollar of GDP. The pace of economic development can be assessed by comparing the growth rates of GDP per capita – a function of both GDP growth and population growth – among regions within a given model, and in relation to historical trends.

One of the most influential forecasts of future economic growth is published by the International Energy Agency (IEA) in its annual World Energy Outlook (WEO) (International Energy Agency 2010b). Many models of energy, climate and economy follow these IEA projections, among them the McKinsey and Company (2009) marginal abatement pathways[2] and the IEA's own Energy Technology Perspectives (International Energy Agency 2010a) and BLUE Map scenario. GDP and population forecasts are described in detail in the Appendix.

In this chapter, countries are divided into four groups based on their 2005 PPP[3] per capita income, as follows:[4]

- High-income group: 55 countries with 18 percent of the 2005 global population; PPP incomes in 2005 range from $68,500 in Luxembourg to $12,300 in Mexico
- High-middle-income group: 53 countries, including China, with 38 percent of population; incomes range from $12,200 in Chile to $4,000 in Syria
- Low-middle-income group: 23 countries, including India, with 29 percent of population; incomes range from $3,900 in Paraguay to $2,100 in Pakistan
- Low-income group: 45 countries with 15 percent of population; incomes range from $1,900 in Uzbekistan to $202 in the Republic of the Congo

Thirty-four of the low-income countries are in Sub-Saharan Africa, representing 66 percent of the group's population in 2005 and 84 percent in 2105. One country, the Sudan, is in North Africa. Another nine low-income countries are in Asia and the Pacific, including Bangladesh, which by itself accounts for 16 percent of the low-income countries' current population. The final country in this group is Haiti, by far the poorest country in the Americas; the most recent World Bank data indicates that Haiti's per capita income – $1,016 in 2005 – shrank to $996 in 2010, no doubt in part due to the tragic and ongoing aftermath of its 2010 earthquake.[5]

In the model used for this chapter, GDP per capita is projected by decade from 2005 to 2105 as the ratio of real GDP and population, where population follows the medium variant of the United Nations Department of Economic and Social Affairs' (UNDESA's) 2010 revision (see Appendix). For the period from 2005 to 2035, real GDPs (in PPP terms) are the WEO 2010 projections. After that point, countries have continued GDP growth at their 2020–35 WEO 2010 rate until their per capita output exceeds $20,000. Countries with per capita output between $20,000 and $35,000 are assigned a 2.0 percent rate (in the WEO projections, the only country with GDP per capita greater than $20,000 that exceeds this rate of growth is Canada). Once a country reaches real GDP per capita of $35,000 it is assigned a 1.5 percent long-term real

GDP growth rate, chosen as a rough average of the WEO's projected rates for high-income countries. The GDP per capita projections generated from these assumptions are referred to throughout this chapter as the "standard" or WEO 2010 extended projections.

As Table 3.1 demonstrates, these standard WEO-based GDP projections are at the high end of the ranges used in the Energy Modeling Forum's (EMF) 2009 comparison of twelve climate economics models[6] and the Potsdam Institute for Climate Impact Research's (PIK) 2010 five model comparison,[7] and closer to the middle of the range used in the IPCC's Special Report on Emissions Scenarios (SRES).[8] Both the EMF and PIK model comparisons project lower world GDP per capita. In many of the EMF models with high GDP growth this difference is due, in part, to high population projections for China and India. SRES projections are designed to represent a diversity of possible socioeconomic futures and therefore include a larger range of per capita incomes.

WEO 2010 extended GDP per capita projections show limited convergence over time, leaving a big gap between incomes in the richest and poorest countries (see Table 3.1). When disaggregated projections are applied to individual countries (see Appendix), the ratio of per capita income in high-income countries to that in low-income countries shrinks from 27–1 today down to 20–1 in 2105 (see Figure 3.1). Average per capita income in high-income countries grows four times larger; in high-middle-income countries, 14 times larger; and in low-middle-income countries, 21 times larger – but economic development in low-income countries lags behind. Average per capita income in the poorest countries grows just six-fold, from $1,100 in 2005 to $6,500 in 2105.

The 45 countries with the lowest average incomes (the low-income group) are expected to have much more rapid population growth than the rest of the world and to have real per capita GDP growth rates that average 1.6 percent per year over the century (compared to 2.7 percent for high-middle-income countries and 3.1 percent for low-middle-income countries). According to UNDESA's medium-variant population projections, these 45 countries will contribute 73 percent of global population increase during the 21st century, growing from 0.9 billion people to 3.5 billion people.

The result of combined standard real GDP growth and population growth is per capita income that rises slowly in today's low-income countries, and much more quickly in middle-income countries. Generalizing across the climate economics models reviewed here, emissions forecasts assume that at the end of this century the 45 low-income countries as a group will have real average per capita incomes of $6,500 a year – matching those of Tunisia, Belize or Serbia in 2005. The bottom end of national average incomes in this

Table 3.1. Socioeconomic growth in climate-economic models

Model	2100–2105 Real GDP		2100–2105 Population (billions)	2100–2105 Real GDP per capita	
	(trillions 2005 US$ PPP)	Average Annual Growth		(2005 US$ PPP)	Average Annual Growth
Extended WEO 2010					
World	$537	2.3%	9.8	$54,000	1.8%
China	$101	3.0%	0.9	$106,000	3.3%
India	$102	3.8%	1.6	$65,000	3.4%
United States	$65	1.7%	0.5	$139,000	1.2%
European Union	$63	1.6%	0.5	$128,000	1.6%
OECD	$176	1.6%	1.4	$124,000	1.4%
Non-OECD	$362	2.9%	8.4	$43,000	1.8%
EMF 12-Model Comparison					
World	$258–$528	1.8–2.5%	8.7–10.6	$22,000–$46,000	1.3–2.1%
China	$27–$115	2.8–4.0%	1.1–1.7	$15,000–$76,000	1.2–4.3%
India	$18–$63	3.1–4.4%	1.5–2.6	$14,000–$29,000	2.6–3.5%
United States	$40–$99	1.2–2.0%	0.3–0.5	$96,000–$150,000	1.0–1.5%
European Union	$40–$67	1.2–1.4%	0.4–0.6	$68,000–$127,000	1.2–1.6%
PIK 5-Model Comparison					
World	$236–$446	1.8–2.5%	9.2	$21,000–$39,000	1.4–2.1%
IPCC SRES Emissions Scenarios					
World	$350–$820	2.1–3.1%	7.0–15.1	$24,000–$116,000	1.4–2.9%
OECD	$84–$185	1.0–1.8%	0 9–1.5	$87,000–$167,000	1.0–1.6%
Non-OECD	$231–$634	2.1–3.1%	5.9–13.6	$17,000–$107,000	2.2–4.2%

Figure 3.1. Real GDP per capita by income group in 2005 and 2105

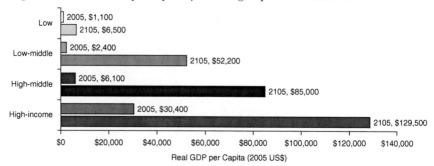

Table 3.2. Scenario assumptions

Scenario	Scenario Type	Economic Growth	Emission Intensity Reductions
Without Development	Business-as-usual	Standard	Slow
Development with Carbon	Business-as-usual	High	Slow
Development without Carbon	Policy	High	Fast

low-income group ranges as low as $1,100 a year – matching those of Zambia, Bangladesh and Haiti today. In these forecasts, middle-income countries' 2105 per capita income surpasses high-income countries' 2005 levels, and the development gap between middle- and high-income countries is greatly reduced. But the 45 poorest countries – 15 percent of 2005 global population rising to 35 percent in 2105 – are left behind.

Modeling Income Convergence

The integrated assessment models reviewed here tend to presuppose a slow pace of economic growth in most developing countries. This section presents a simple, scenario-driven modeling exercise for the purpose of illustrating the impact of very slow development assumptions on the policy recommendations derived from climate economics analysis. End of the century per capita GDP and cumulative twenty-first century greenhouse gas emissions are estimated for three stylized futures (see Table 3.2):

- Without Development: This business-as-usual scenario models standard economic growth with slow reductions in emissions per dollar of GDP; there are no policy-driven emission reductions

- Development with Carbon: Faster economic growth brings all countries out of poverty, again with no policy-driven emissions reductions. This scenario represents an alternate vision of business-as-usual
- Development without Carbon: Fast economic growth is coupled with strong decarbonization policies in developing and developed countries alike

Standard economic growth refers to the extended WEO 2010 projections described above. In high economic growth scenarios the following changes are made to the standard growth assumptions: all GDP per capita growth rates in all periods are set to 5.0 percent per year in countries with incomes below $20,000, 3.0 percent per year in countries with incomes between $20,000 and $35,000 and to 1.5 percent in countries with incomes above $35,000. (Using standard growth, GDP grows at 1.5 percent in countries with average incomes above $35,000; using high growth, GDP per capita grows at 1.5 percent for average incomes over $35,000.) Slow and fast emissions intensity reductions are described in the next section.

Modeling changes in emissions intensity

Projections of future annual greenhouse gas emissions are based not only on assumptions regarding real GDP growth, but also on expected changes in emissions intensity (or emissions per dollar of GDP). In 2005, emissions intensities ranged from 23 kg CO_2-e per dollar (kg/$) in the Central African Republic and the Republic of the Congo (both dominated by non-CO_2 emissions) to 0.2 kg/$ in Switzerland and Norway.[9] In very general terms – and with many important exceptions – higher per capita income is associated with lower emissions intensity and vice versa. On average, high-income countries' emission intensity in 2005 was 0.5 kg/$; middle-income countries, 1.2 kg/$; and low-income countries, 2.1 kg/$.

Emissions intensities are not expected to stay steady over time. Instead, emissions per dollar tend to fall as technology improves and incomes rise (making relatively expensive low-carbon technology more affordable). From 1980 to 2005, emissions intensities fell with rising income in 44 out of the 53 high-income countries and in all but six OECD countries.[10] Overall, during this period emissions intensities fell as income rose in 108 out of the 174 countries modeled for the historical period, representing 86 percent of today's global GDP and 77 percent of today's greenhouse gas emissions.

The assumption that emissions intensities will decrease over time is well entrenched in climate economics modeling; the mechanisms and causes of that reduction much less so (a topic revisited below). According to the IPCC's Special Report on Renewable Energy Sources and Climate Change

Mitigation, "economic growth can largely be decoupled from energy use by steady declines in energy intensity as structural change and efficiency improvements trigger the 'dematerialization' of economic activity" (Sathaye et al. 2011). Sathaye et al. caution, however, that successful reduction of emissions intensity in rich countries has been due in part to the outsourcing of energy intensive industries to poorer countries.

The final impact on emissions themselves is, however, ambiguous. Higher incomes both raise GDP and lower emissions intensity, so the impact on emissions, the product of GDP and emission intensity, is uncertain. The former linkage – higher incomes raise emissions – is often referred to as the scale effect, while the latter – higher incomes lower emissions – represents the combination of two linkages, both of which work to reduce emissions intensities: the technique effect caused by technological improvement; and the composition effect caused by changes to the sectoral composition of the economy (Tsurumi and Managi 2010). In principle, it is possible for either the scale effect or the technique-composition effects to dominate.

Emissions for future years are projected here using either of two methods: slow or fast. In both methods, emissions are modeled as the product of real national GDP (PPP) and national emissions intensity (CO_2-e emissions per dollar of GDP) for each country in the data set. Base year 2005 emissions are total greenhouse gases, including non-CO_2 gases, from the World Resources Institute's Climate Analysis Indicators Tool.[11]

The "slow" reduction in emissions intensity assumes that from 2045 onward, each country's emissions intensity is the smaller of its 2005 intensity, or the projection from a cross-section analysis of emissions intensity versus income. A linear transition is assumed from 2005 to 2045 intensity levels. From 2045 forward slow emissions intensity reductions are projected as follows:

$$\ln Intensity_k = a + (b * \ln Income_k)$$

where k is the country, and a and b are the intercept and coefficient, respectively, of a log-log regression of 2005 national GDP per capita on 2005 national emissions intensity: a is 2.77 and b is 0.34. Both a and b are statistically significant at the 99 percent confidence level; the regression has an adjusted r-squared value of 0.31. Empirically, there is a clear relationship between countries' 2005 per capita income and emissions intensity: on average, a 1 percent increase in per capita income is correlated with a 0.34 percent drop in its emissions intensity.

Assuming that this cross-section relationship applies over time, this can be viewed as a pattern for potential future autonomous reductions to emissions intensity, which occur solely as a result of economic growth. That pattern is referred to here as the "income-driven" intensity reduction pattern. Income-driven reductions can be contrasted to policy reductions, which occur as a result of deliberate policy actions. (Note that this may be a conservative assumption with regard to emissions projections. If emissions intensity is less sensitive to incomes than predicted, or if in some countries, it follows an inverted U-shaped path – at first increasing with economic development but eventually decreasing after a threshold per capita income is reached[12] – cumulative emissions will be higher.)

"Fast" emissions intensity reductions are projected in an identical manner, save for one change: the parameter b is modeled at 0.68, doubling the "slow" reduction pace of income-driven intensity reduction. Multiples of parameter b higher than 2 do little to further reduce the emissions intensity – in effect, an elasticity of emissions intensity with respect to income of 0.68 brings national emissions intensities very close to their minimum values (in accordance with the statistical relationship presented above) and, indeed, close to zero. Here, no argument is made about the likelihood of this rapid pace of emissions reductions (although some countries have met or exceeded it in the recent past – see more explanation of this below); the "fast" pattern of reductions is presented rather as an illustration of the speed at which intensities must fall to achieve the twenty-first century budget for avoiding dangerous climate change.

As a simple model of an ambitious climate policy, this "fast reduction" relationship represents a global standard in which countries must by a given date conform to a schedule of allowable emissions intensity per dollar of per capita income. (Before that date, this model assumes that countries are, with perfect foresight, reducing emissions linearly to achieve a target emissions intensity set according to their future per capita income.) A policy target date set far into the future allows countries with emissions intensities higher than the accepted pattern a long period during which their emissions per dollar, although dropping, are higher the most other countries. In policy circles, this effect is often referred to as "grandfathering," when regulations include allowances for future emissions based on each agent's past emissions.

The further into the future the policy target date is set, the less equitable – from the point of view of countries with low historical emissions – the distribution of future emissions. Four policy target dates were modeled: 2045, 2065, 2085 and 2105. Of course, under both the slow and fast emissions intensity reductions, the later the policy target date, the higher the cumulative emissions. Scenarios' success in reducing emissions may be judged against Bowen and Ranger's (2009) estimated budget for keeping global average temperature increases below 2°C: 2,000Gt CO_2-e emitted cumulatively during the 21st century, including both CO_2 and other non-CO_2 greenhouse gases.[13]

Table 3.3. Scenario results with 2045 policy target date

	2105 GDP per capita (PPP 2005 US$)		Cumulative 21st Century Emissions (Gt CO$_2$-e)		
	Without Development	Development with and without Carbon	Without Development	Development with Carbon	Development without Carbon
High-Income	$128,500	$158,600	3,350	3,840	590
High-Middle-Income	$85,000	$92,200	4,150	4,700	870
Low-Middle-Income	$52,200	$71,700	2,940	3,820	370
Low-Income	$6,500	$55,300	720	2,900	220
World	$54,400	$83,000	11,150	15,270	2,060
Mitigation Target			9,150	13,270	60

Findings

The Without Development emissions projections (see Table 3.3, which assumes a 2045 policy target date throughout) are slightly above the high end of the range used in climate economics models' business-as-usual scenarios (indicating that these models, which have similar income per capita projections, employ even more optimistic assumptions of income-driven reductions to emissions intensity). In this scenario, twenty-first century cumulative emissions reach 11,150 Gt CO$_2$-e, with low-income countries contributing just 6 percent of the total. Twenty-first century cumulative emissions range from 4,700 to 9,100 Gt CO$_2$-e in the EMF and PIK model comparisons, and SRES emissions scenarios.[14]

In the Development with Carbon and Development without Carbon scenarios incomes converge. With faster economic growth per capita incomes reach $158,600 per year in high-income countries, $92,200 in high-middle-income countries, $71,700 in low-middle-income countries and $55,300 in low-income countries in 2105. The end of the century ratio of high-income to high-middle-income countries per capita income is 1.7:1; and for high- to low-middle-income countries, 2.2:1. The ratio of high to low-income countries is 2.9:1 with faster economic growth, compared to 20:1 with standard growth.

With the 2045 policy target date, in the Development with Carbon scenario, twenty-first century cumulative emissions reach 15,270 Gt CO_2-e, 19 percent of which originates in the poorest countries. In this scenario, low-income countries emit a cumulative 2,900 Gt in the 21st century, exceeding the entire global 2,000 Gt budget for avoiding dangerous climate change. In the Development without Carbon scenario, economic growth remains high in the poorest countries, but policy measures supplement income-driven emissions intensity reductions, outrunning economic growth. Cumulative twenty-first century emissions are limited to 2,060 Gt CO_2-e, including 220 Gt emitted by the low-income group.

The importance of the policy target date (and, therefore, the degree of grandfathering of past emissions intensities) to cumulative twenty-first century emissions is displayed in Table 3.4. In the Development without Carbon scenario, with its fast pace of emissions intensity reductions, only the 2045 policy target date succeeds in keeping emissions close to the 2,000 Gt budget for keeping temperatures below 2°C.

Table 3.4. Cumulative twenty-first century emissions with varying policy target dates

	Policy Target Date			
	2045	2065	2085	2105
Development with Carbon	15,270	16,090	17,710	20,480
Development without Carbon	2,060	4,070	7,350	12,270

Table 3.5 puts the 2045 policy target date scenarios' emissions in what may be a more familiar context, reporting the results for the United States and India, in addition to the income groups, as points of reference. Per capita emissions, higher in richer countries today, would grow in every region in the Without Development scenario while still maintaining that basic pattern. The Development with Carbon scenario results in per capita emissions that are still higher in almost every country. In the Development without Carbon scenario, per capita emissions must be ratcheted down in every region to stay within the emissions budget; in per capita terms, these reductions are smallest in the case of the lowest-income countries. Under the Development with Carbon scenario, speeding up growth but keeping the pattern of income-driven emissions intensity reductions the same, results in an enormous increase to cumulative twenty-first century total emissions (shown in Table 3.3), and an increase in annual per capita emissions in every income group (shown in Table 3.5). If climate economics models are underestimating economic growth in

Table 3.5. Per capita emissions by scenario with 2045 policy target date

	Per Capita Emissions in 2005 (tons CO_2-e /person)	Per Capita Emissions in 2105 (tons CO_2-e/person)		
		Without Development	Development with Carbon	Development without Carbon
High-Income	15.0	44.3	44.3	0.8
High-Middle-Income	7.3	31.0	31.0	0.7
Low-Middle-Income	2.9	26.3	26.3	0.6
Low-Income	2.4	22.1	22.1	0.6
World	6.7	28.5	28.5	0.6
United States	22.9	49.2	49.2	0.8
India	1.7	26.4	26.4	0.6

low-income countries, expected business-as-usual cumulative emissions are too low, and emission reduction targets in richer countries will be grossly insufficient to meet policy goals. If successful, rapid development were modeled (as in the Development with Carbon scenario), the gap between business-as-usual emissions and the allowable budget (2,000 Gt) – and, consequently, the global target for emissions reductions – would be 13,270 Gt. When, instead, conventional, weak development is modeled (as in the Without Development scenario), the target for emissions reductions falls to 9,150 Gt.

Pessimistic economic development assumptions in climate economics models have the effect of lowering high income and emerging economies' goals for emissions reductions. Poor foresight leads to poor planning.

Policy Measures to Reduce Emissions Intensity

Without some policy-driven assistance, real economic development drowns out income-driven emissions intensity reductions.[15] A successful Development Without Carbon strategy requires both economic development – including policies to address energy poverty – and emissions mitigation policy. Climate policy needs to support and accelerate income-driven intensity reductions by improving countries' adherence to the income-driven pattern, offering additional support to countries with anomalously high emissions intensities, and driving the innovation of low-cost, low-carbon technologies forward in order to speed up emissions reduction.

Policy measures to improve adherence to the income-driven intensity reduction pattern include supporting emissions intensity reduction in countries at risk of exhibiting rising emissions per dollar as incomes grow. The experience of El Salvador, where per capita GDP was $4,400 in 2005, is illustrative. El Salvador's per capita GDP (PPP) grew 30 percent from 1985 to 2005, while its emissions intensity more than doubled from 0.09 kg CO_2/$ in 1985 up to 0.19 kg/$ in 2005. El Salvador's emission intensity in this period may be interpreted as being on the upswing of an inverted U-shaped path, or so-called Environmental Kuznets Curve (EKC).[16] In the EKC pattern, countries are expected to see emissions, or other forms of environmental degradation, rise and then fall as their income per capita grows.[17]

Without policy measures designed to connect energy poverty reduction and other forms of economic development with emissions reduction, there is a strong potential for low-income countries' emissions intensities to increase with rising incomes, as they did in El Salvador, among many other examples. The EKC, which is sometimes used to suggest an inevitable relationship between development and environmental quality, however, has been widely critiqued. Conflicting empirical results show that the relationship, when and where it exists, may not be robust, and some research suggests that the pattern may be caused by an induced policy response (Dasgupta et al. 2002; Munasinghe 1999; Torras and Boyce 1998).

Lindmark (2004) provides examples of both high- and low-income countries that have experienced first rising and then falling CO_2 emissions with income growth, finding that high-income countries are more likely to have a history of an inverted U-shaped, or EKC-like, emissions intensity transitions than are low-income countries. The experience of El Salvador and a number of other low- and middle-income countries suggests, however, that an inverted U-shaped emissions intensity could be a real possibility for these countries as well. In some countries, public policy measures, together with international assistance, may be necessary to make the income-driven intensity reduction pattern more robust.

Successful emissions intensity reduction policies also will need to offer additional support to countries with anomalously high emissions intensities. The autonomous, income-driven intensity reduction pattern requires countries with especially high emissions intensities to jump from their current technology to the expected technology for their income level within a few decades. Most countries in which actual intensity exceeds expected intensity are in the low- and low-middle-income groups (including many of the ex-Soviet Republics), or are major fossil fuel exporters.

The low-income countries with the highest emissions intensities are the Central African Republic (almost entirely due to methane and nitrous oxide emissions from agriculture) and Cambodia (primarily due to CO_2 emissions from deforestation).[18] Countries with higher than expected emissions intensities may need special assistance or incentives to kick-start income-driven intensity reductions. The examples of the Central African Republic and Cambodia suggest that some low-income countries may need additional technical support in reducing land-use emissions.[19]

Finally, successful global emissions abatement will require policy measures to support the innovation of low-cost, low-carbon technology, thereby enhancing the existing income-driven intensity reduction pattern. Low-cost alternative electricity generation and heating and cooking fuels are critical components of energy poverty reduction. From 1980 to 2005, twelve countries, including Mozambique, exceeded the "fast" pace of emissions reductions (a 0.68 percent drop in emissions intensity for every 1 percent decrease in income per capita) necessary to the success of the Development without Carbon scenario; 29 countries exceeded the "slow," income-driven pace of emissions reductions.

The low-income countries that have reduced intensities most, in relation to their economic growth, are Burkina Faso and Mozambique. Among middle-income countries, Colombia and Belize provide examples of a strong relationship between increasing per capita income and decreasing emissions intensity. For Mozambique and Colombia, part of this success can be attributed to significant investment in hydroelectric generation; for Burkina Faso and Belize – where land-use emissions dominate – the causes are less clear. Affordable low-carbon technology is crucial to fostering and increasing the pace of the income-driven intensity reduction pattern, and public policy has an important role to play in supporting and disseminating technological innovations.

Discussion and Recommendations

Standard projections used in climate economics models show strong economic growth in many of the middle-income countries over the next century, but much weaker growth in low-income countries. This assumption – that economic development will fail in the poorest countries – results in lower business-as-usual global emissions, allowing emissions reduction targets to be less stringent in richer countries. But what if pessimistic assumptions about economic development turn out to be wrong?

What if low-income countries experience genuine economic development? In 1985, India's real per capita income (in PPP 2005) was $1,035 – very similar to that of Haiti before the 2010 earthquake. In 20 years, India's per capita income more than doubled, reaching $2,300 in 2005.[20] Standard growth projections described above have India's per capita income exceeding $9,300 by 2035, and reaching $45,900 by 2085, the result of 3.9 percent average annual growth over the 100-year period. Contrast this to the implied twenty-first century per capita income growth expected for Haiti by climate economics models, on average just 2.0 percent per year over the 100-year period, reaching $7,200 in 2105.

Economic growth is by no means guaranteed, especially in the absence of sufficient international aid, but what if economic development for the poorest countries can and does occur? What if Haiti (and every low-income country) can match the success of India and China? In the Development with Carbon scenario modeled for this chapter, more optimistic assumptions about economic development lead to higher expected cumulative greenhouse gas emissions from low-income countries, higher global business-as-usual emissions and, therefore, a need for more stringent emissions reductions goals. Even if poverty eradication is regarded as unlikely, climate policy should be designed to allow for the best-case possibility that every Haiti could grow like India.

Chapter 4

THE TRAGEDY OF MALDISTRIBUTION: CLIMATE, SUSTAINABILITY AND EQUITY

Elizabeth A. Stanton

This essay is an initial exploration of the dimensions of the equity/sustainability linkage from the perspective of public goods analysis. Sustainability requires an abundance of public goods. Where these commons lack governance, sustainability is at risk. Equity is a critical component of sustainability that can itself be viewed as a public good, subject to deterioration (maldistribution) when left ungoverned. As is the case for so many forms of environmental degradation, the private benefits of maldistribution tend to overshadow the larger social costs, and the result is a degradation of equity. This chapter sketches out the analogy of equity as a public good by: examining the evidence regarding current and historical income equality within and between countries; introducing the characteristics of public goods and grounding equity in this idiom; reviewing several theories explaining the suboptimal provision of environmental goods; applying these theoretical frameworks to the case of equity, with an examination of the potential causes of, and solutions to, maldistribution; and, finally, addressing equity's critical role as a component of sustainability in the case of climate change, with implications for climate policy.

Introduction: Equity and Sustainability

Analysis of public goods has long dwelled within the purview of environmental economics. But the breadth of the commons extends far beyond natural resources and pollution sinks to radio frequencies, the collected works of Shakespeare and ownership of the moon (Barnes 2006). Even starting from the more narrow vantage point of environmental amenities, the language and logic of sustainable development connects environmental protection with the broader set of public goods related to the advancement of social welfare. The Brundtland Commission's (World Commission on Environment and

Development 1987) definition of sustainable development as meeting "the needs of the present without compromising the ability of future generations to meet their own needs" explicitly referenced the central role of access to and distribution of resources, noting that "physical sustainability implies a concern for social equity between generations, a concern that must logically be extended to equity within each generation."

Sustainability requires a robust commons (or an abundance of public goods). Where these commons lack governance, sustainability is at risk. Equity is a critical component of sustainability and can, itself – as I argue in this initial exploration – be viewed as a public good, subject to degradation when left ungoverned.

As is the case for so many forms of environmental degradation, the private benefits of maldistribution tend to overshadow the larger social costs, and the result is a degradation of equity. This essay explores the dimensions of the equity/sustainability linkage from the perspective of public goods analysis. The thoughts presented here are best approached as a first exploration of an interesting analogy – equity as a public good – and not as any attempt to form a completely developed theory or model.

The remaining sections of this chapter sketch out the analogy of equity as a public good. The next section examines the evidence regarding current and historical income equality within and between countries, establishing an empirical basis for maldistribution. Then, I introduce the characteristics of public goods and grounds equity in this idiom. The following section reviews several theories in environmental economics literature regarding how and why the actual quantity of an environmental good might be less than optimal, and, conversely, how an optimal quantity may be achieved. I then apply these theoretical frameworks to the case of equity, examining the potential causes of and solutions to maldistribution. Finally, the last section returns to equity's critical role as a component of sustainability in the case of climate change; this section discusses the implications of maldistribution and proffers several related policy conclusions.

Measuring Equity

Equity can be understood broadly, as a general sense of egalitarianism – the application of the same rules, rights and responsibilities to all individuals in a society – or narrowly, as strict equality of income and wealth. Maldistribution is here defined as failure to achieve potential enlargements of social welfare via a more equal distribution of income or other resources; the determination of "potential enlargements" may include both positive and normative criteria.

The existence of a wide range of collective goods and services suggests that income distribution is a necessary but insufficient metric of equity. Redistribution of income and other resources in the direction of greater equality not only has private costs and benefits to individuals – some must gain and some must lose – but also has some less obvious benefits to the society at large. Greater income equality has been associated with better environmental, health and education outcomes, lower crime rates and more robust overall social capital (Marmot 2005; Kawachi and Kennedy 1997; Boyce 1994)[1]. Together, these benefits demonstrate the public goods character of equity.

Nonetheless, the distribution of income is by far the best-measured component of equity, an indispensible first cut at the adequacy of resources. The main imperfections of this metric come in three broad categories: the nonmonetized, the indivisible and the ill-measured.

- Nonmonetized aspects of wellbeing: So much of what we value most in life defies monetization. Income captures neither our family's health nor the health of our local environments (Ackerman and Heinzerling 2004; Sen 2000).
- Indivisible household resources: The measurement of distribution is greatly complicated by fundamental ambiguity regarding the basic unit of analysis: household income is not readily divisible into individual income. In a multi-person household, individual earnings do not represent the money available for consumption, which is almost always a function of household income and power dynamics within the household (Waring 1990; Folbre 1982).
- Ill-measured income data: No data set exists recording the income of every person (or household) in the world. Indeed, such data exist for very few countries. Instead, income distribution between countries is often estimated from small samples or imputed from data on consumption, while income distribution between countries compares per capita gross domestic product (GDP) (itself, infamous for its omissions and myopic focus on the formal market) across countries (Milanovic 2005).

However imperfectly measured, income distribution is one of the most important markers in gauging the scale of global maldistribution. Global income inequality can be decomposed into two elements: between-country inequality (or differences in per capita GDP among all the nations of the world) and within-country inequality (or differences in household income among all of the households of a single nation). The former, when considered in isolation, sometimes incorporates population weights (Milanovic 2005). Both elements are commonly summarized using one or more of the following methods: the percentile ratio, for example, the ratio of the income of the top

10 percent to that of the bottom 10 percent; the Gini coefficient; or the Theil index.[2] Recent research from Branko Milanovic, a World Bank economist and the author of a large body of research on current and historical income inequality, reports that global inequality has worsened from 1988 to 2002 (the latest year for which data are broadly available). In 1988, the 10 percent of world population with the highest incomes received 51 percent of global income; in 2002, the top decile received 57 percent (Milanovic 2009). World Bank data have demonstrated that the bulk of this global inequality exists between countries and not within them. Using the Gini coefficient (which ranges from 0, perfect equality, to 100, perfect inequality), global inequality for 1998 was 64, of which 11 points derived from within-country inequality and 53 points from between-country (Milanovic 2005). Over an assortment of measures, Milanovic finds that 71 to 83 percent of global inequality is the result of differences in per capita income among countries.

Bourguignon and Morrisson's (2002) construction of global inequality measures for selected years from 1820 to 1992 shows the global Gini rising steadily (if not quite monotonically) over time. Their work also reveals the importance of changes in the regional (and national) composition of world income quantiles. In 1950, Europe and its "offshoots" (defined as "European-populated" countries in the Americas and the Pacific) accounted for 81 percent of the top income decile; by 1992, this figure had fallen to 66 percent, while Japan, Korea and Taiwan climbed from 2 to 18 percent.[3]

Within-country Gini coefficients recorded from 2000 to 2009 ranged from 16.8 in Azerbaijan in 2005 to 65.8 in Seychelles in 2007. Countries with the most equal distributions of income cluster in Scandinavia and the former Soviet Republics. The nations with the greatest divergences in income include: Angola, Brazil, Colombia, Comoros, Ecuador, Haiti, Micronesia and South Africa (World Bank 2011). Many countries in the World Bank data set have Gini coefficients for either one year, or no Gini data whatsoever; among countries with Ginis for multiple years, some have risen over time while others have fallen.[4]

The well-known Kuznets curve maps national Gini coefficients against per capita income. Kuznets identified an inverted U-shaped pattern in this relationship (equality rising and then falling with income) in the United States, United Kingdom and Germany from the late 19th century through 1950 (Kuznets 1955); he later repeated the analysis, finding a similar pattern for a larger set of countries (Kuznets 1963; Kuznets 1957). A substantial body of literature rejects the Kuznets hypothesis, finding that the relationship between inequality and growth is both more complex and more idiosyncratic (Taylor 1996; Randolph and Lott 1993; Deininger and Squire 1998).

The conclusions drawn from Kuznets' putative pattern have resulted in some troubling policy advice: policy makers need not concern themselves with a decline in equity related to income growth; further growth will bring a more equal income distribution. In development economics literature "growth first" policies emphasizing the importance of economic growth over broader investment in sustainable development are thought by some scholars to have resulted in "immiserizing growth," where increased output degrades the terms of trade, resulting in a reduction in per capita income (Bhagwati 1958, 1968).

Global income inequality between individuals, which includes both the between- and within-country components, is large in scale and growing over time. The question of whether 10 percent of global population receiving 57 percent of all income is too much inequality is, of course, a subjective one. The determination of maldistribution is qualitative and is a product, at least in part, of the observer's own place in the income distribution. This led Rawls (1971) to ground his theory of justice on an idealized "original position" in which people sit behind a "veil of ignorance" that prevents them from knowing their own situation before choosing distributive principles for society. The remaining sections of this chapter make the case that a redistribution of income towards greater equality, along with the equalization of access to other key resources, would represent an improvement in social welfare.

Equity as a Public Good

Pure public goods are defined, in economics, as goods that are nonrival and nonexcludable (Newman 1987; Samuelson 1954). An example may help to clarify: a sandwich is a private good, but a traffic light is a public good. A sandwich is rival (one person's enjoyment of the sandwich clearly impedes others' ability to enjoy that same sandwich) and excludable (it is, in principle, quite feasible for one person to exclude others from eating her sandwich). In contrast, a traffic light is nonrival (many people enjoy the benefits of the traffic light simultaneously without impeding one another's use) and nonexcludable (barring some from the traffic light's benefits while still retaining those benefits for oneself would be infeasible). Many public goods exist on the continuum between the purely private and purely public; rivalness in the use of a public park, for example, abounds, and the enclosure of a public space for private use is all too familiar.

The degradation of environmental amenities – clean air and water, the wealth of natural resources, healthy and biodiverse ecosystems – can often be taken as evidence that a good is not purely public, and that private, rival concerns compete for its use. Analysis of the privatization of publicly controlled goods has a long tradition in political economy and natural philosophy. Thomas More's *Utopia* (1909 [1516]) documents the enclosure (or privatization) of English common land for sheep farming. More described the destitution caused by losing access to the commons, writing that rich farmers' "sheep [...] devour men and unpeople, not only villages, but towns." By the 18th century, the British parliament had adopted legislation enforcing this privatization. Marx (1967 [1867]) wrote of the "expropriation of the agricultural population from the land," and the coincidence of the creation of this landless class with industrialists' need for wage laborers.

Hardin (1968) viewed the destruction of environmental "public" goods as inevitable for any finite resource. His well-known "tragedy of the commons" – the argument that in utilizing a common good one reaps the full benefits of one's actions, but only suffers a fraction ($1/x$, where x is the number of people sharing the commons) of the costs of resource depletion, and that, by ignoring costs felt by others, each individual's net incentive will lead to a destruction of the commons – is a treatise on the need to protect public goods through privatization and state control. (It should be noted that the central focus of Hardin's argument is not resource use but population growth. Hardin associates commonly owned property with overuse by arguing that environmental resources are finite but that the potential population, while not infinite, reaches a maximum at a level that would dictate great deprivation in terms of per capita resource use. A commons therefore, he writes, is "too horrifying to contemplate" and "Injustice is preferable to total ruin." Hardin's solution to the perceived problem of over-population was "mutually agreed coercion.") Ostrom et al. (1999) recast Hardin's tragedy as the fate not of all commons, but instead of a particular class of "open-access" commons: "When valuable [public goods] are left to an open-access regime, degradation and potential destruction are the result." Ostrom and her coauthors emphasize the importance of distinguishing between ungoverned, open-access commons, and commons that are governed by a set of effective rules. Governance rules define rights and duties with regard to the public good, and prevent both overuse and insufficient contribution to resource maintenance. Open-access commons are nonexcludable but rival and, as such, are indeed tragically vulnerable to depletion.

Boyce (2002) points out that in the power to cause a tragedy of the commons, "some are more equal than others [...] Everyone may have the same right to pollute the air and water, but not everyone has equal means to do so." One's ability to pollute or to extract natural resources is mediated by one's power, broadly defined to include income (or purchasing power), political power and status. With open-access public goods at least two types of tragedies are possible: overuse, and consequent degradation, by coequal users of the commons, and the appropriation of the commons by more powerful users, transforming it into a private resource. In both cases, the public good is eradicated. Where Hardin saw private property rights as a bulwark between the indefensible commons and its own demise, Boyce and coauthors offer the democratization or communal appropriation of open-access commons as a solution – "establishing the rights of the poor to environmental sinks and raw materials that previously were treated as open-access resources" (Boyce 2003; Boyce et al. 2007).

Like so many of the environmental amenities that underpin sustainability, equity may be viewed as a public good with important social benefits (Thurow 1971). Equity is an attribute of a group as a whole – any attempt to define it for an individual divests the term of its meaning. Equity is nonrival (many people enjoy the benefits of equity simultaneously without impeding one another's use) and nonexcludable (it would be infeasible to bar some from the benefits of equity while retaining those benefits for oneself). In light of the preceding review, it seems apparent that equity, as a public good, lacks governance – that is, it shares an important characteristic with open-access commons: private interests can reduce the degree of equity.

While the equity commons cannot be privatized or overused to the point of destruction, per se, it is nonetheless subject to its own particular vulnerability: a tragedy of maldistribution. In this tragedy, one can only increase one's income or other private benefits at the expense of others. And, indeed, in macroeconomic literature there seems to be little or no positive relationship between growth and inequality (Banerjee and Duflo 2003; Barro 2000), and a good case has been made in numerous studies for a strong negative relationship (Persson and Tabellini 1994; Alesina and Rodrik 1994; Woo 2009; Voitchovsky 2009).

Abstracting, for simplicity's sake, from the effects of progressive taxation, the full benefits of a higher-than-average income accrue to individuals who suffer only a fraction ($1/x$, where x is the number of people in the society) of the social costs of maldistribution (higher crime rates, less social cohesion, etc.). By ignoring costs felt by others, each individual's net incentive drives society towards a depletion of equity.

Suboptimal Levels of Environmental Public Goods

One of the best-known economic analyses of natural resource degradation is the Environmental Kuznets Curve (EKC), which has its origins in the Kuznets hypothesis regarding inequality and per capita income discussed above. EKC literature looks for, and sometimes finds, an inverted U-shaped relationship between various forms of environmental degradation and per capita income levels, such that pollution levels first rise and then fall with economic growth (Grossman and Krueger 1995, 2008; Stern 2004; Dasgupta et al. 2002).

Evidence for the EKC is mixed, often depending on the choice of pollutant, selection of countries and years and the range of incomes considered.

The literature critiquing the EKC focuses on the same sort of unfortunate policy implications that are taken from Kuznets' inverted-U shape between inequality and per capita income. The existence of this pattern is not evidence of its inevitability (Munasinghe 1999); the eventual reduction in environmental degradation at a given income threshold is better explained as an induced policy response (Grossman and Krueger 1995). Like the Kuznets' curve, the EKC has led to what Torras and Boyce term as an "incautious policy inference," noting that "distribution concerns were subordinated to growth by proponents of "trickle-down" economic development, so environmental concerns may be downplayed as a transitional phenomenon that growth will resolve in due course" (Torras and Boyce 1998).

EKC analysis builds on a much larger body of literature examining the socioeconomic factors affecting environmental quality. A review of environmental economics literature reveals three main causes for environmental degradation, where the actual quantity of environmental public goods is lower than the optimal quantity: social costs that are external to market transactions; a narrow, and perhaps biased, focus on monetary costs and benefits; and an invisible fist – power relationships that dominate social welfare decisions.

Externalities

In environmental economic theory, optimal quantity of an environmental public good is determined by the intersection of the marginal benefit and marginal cost of that good:

$$(4.1) \qquad \frac{dB_t}{dQ} = \frac{dC_t}{dQ}$$

where B_t is the total benefit, C_t is total cost, and Q is the quantity of the environmental good. These marginal benefits and costs include both private benefits and costs, received and spent by consenting agents in a market transaction, and external, or social, benefits and costs. The latter class is often referred to as externalities: impacts of a market transaction on parties not participating in that transaction.

Air pollution is a classic example. The purchase of gasoline (a market transaction between the car driver and the petroleum company) has both private benefits and costs, determining the price of gasoline and quantity sold in the marketplace, and negative externalities. Carbon dioxide emissions, particulates and other pollutants affect public health in communities where the gasoline is refined and where the car is driven, as well as increasing the atmospheric concentration of greenhouse gases, with far-reaching consequences for global temperatures and weather patterns. These costs are external to the market for gasoline; while their impacts are felt, no one need pay for having caused this damage. The optimal level of gasoline use is determined by the intersection of its marginal total benefits and marginal total costs, but the actual level is set by marginal private benefits (dB_p/dQ) and costs (dC_p/dQ):

$$(4.2) \qquad \frac{dB_p}{dQ} = \frac{dC_p}{dQ}$$

When marginal total costs exceed marginal private costs $(dC_t/dQ > dC_p/dQ)$, a negative externality exists.

The puzzle of externalities – damages no one need pay for – has long been understood in terms of an absence of governance. Coase (1960) explained that where property rights were incomplete – as is the case with many public goods including the atmosphere – costs could be imposed without recourse. Boyce (2002) extends this analysis, suggesting that the "winners" from environmental degradation are able to impose costs on the "losers" because the losers may belong to future generations, may be unaware of their losses or may lack the power necessary to impede the winners' actions. When total costs are greater than private costs the result is too little of an environmental good or too much of an environmental bad.

In applied environmental economics, the cure for a negative externality is to internalize it by placing a price on environmental degradation. Pigou (1952 [1920]) first identified "divergences between marginal social net product and marginal private net product" and suggested a remedy known as the Pigovian tax or "polluter pays principle": simply put, the polluter is made to pay the value of the environmental damage caused. This raises private costs to equal total social costs, such that – given the right price – the market clears at the optimal level. The so-called Coase Theorem (Coase 1960) states that as long as property rights are well-defined (*i.e.*, no open-access or governance problems) and transaction costs are very low, bargaining among the parties causing and affected by the externality will lead to an optimal allocation of the environmental good. (Coase's (1991) point was that transaction costs – lawyers, information, negotiation, contracting and enforcement – are often prohibitively high, impeding an optimal outcome.) Difficulties arise when, as with so many environmental public goods, property rights are incomplete and transaction costs are high for some affected parties. Coase's analysis suggests two complementary solutions to suboptimal levels of environmental goods: clarifying ownership and control of the goods (either by Hardin's privatization or by Boyce's democratization, as discussed in the previous section) and reducing transaction costs (a topic for which extensive literature exists in development and environmental economics).

Cost–benefit analysis

A second cause of a suboptimal level of environmental public goods is the conflation of utility with income. In modern theoretical welfare economics, individual utility cannot be summed to arrive at a measure of social welfare because it had been deemed impossible to compare the utility experienced by different individuals. The aim of maximizing social welfare was replaced by Pareto improvement – making one person better off without making anyone else worse off – in the first half of the twentieth century. (This avoids a politically controversial conclusion: transferring income from the rich to the poor improves social welfare. The history of thought of these ideas is discussed in Stanton (2011c).) Modern applied welfare economics, however, takes a different point of view. Cost–benefit analysis sums up not utility but income to arrive at social welfare, neatly sidestepping diminishing marginal utility and welfare improvement from redistribution. The "compensation test," introduced by Kaldor (1939) and Hicks (1940), connects cost–benefit analysis to Pareto optimality by introducing the concept of a "potential Pareto improvement," which occurs when the beneficiaries of an action could in principle compensate those harmed and still be better off. They need not actually compensate anyone; merely the potential for such compensation is sufficient to declare the underlying action a benefit to society.[5]

While the compensation test may leave noneconomists scratching their heads (by this criteria, anything that increases GDP is a social good!), it is nonetheless a basic tenet in the cost–benefit analysis that has become the litmus test for so much public policy (Sen 2000).[6] The "optimal" quantity of an environmental good is determined by the intersection of its marginal benefit and marginal cost (as in Equation 4.2 above), but the benefits of that good are strictly defined in terms of their effect on income. With the interesting exception of a class of optimization models used in climate analysis – discussed below – applied economic analysis proceeds as if utility were purely a function of income $(u(y))$ and were neither concave nor convex $(u''(y) = 0)$.

Of course, in broader literature, environmental amenities are widely understood to have nonmonetary benefits and costs (Arrow et al. 1993). But the tightly circumscribed set of values considered in cost–benefit analysis excludes goods that are not easily valued in money terms and means that optimal quantities of environmental goods do not correspond with actual quantities (Ackerman and Heinzerling 2004). In analysis of regulations with environmental impacts these omissions often follow a particular pattern: costs are documented completely and accurately, based on engineering models and actual market values, but the benefits of environmental regulation are incomplete, poorly documented and under-valued. Environmental benefits include lower cancer risks, more abundant wildlife and the knowledge that a particular ecosystem or natural setting will survive for posterity. Too often the solution to including such priceless amenities in a dollars-and-cents cost–benefit analysis is to acknowledge their importance in an aside without assigning them prices – or, effectively, assigning these amenities a price of zero (Ackerman and Stanton 2010b, 2011b). This imbalance results in a bias against strong environmental regulations.

Solutions to the deficiencies of cost–benefit analysis include decision making based on multi-criteria and cost-effectiveness analyses. Multi-criteria analysis combines parallel quantitative assessments using multiple metrics – money, disability-adjusted life years, indices of biodiversity or ecosystem health – with a final qualitative policy decision (Scrieciu 2011; Stirling 2006; Janssen 2001). Cost-effectiveness analysis begins with a threshold taken from a science- or value-based policy decision – this much pollution and no more – and recommends the most economically efficient means of staying below that threshold (Ackerman and Heinzerling 2004).

Power-weighted decision rule

Boyce's (2002, 1994) political economy analysis of environmental issues includes the introduction of the "power-weighted decision rule," in which the total impacts of a market activity or environmental regulation are divided up not by separating benefits from costs (the customary division used in analysis of externalities) but instead by separating net winners from net losers. While there may be multiple categories of benefits and costs from a given action, each individual will experience either a negative, zero or positive net balance of impacts. The optimal quantity of an environmental good is determined by the intersection of net winners' positive marginal net impacts and net losers' negative marginal net impacts.

Unlike the cost–benefit approach, which identifies optimal outcomes in a normative framework, Boyce's model is descriptive, and seeks to explain actual, but suboptimal, outcomes. Boyce's model is similar to a model of political negotiation elaborated by Bueno de Mesquita (2002) in which each actor has an effective "vote" for each potential outcome that is equal to the product of the utility the actor would derive from that outcome, the actor's power and the salience of the issue to the actor. Using this new conceptualization of Pigou's classic externality analysis, Boyce explains divergences from the optimal result as the effect of power weights in the objective function for the social decision rule (Equation 4.3 is a variant of Boyce's objective function in which net benefits, in monetary units, have been replaced by utility):

$$(4.3) \qquad\qquad Z = \sum_i \left[\pi_i * u_i(y, z) \right]$$

where Z is the decision rule such that the policy is adopted if and only if $Z > 0$, π is relative power, and z is a vector of other factors. Each person's contribution to the objective function is weighted by her relative power in society (broadly defined to include purchasing as well as political and social power). When net winners from environmental degradation are more powerful than net losers, the degree of degradation will be higher than optimal (and the quantity of the public good will be lower than optimal); when net losers are more powerful, the degree of degradation will be lower than optimal.

While the latter circumstance is possible (Boyce gives the example of urban "beautification" displacing slum dwellers), there are compelling reasons to expect benefits from environmental degradation to be positively correlated with income and other forms of power. Richer, more powerful people both consume more and control more productive assets, affording them disproportionately large incentives and ability to cause environmental degradation (Torras and Boyce 1998; Boyce 1994).

If public policy is determined by a power-weighted decision rule, then solutions to suboptimal quantities of environmental public goods include the redistribution of income and other determinants of power. The more equal the distribution of power between the net winners and net losers, the more closely actual levels of environmental goods will resemble optimal levels.

Strengthening the Equity Commons: Obstacles and Strategies

The same explanations for suboptimal levels of environmental public goods can also be applied to maldistribution, or the degradation of the equity commons. The problem of defining an "optimal" level of equity, absent some political analog to the veil of ignorance, is an important concern for a more complete treatment of the practical considerations of basing public policy objectives on equity measurements. In the analogy presented here, however, an "optimal" level of equity can be given a similar treatment to an "optimal" level of environmental quality: debate regarding how to identify an optimum need not impede a general discussion of obstacles to and strategies for moving closer to that optimum.

Redistribution of income in the direction of greater inequality has private benefits and costs – some people grow richer while others grow poorer. But the total marginal benefits and costs that determine the presumed "optimal" level of equity comprise both private and social costs. The negative externalities associated with an erosion of equity include worsening health outcomes, higher crime rates and a decline in social cohesion. Total marginal costs exceed private marginal costs and, as a result, the actual level of equity is lower than the optimal level.

Cost–benefit analyses of public policies with equity implications consider only the aggregate effects of distributive changes. For a single period, the results of a cost–benefit analysis are neutral to changes in the income distribution: the sum of income does not vary with its distribution. Often, the social impacts of maldistribution do not have monetary values and therefore would not be included in a standard cost–benefit analysis. Because of these limitations, such an analysis would never recommend against a public policy on equity grounds.

The power-weighted decision rule takes a different path to the same conclusion (regarding what will happen, as opposed to what should happen); it acknowledges the presence of winners and losers and assumes that power dynamics determine public policy decisions and the outcome of market activities. The winners from maldistribution are richer and more powerful than the losers, and the result is a lower than optimal level of equity.

As a public good, equity is vulnerable to a similar set of deprivations as many environmental amenities. Taken together, suboptimal levels of equity may be caused by any and all of the following: social benefits (better health outcomes and greater social cohesion) that are external to market transactions; benefits that are priceless (longer and better quality of life, and more robust natural ecosystems) and therefore difficult to assign a monetary value to; and structures of decision making that weight winners' net benefits and losers' net costs from greater equity with the relative power of those winners and losers, together with an unequal distribution of power in favor of the winners. While the tragedy of maldistribution may be taken to imply the inevitability of suboptimal equity, there are – just as with solutions for the degradation of environmental public goods – strategies to protect and enhance the equity commons.

Drawing from the solutions for raising levels of environmental goods towards the optimum, discussed in the previous section, strategies for fortifying and increasing equity may include clarifying property rights, reducing transaction costs, multi-criteria analysis, cost-effectiveness analysis, redistribution of income or wealth and redistribution of political and social power.

Clarifying property rights

Equity is "owned" collectively, and its social benefits accrue to all. But, just as is the case with many environmental public goods, the lack of a well-articulated, well-respected set of governance rules leaves the rights and responsibilities associated with maintaining an egalitarian society undefined, and leaves the equity commons open to predation (Arrow et al. 2000). Public recognition of equity as a critical component of social welfare and key element in sustainable development would improve governance and make the benefits that derive from equity more explicit.

Reducing transaction costs

The costs of assuring a "fair" market outcome can be high. In making the point that positive transaction costs, and in particular legal costs and access to the legislature, are important considerations in any market analysis, Coase (1991) notes that, "the rights which individuals possess, with their duties and privileges, will be, to a large extent what the law determines. As a result the legal system will have a profound effect on the working of the economic system and may in certain respects be said to control it." Legal defense of the equity commons – and, similarly, the quality of its political representation – is highly circumstantial (Friedman 2003), and each individual's or community's access is, regrettably, a function of income.

Multi-criteria analysis

In describing the rationale behind its use of multi-criteria analysis in climate modeling, a United Nations Environment Programmed (UNEP) analysis states that, in contrast to cost–benefit analysis, the multi-criteria method "does not impose limits on the forms of criteria or pre-ordain objectives, allowing for consideration of social objectives and other forms of equity rather than focusing only on efficiency" (Scrieciu 2011). Where cost–benefit analysis can only see value that is easily expressed in monetary terms, multi-criteria analysis has the potential to measure the broader spectrum of values generated by improved equity, including nonmonetary and collective benefits.

Cost-effectiveness analysis

The determination of the most cost-effective approach to a public policy decision related to the equity commons would call for the declaration of a threshold for maldistribution together with analysis identifying the most efficient way to avoid passing that threshold (Beckman 2004). Criteria establishing an appropriate level of equity would require a normative standard and are therefore underexplored in social science literature, but there exist numerous criteria setting thresholds for low incomes; a poverty line can be based on positive standards, such as the cost of a subsistence-level basket of market goods (Coudouel et al. 2002). Cost-effectiveness analysis' efficacy in contributing to a more robust equity commons would depend strongly on the chosen income threshold.

Redistribution of income and wealth

Given the definition of equity chosen for this analysis, income redistribution's impact on social welfare is axiomatic. Arrow (2002) emphasizes government's critical role in reducing inequality, noting the special case of "fugitive" resources – public goods that resist Hardin's protection by privatization – for which "government intervention may be practically unavoidable." As a purely collective public good, equity resists privatization, but, like other fugitive resources, this quality does not protect it from degradation. Government redistribution of income and wealth can take the form of a progressive system of taxation or of the socialization of private assets concentrated in the hands of the most wealthy.

Redistribution of political and social power

A shift in the balance of power – redistribution of political and social power – is central to each of the preceding proposed solutions; each solution corresponds to one of the five dimensions of power outlined by Boyce (2002). *Value power* is the ability to influence the preferences of others, critical in any effort to reform the public perception of equity. *Event power* is the ability to determine the set of choices available to others; this power makes it possible to influence our system of jurisprudence, its treatment of equity concerns, and the transactions costs associated with redistribution. *Agenda power* is the ability to decide what issues will or won't be the subject of public policy, for example, determining the elements included in a multi-criteria analysis. *Decision power* is the ability to dictate the outcome of a choice involving multiple parties; the power to set an income or inequality target, and to use public policy to assure that it is met, is essential to a cost-effectiveness approach to equity enhancement. Finally, *purchasing power* is the ability (and willingness) to pay for a particular good or service. The redistribution of income and wealth depends on the balance struck between purchasing power and other forms of political and social power.

Like other public goods, equity, when not well-governed, can easily be degraded. Solutions to the tragedy of maldistribution require a shift in the distribution of power, so that both income and decision making power are held more equally. The final section of this chapter examines the role of equity both in the emissions of the greenhouse gases that cause climate change and in climate policy solutions.

Equity for Sustainability: The Case of Climate Change

The relationship between equity and sustainability is multi-faceted. As the Brundtland Commission suggested, meeting the needs of the present without compromising future generations' ability to meet their own needs requires an equitable distribution of economic and political power. Public goods, both environmental and social, have essential roles to play in maintaining and enhancing sustainability. The direct role of the atmospheric commons may be obvious: current-day greenhouse gas emissions are sustainable only when they do not compromise future generations' standard of living.

But another public good, the equity commons, has two less direct but no less important roles in making climate sustainability possible. First, income levels determine emissions. From 1980 to 2007, the 55 countries with the highest incomes (with 18 percent of 2005 global population) contributed 62 percent of cumulative global emissions, while the 45 countries with the lowest incomes (with 15 percent of 2005 population) contributed 2 percent (Stanton 2011a). Between-country inequality – divergence in GDP per capita – goes a long way towards explaining who will use up how much "emissions space" (Stanton 2011b). (Several researchers have identified an EKC-like curve for carbon dioxide emissions for high-income countries, but not for developing countries (Galeotti et al. 2006; Lindmark 2004). The goal of maintaining a good chance of avoiding dangerous climate change imposes a finite global emissions budget (German Advisory Council on Global Change 2009), implying that emissions allocations are a zero-sum game.

Similarly, within-country inequality reflects the pattern of greenhouse gas emissions across each national population, with richer individuals emitting more than their poorer neighbors (Boyce and Riddle 2009; Ananthapadmanabhan et al. 2007). Greater income equality both within and between nations – in the absence of new measures to reduce emissions – would increase global emissions, suggesting a trade-off between climate protection and redistributive improvements to social welfare. (This conclusion also requires that the income elasticity of emissions be less than one (Ravallion et al. 2000).

Second, income levels determine mitigation. Each country's (and each household's) capacity to engage in emissions reductions is a function of its income. Baer et al. (2008) find that the 70 percent of global population with the lowest incomes are responsible for only 15 percent of cumulative emissions, and have very little capacity for investing in emissions mitigation. Even so, Baer and coauthors identify viable solutions to the climate crisis that take emissions growth from economic development into account and rely only on the actions of those individuals exceeding a given development threshold. With greater income equality, the responsibility of mitigation could be shared more evenly across the world population.

As with the dubious development and environmental policies that have resulted from Kuznets curve and EKC evidence, it is of paramount importance that historical patterns not be mistaken for destiny. If maldistribution dictates both the cause of and the solution to climate change – the rich made this mess and the rich must clean it up – than what role is left for the rest of humanity?

Boyce (1994) provides several reasons to expect that greater equity would result in better (and not, as Ravallion et al. (2000) have suggested, worse) environmental outcomes, as predicted by the power-weighted social decision rule: greater income and power are associated with better access to information about environmental outcomes, and technology is subject to social and political influences, which in turn are shaped by the distribution of decision making power. Income redistribution would lift emissions for the poor by more than it lowers them for the rich – but it could also shift the balance of power in climate policy negotiations, both domestic and international, toward a greater urgency in preventing climate change. It is not obvious which of these effects would dominate and over what time period.

The notion that policies based on equating marginal total costs with marginal total benefits depend strongly on the distribution of income – notably absent in much of environmental economics – has received substantial interest from climate economists. Several well-known integrated assessment models depart from standard applied welfare economics by optimizing utility and not income (Stanton 2011c), and the question of income inequality's effect on a worldwide carbon price has been well explored (Sheeran 2006; Chichilnisky and Heal 1994).

The solutions to the twin tragedies of open-access resources and maldistribution – clarifying property rights, reducing transaction costs, adopting multi-criteria analysis and cost-effectiveness analysis; redistribution of income, wealth and political and social power – are also, necessarily, solutions for preventing dangerous climate change:

• Clarifying property rights and reducing transaction costs improve the governance of public goods. For the atmosphere this may mean formalizing its collective ownership and the principle of equal per capita rights to its carbon-storage capacity (Narain and Riddle 2007). For equity, as it relates to climate policy, a concrete representation of "common but differentiated responsibilities" for rich and poor nations in international law would be facilitated by the basic principles set out in several, well-known, equity-centered emission allocation proposals (Winkler et al. 2011; Baer et al. 2008; Government of India 2008; Agarwal and Narain 1991).

• Multi-criteria and cost-effectiveness analyses incorporated into integrated climate and economics modeling allow nonmonetized, collective public goods, such as the atmosphere and equity, to enter into policy recommendations for emission reductions. UNEP's MCA4climate initiative has the explicit goal of using multi-criteria analysis to incorporate nonmonetary impacts of climate policies into decision making (Scrieciu 2011). Cost-effectiveness analysis of emission reduction measures is already common among European researchers, although some of the simplest – but best-known – climate economics models still engage in cost–benefit analysis (Ackerman and Stanton 2009, 2011a; Stanton et al. 2009).

• And the redistribution of income, wealth and political and social power toward greater equality? Evidence assembled by Milanovic and others (cited above) indicates that, at least through 2002, the world income was becoming more, not less, unequally distributed. Boyce's power-weighted social decision rule suggests both that if those most affected by climate damages had more power – whether economic or political – there would be a greater likelihood that emissions would be kept in check, and that the poor will suffer most from climate change. As matters stand today, the rich seem to hold all the cards, possessing the capacity both to emit disproportionate amounts of greenhouse gases and to pay for emissions mitigation measures.

Equity is one of the many public goods on which sustainability depends. In the analysis of the causes of and solutions to climate change, the quality of the equity commons and the governance rules that protect and enhance it are key elements in crafting a viable international agreement on future emissions allocation and burden-sharing of emissions mitigation and climate adaptation costs. More broadly, equity – together with so many of the public goods that provide the foundation for environmental sustainability and sustainable development – is vulnerable. Deliberate policies in favor of increasing equity over time not only improve social welfare, but also act to shore up the foundations for the equity commons of the future, by establishing and strengthening rules for its governance.

Part II

ANALYSES OF CLIMATE DAMAGES

Chapter 5

CLIMATE IMPACTS ON AGRICULTURE: A CHALLENGE TO COMPLACENCY?

Frank Ackerman and Elizabeth A. Stanton

Unduly optimistic views of the impacts of climate change on agriculture, drawing on the research of the 1990s, have helped to justify relatively complacent approaches to climate policy. In the last decade, newer research has identified more ominous climate threats to agriculture – which should call for a revised perspective on climate policy. We review three categories of climate impacts on agriculture. Carbon fertilization, while still seen as a benefit to most crops, is now estimated to be smaller than in earlier research. The effect of temperature increases on crops is now recognized to involve thresholds, beyond which yields per hectare will rapidly decline. Finally, changes in precipitation can be crucial – not only in cases of drought, but also in subtler shifts in timing and intensity of rainfall. Response to the climate crisis in agriculture will require adaptation to inescapable near-term trends, via the creation of heat-resistant and drought-resistant crops and cultivars whenever possible. Yet unchecked climate change would quickly reach levels at which adaption is no longer possible; it is also urgent to reduce greenhouse gas emissions as rapidly as possible, to limit future climate-related damages.

Introduction: The Foundations of Inaction

Climate policies rely, explicitly or implicitly, on estimates of the damages that will be caused by climate change. This dependence is explicit when policy recommendations draw on the results of formal economic models. Such models typically weigh the costs of policy initiatives against the benefits. The costs of emission reduction are the incremental expenditures for renewable electricity generation, low-emission vehicles and the like, compared to more conventional investments in the same industries. The benefits are the future climate damages that can be avoided by emission reduction. The greater the expected damages, the more it is "worth" spending to avoid them.

As explained below, many of the best-known and most widely used models are significantly out of date in their damage estimates, in agriculture among other areas.

Often, of course, policy decisions are not based on formal models or explicit economic analysis. Yet even when politicians and voters decide that climate action is simply too expensive, they may be relying on implicit estimates of damages. Declaring something to be too expensive is not solely a statement of objective fact; it is also a judgment that a proposed expenditure is not particularly urgent. Protection against threats of incalculable magnitude – such as military defense of a nation's borders, or airport screening to keep terrorists off of planes – is rarely described as "too expensive."

The conclusion that climate policy is too expensive thus implies that it is an option we can do without, rather than a response to an existential threat to our way of life. Can we muddle along without expensive climate initiatives, and go on living – and eating – in the same way as in the past? Not for long, according to some of the new research on climate and agriculture.

What We Used to Know about Agriculture

Agriculture is one of the most climate-sensitive industries, with outdoor production processes that depend on particular levels of temperature and precipitation. Although only a small part of the world economy, it has always played a large role in estimates of overall economic impacts of climate change. In monetary terms, agriculture represents less than 2 percent of GDP in high-income countries, and 2.9 percent for the world as a whole.[1] It is more important to the economies of low-income countries, amounting to almost one-fourth of GDP in the least developed countries. And its product is an absolute necessity of life, with virtually no substitutes.[2]

In the 1990s, it was common to project that the initial stages of climate change would bring net benefits to global agriculture (e.g., Mendelsohn et al. 1994). As late as 2001, the US Global Change Research Program still anticipated that US agriculture would experience yield increases due to climate change throughout this century (Reilly et al. 2001). Warmer weather was expected to bring longer growing seasons in northern areas, and plants everywhere were expected to benefit from carbon fertilization. Since plants grow by absorbing CO_2 from the air, higher CO_2 concentrations might act as a fertilizer, speeding the growth process.

Simple and dated interpretations of climate impacts on agriculture continue to shape relatively recent economic assessments of climate damages. Widely used integrated assessment models such as DICE and FUND are still calibrated to relatively old and optimistic agricultural analyses.[3] Even the more sophisticated and detailed PESETA (Projection of Economic impacts of climate change in Sectors of the European Union based on bottom-up Analysis) project, analyzing climate impacts throughout Europe, assumed linear relationships between average temperatures and crop yields.[1] It projected that temperature changes through the end of this century would cause yield declines in Mediterranean and southern Atlantic Europe, and yield increases elsewhere (Iglesias et al. 2011). For Europe as a whole, PESETA estimated little change in crop yields for average European temperature increases up to 4.1°C, with a 10 percent yield decline at 5.4°C, the highest temperature analyzed in the study (Ciscar et al. 2011).

Such estimates have fallen well behind the state of the art in the research literature. There are three major areas in which recent results and models suggest a more complex relationship between climate and agriculture: the revised understanding of carbon fertilization, the threshold model of temperature effects on crop yields and the emerging analyses of climate and regional precipitation changes.

The best-known of the new areas of research is the empirical evidence that carbon fertilization benefits are smaller than previously believed. Plants grow by photosynthesis, a process that absorbs CO_2 from the air and converts it into organic compounds such as sugars. If the limiting factor in this process is the amount of CO_2 available to the plant, then an increase in the atmospheric concentration of CO_2 could act as a fertilizer, providing additional nutrients and allowing faster growth.

Almost all plants use one of two styles of photosynthesis.[5] The majority of food crops and other plants are C_3 plants (so named because a crucial molecule contains three carbon atoms), in which growth is limited by the availability of CO_2, so that carbon fertilization could be beneficial to them. In contrast, C_4 plants have evolved a different photosynthetic pathway that uses atmospheric CO_2 more efficiently. C_4 plants, which include maize, sugarcane, sorghum and millet (as well as switchgrass, a potentially important biofuel feedstock), do not benefit from increased CO_2 concentrations except in drought conditions (Leakey 2009).

Initial experimental studies conducted in greenhouses or other enclosures found substantial carbon fertilization effects. The 2001 US National Assessment summarized the experimental evidence available at that time as implying yield gains of 30 percent in C_3 crops and 7 percent in C_4 crops from a doubling of CO_2 concentrations (Reilly et al. 2001). More recently, Free-Air CO_2 Enrichment (FACE) experiments have allowed crops to be grown in outdoor environments with a greater resemblance to the actual conditions of production. According to a widely cited summary, the effects of CO_2 on yields for major grain crops are roughly 50 percent lower in FACE experiments than in enclosure studies (Long et al. 2004).[6] Another literature review reaches similar conclusions, offering "important lessons from FACE," one of which is that "the [CO_2] 'fertilization' effect in FACE studies on crop plants is less than expected" (Leakey 2009).

One summary of the results of FACE experiments reports that an increase in atmospheric CO_2 from 385 ppm (the actual level a few years ago) to 550 ppm would increase yields of the leading C_3 crops, wheat, soybeans and rice, by 13 percent and would have no effect on yields of maize and sorghum, the leading C_4 grains (Ainsworth and McGrath 2010). Cline (2007) develops a similar estimate; because C_4 crops represent about one-fourth of world agricultural output, he projects a weighted average of 9 percent increase in global yields from 550 ppm.

While research on carbon fertilization has advanced in recent years, there are at least three unanswered questions in this area that are important for economic analysis. First, there is little information about the effects of very high CO_2 concentrations; many studies have only examined yields up to 550 ppm, and few have gone above 700 ppm. Long-term projections of business-as-usual emissions scenarios, however, frequently reach even higher concentrations. Does CO_2 fertilization continue to raise yields indefinitely, or does it reach an upper bound?

Second, most studies to date have focused on the leading grains and cotton; other plants may have different responses to increases in CO_2. For at least one important food crop, the response is negative: Cassava (manioc), a dietary staple for 750 million people in developing countries, shows sharply reduced yields at elevated CO_2 levels, with tuber mass reduced by an order of magnitude when CO_2 concentrations rise from 360 ppm to 710 ppm (Gleadow et al. 2009; Ghini et al. 2011). This result appears to be based on the unique biochemistry of cassava, and does not directly generalize to other plants. It is, nonetheless, a cautionary tale about extrapolation from studies of a few plants to food crops as a whole.

Third, carbon fertilization may interact with other environmental influences. Fossil fuel combustion, the principal source of atmospheric CO_2, also produces tropospheric (ground-level) ozone, which reduces yields of many plants (Ainsworth and McGrath 2010). The net effect of carbon fertilization plus increased ozone is uncertain, but it is very likely to be less than the experimental estimates for carbon fertilization alone.

Temperature Thresholds for Crop Yields

Describing climate change by the increase in average temperatures is inescapably useful, but at the same time often misleading. Increases in global average temperature of only a few degrees, comparable to normal month-to-month changes in many parts of the world, will have drastic and disruptive effects. A recent study suggests that it may be easier for people to perceive climate change as reflected in temperature extremes, such as the marked increase in the frequency of temperatures more than three standard deviations above historical summer averages (Hansen et al. 2012).

An important new wave of research shows that crops, too, are often more sensitive to temperature extremes than to averages. In many cases, yields rise gradually up to a temperature threshold, and then collapse rapidly as temperatures increase above the threshold. This threshold model often fits the empirical data better than the earlier models of temperature effects on yields.

It is obvious that most crops have an optimum temperature, at which their yields per hectare are greater than at either higher or lower temperatures. A simple and widely used model of this effect assumes that yields are a quadratic function of average temperatures.[7] The quadratic model, however, imposes symmetry and gradualism on the temperature-yield relationship: yields rise smoothly on the way up to the optimum temperature, and then decline at the same smooth rate as temperatures rise beyond the optimum.

The threshold model makes two innovations: it allows different relationships between temperature and yield above and below the optimum, and it measures temperatures above the optimum in terms of the growing-season total of degree-days above a threshold, rather than average seasonal or annual temperatures.[8] Perhaps the first use of this model in recent agricultural economics was Schlenker et al. (2006), drawing on earlier agronomic literature. This approach has a solid grounding in plant biology: many crops are known to have temperature thresholds, in some cases at varying temperatures for different stages of development (Luo 2011).

The threshold model has been widely used in the last few years. For instance, temperature effects on maize, soybean and cotton yields in the United States are strongly asymmetric, with optimum temperatures of 29–32°C and rapid drops in yields for degree-days beyond the optimum. For maize, replacing 24 hours of the growing season at 29°C with 24 hours at 40°C would cause a 7 percent decline in yields (Schlenker and Roberts 2009).

A very similar pattern was found in a study of temperature effects on maize yields in Africa, with a threshold of 30°C (Lobell et al. 2011). Under ordinary conditions, the effects on yields of temperatures above the threshold were similar to those found in the United States; under drought conditions, yields declined even faster with temperature increases. Limited data on wheat in northern India also suggests that temperature increases above 34°C are more harmful than similar increases at lower levels (Lobell et al. 2012).

A study of five leading food crops in sub-Saharan Africa found strong relationships of yields to temperatures (Schlenker and Lobell 2010). By mid-century, under the A1B climate scenario (a mid-range SRES scenario), yields are projected to drop by 17 to 22 percent for maize, sorghum, millet and groundnuts (peanuts), and by 8 percent for cassava. These estimates exclude carbon fertilization, but maize, sorghum and millet are C_4 crops, while cassava has a negative response to increased CO_2, as noted above. Negative impacts are expected for a number of crops in developing countries by 2030. Among the crops most vulnerable to temperature increases are millet, groundnut and rapeseed in South Asia; sorghum in the Sahel; and maize in Southern Africa (Lobell et al. 2008).

Other crops exhibit different, but related, patterns of temperature dependence; some perennials require a certain amount of "chill time," or annual hours below a low temperature threshold such as 7°C. In a study of the projected loss of winter chilling conditions in California, Germany and Oman, fruit and nut trees showed large decreases in yield due to climate change (Luedeling et al. 2011). In this case, as with high-temperature yield losses, the relevant temperature variable is measured in terms of threshold effects, not year-round or even seasonal averages. Small changes in averages can imply large changes in the hours above or below thresholds, and hence large agricultural impacts.

Studies of temperatures and yields based on recent experience, including those described here, are limited in their ability to project the extent of adaptation to changing temperatures. Such adaptation has been important in the past: as North American wheat production expanded into colder, drier regions, farmers adapted by selecting different cultivars that could thrive in the new conditions; most of the adaptation occurred before 1930 (Olmstead and Rhode 2010). On the other hand, regions of the United States that are well above the optimum temperatures for maize, soybeans and other major crops have grown these crops for many years, without any evidence of a large-scale shift to more heat-resistant crops or cultivars; temperature-yield relationships are quite similar in northern and southern states (Schlenker and Roberts 2009). Thus adaptation is an important possibility, but far from automatic.

A third area of research on climate and agriculture has reached less definite global conclusions, but it will be of increasing local importance. As the world warms, precipitation patterns will change, with some areas becoming wetter, but some leading agricultural areas becoming drier. These patterns are difficult to forecast; climate model predictions are more uncertain for precipitation than for temperature, and "downscaling" global models to yield regional projections is only beginning to be feasible. Yet recent droughts in many parts of the world underscore the crucial role of changes in rainfall.

Even if total annual precipitation is unchanged, agriculture may be harmed by changes in the seasonality or intensity of rainfall.

Overall, warming is increasing the atmosphere's capacity to hold water, resulting in increases in extreme precipitation events (Min et al. 2011). Both observational data and modeling projections show that with climate change, wet regions will generally (but not universally) become wetter, and dry regions will become drier (Sanderson et al. 2011; John et al. 2009). Perceptible changes in annual precipitation are likely to appear in many areas within this century. While different climate models disagree about some parts of the world, there is general agreement that boreal (far-northern) areas will become wetter, and the Mediterranean will become drier (Mahlstein et al. 2012).

With 2°C of warming, dry-season precipitation is expected to decrease by 20 percent in northern Africa, southern Europe and western Australia, and by 10 percent in the southwestern United States and Mexico, eastern South America and northern Africa by 2100 (Giorgi and Bi 2009).[9] In the Sahel area of Africa, the timing of critical rains will shift, shortening the growing season (Biasutti and Sobel 2009), and more extensive periods of drought may result as temperatures rise (Lu 2009).[10] In the Haihe River basin of northern China, projections call for less total rainfall but more extreme weather events (Chu et al. 2009). Indian monsoon rainfall has already become less frequent but more intense, part of a pattern of climate change that is reducing wet-season rice yields (Auffhammer et al. 2011).

The relationship of crop yields to precipitation is markedly different in irrigated areas than in rain-fed farming; it has even been suggested that mistakes in analysis of irrigation may have accounted for some of the optimism about climate and agriculture in the 1990s literature (Schlenker et al. 2005). In California, by far the leading agricultural state in the United States, the availability of water for irrigation is crucial to yields; variations in temperature and precipitation are much less important, as long as access to irrigation can be assumed (Schlenker et al. 2007). Yet there is a growing scarcity of water and competition over available supplies in the state, leading some researchers to project a drop in irrigated acreage and a shift toward higher-value, less water-intensive crops (Howitt et al. 2009). An analysis of potential water scarcity due to climate change in California estimates that there will be substantial costs in dry years, in the form of both higher water prices and supply shortfalls, to California's Central Valley agriculture (Hanemann et al. 2006).

In our study of climate change and water in the southwestern US, we found that climate change is worsening the already unsustainable pattern of water use in agriculture (Ackerman and Stanton 2011c).[11] Nearly four-fifths of the region's water is used for agriculture, often to grow surprisingly water-intensive, low-value crops; a tangled system of legal restrictions and entitlements prevents operation of a market in water. If there were a market for water in the Southwest, municipal water systems and power plants would easily outbid many agricultural users. Yet one-fifth of US agricultural output comes from this region, virtually all of it dependent on irrigation.

More than half of the water used in the region is drawn from the Colorado River and from groundwater, neither of which can meet projected demand. The Colorado River is infamously oversubscribed, and is the subject of frequent, contentious negotiations over the allocation of its water. Climate change is projected to cause a decrease in precipitation, runoff, and streamflow in the Colorado River basin, leading to frequent water shortages and decreases in energy production (Christensen and Lettenmaier 2007).[12]

Groundwater supplies are difficult to measure, and there are two very different estimates of California's groundwater reserves. Even assuming the higher estimate, the state's current patterns of water use are unsustainable, leading to massive shortfalls of groundwater within a few decades.

In California, projections of changes in annual precipitation are not consistent across climate models. Even if annual precipitation remains constant, however, climate change can worsen the state's water crisis in at least two ways. On the demand side, higher temperatures increase the need for water for irrigation, and for municipal and other uses. On the supply side, rising temperatures mean that winter snows will be replaced by rain, or will melt earlier in the year – which can have the effect of reducing the available quantity of water.

The mountain regions of the western United States are experiencing reduced snowpack, warmer winters and streamflows coming earlier in the calendar year. Since the mid-1980s, these trends have been outside the past range of natural variation, but consistent with the expected effects of anthropogenic (human-caused) climate change (Barnett et al. 2008). In the past, snowmelt gradually released the previous winter's precipitation, with significant flows in the summer when demand is highest. The climate-related shift means that water arrives, in large volume, earlier in the year than it is needed – and the peak runoff may overflow existing reservoir capacity, leading some of it to flow directly to the ocean without opportunity for human use (Barnett et al. 2005).

We developed a model of the interactions of climate, water and agriculture in California and in the five-state region, assuming constant annual precipitation but modeling temperature-driven increases in demand as well as changes in seasonal streamflows (Stanton and Fitzgerald 2011). We found that climate change makes a bad situation much worse, intensifying the expected gap between water supply and demand. Under one estimate of the cost of supplying water, we found that climate change is transforming the region's

$4 trillion water deficit over the next century into a $5 trillion shortfall (Ackerman and Stanton 2011c). If we had also modeled a decline in annual precipitation, of course, the problem would have been even worse.

To those unfamiliar with the southwestern United States, this may sound like an excursion into hydrology and water management rather than an analysis of agriculture. No one who lives there could miss the connection: most of the region's water is used for agriculture; virtually all of the region's agriculture is completely dependent on a reliable flow of water for irrigation. As climate change presses down on western water, it will start to squeeze a crucial sector of the US food supply. This is a far cry from the optimism of earlier decades about what climate change will mean for agriculture.

Conclusions

The extraordinary proliferation of recent research on climate change has moved far beyond an earlier complacency about agricultural impacts. With better empirical studies, estimates of carbon fertilization benefits have shrunk for C_3 crops (most of the world's food) in general – as well as being roughly zero for maize and other C_4 crops, and negative for cassava. With a better explanatory framework, focused on temperature extremes rather than averages, judgments about temperature impacts on crop yields have become more ominous. With more detailed local research, the regionally specific interactions of climate, water and agriculture are beginning to be understood, often implying additional grounds for concern.

It should not be surprising that even a little climate change is bad for agriculture. The standard models and intuition of economic theory emphasize options for substitution in production – less steel can be used in making cars, if it is replaced by aluminum or plastic – but agriculture is fundamentally different. It involves natural processes that frequently require fixed proportions of nutrients, temperatures, precipitation and other conditions. Ecosystems don't make bargains with their suppliers, and don't generally switch to making the same plants out of different inputs.

Around the world, agriculture has been optimized to the local climate through decades of trial and error. The conditions needed to allow crops to flourish include not only their preferred ranges of average temperature and precipitation, but also more fine-grained details of timing and extreme values. This is true for temperatures, as shown by the existence of thresholds and the sensitivity of yields to brief periods of extreme temperatures beyond the thresholds. It is also true for precipitation, as shown by the harm to Indian rice yields from less frequent but more intense monsoon rains, or by the sensitivity of California agriculture to the delicate timing of snowmelt.

Global warming is now causing an unprecedented pace of change in the climate conditions that affect agriculture – much faster than crops can evolve on their own, and probably too fast for the traditional processes of trial-and-error adaptation by farmers. At the same time, the world's population will likely continue to grow through mid-century or later, increasing the demand for food just as climate change begins to depress yields. To adapt to the inescapable early states of climate change, it is essential to apply the rapidly developing resources of plant genetics and biotechnology to the creation of new heat-resistant, and perhaps drought-resistant, crops and cultivars.

Adaptation to climate change is necessary but not sufficient. If warming continues unabated, it will, in a matter of decades, reach levels at which adaptation is no longer possible. Any long-run solution must involve rapid reduction of emissions, to limit the future extent of climate change. The arguments against active climate policies, based on formal or informal economic reasoning, have been propped up by a dated and inaccurate picture of climate impacts on agriculture, which lives on in the background of recent models and studies. Updating that picture, recognizing and accepting the implications of new research on climate threats to agriculture, is part of the process of creating climate policies that rest soundly on the latest scientific research.

Chapter 6

DID THE STERN REVIEW UNDERESTIMATE US AND GLOBAL CLIMATE CHANGE?

Frank Ackerman, Elizabeth A. Stanton, Chris Hope and Stephane Alberth

The Stern Review received widespread attention for its innovative approach to the economics of climate change when it appeared in 2006, and generated controversies that have continued to this day. One key controversy concerns the magnitude of the expected impacts of climate change. Stern's estimates, based on results from the PAGE2002 model, sounded substantially greater than those produced by many other models, leading several critics to suggest that Stern had inflated his damage figures. We reached the opposite conclusion in a recent application of PAGE2002 in a study of the costs to the US economy of inaction on climate change. This chapter describes our revisions to the PAGE estimates, and explains our conclusion that the model runs used in the Stern Review may well underestimate US and global damages. Stern's estimates from PAGE2002 implied that mean business-as-usual damages in 2100 would represent just 0.4 percent of GDP for the United States and 2.2 percent of GDP for the world. Our revisions and reinterpretation of the PAGE model imply that climate damages in 2100 could reach 2.6 percent of GDP for the United States and 10.8 percent for the world.

Introduction

The Stern Review received widespread attention for its innovative approach to the economics of climate change when it appeared in 2006. It represented a break with conventional analyses in several respects, generating debates about climate economics that have continued to this day. One of the foundations of the Stern analysis was the use of the PAGE2002 model (Alberth and Hope 2007; Hope 2006a; Wahba and Hope 2006) to estimate the damages that would be expected under business-as-usual conditions (i.e., in the absence of effective new climate policies). Based on PAGE, Stern estimated that the present welfare cost of climate damages through 2200 could amount to 5 percent of world output under a relatively narrow definition of damages, up to as much as 20 percent under the broadest definition. These estimates were substantially greater than those produced by many other models, leading several critics to suggest that Stern had inflated his damage figures (Byatt et al. 2006; Lomborg 2006; Mendelsohn 2006; Nordhaus 2007c; Tol and Yohe 2006).[1]

We reached the opposite conclusion in a recent application of the PAGE2002 model. In a study of the costs to the US economy of inaction on climate change, we had initially planned to use the US estimates from Stern's PAGE runs. These estimates, however, turned out to be surprisingly small, and seemingly inconsistent with other, bottom-up calculations of climate damages in the United States. Our recent study of the costs to the US economy of inaction on climate change takes a different approach, building up damage estimates for specific sectors where data and analyses are available (Ackerman and Stanton 2008). That study projects annual damages equal to 1.8 percent of US GDP by 2100 from just four economic sectors: hurricane damages, residential real estate losses due to sea-level rise, energy sector costs and water supply costs.

This chapter describes our revisions to the PAGE estimates for the United States, and explains our conclusion that the model runs used in the Stern Review may well underestimate US and global damages. (Note that we are using PAGE and PAGE2002 interchangeably; there are no references to other versions of PAGE in this chapter.) We first describe the PAGE model and then present the model results used in the Stern Review – including disaggregation by region, a feature that was not highlighted by Stern. The next sections of this chapter explain three principal reasons why the results may be too low for some or all regions: extensive and nearly costless adaptation was assumed to occur, especially in high-income countries; the risk of discontinuous, catastrophic losses was treated more timidly in the model than in the text of the Stern Review; and the overall shape of the (noncatastrophic) damage function was based on very conservative guesses.

We then introduce the problem of uncertainty and worst-case risks, as raised in recent work by Martin Weitzman, and suggest a partial response to this problem, leading to a further increase in the damage estimates that are relevant for policy purposes. The final section of this chapter briefly concludes.

The PAGE2002 Model

PAGE2002 is a simulation model, estimating the climate consequences and damage costs that result from a user-specified emissions scenario. It uses a number of simplified formulas to represent the complex scientific and economic interactions of climate change. A full description of the model can be found in Hope (2006a). Most of the model's coefficients and data ranges are calibrated to match the projections of the Third Assessment Report of the Intergovernmental Panel on Climate Change (IPCC 2001c). Projections of GDP, population and emissions of greenhouse gases are taken from the 2001 version of IPCC Scenario A2.[2] Since many aspects of climate change are subject to uncertainty, PAGE uses probability distributions, based on the best available estimates found in the literature, to represent 31 key inputs to the calculations. Using these input distributions, PAGE performs a Monte Carlo analysis; the most frequently reported results from PAGE are the mean outcomes from 5,000 runs of the model. (Alternative approaches to uncertainty are discussed later in this chapter.)

The model includes ten time intervals spanning 200 years, divides the world into eight regions and explicitly considers three different greenhouse gases (carbon dioxide, methane and sulfur hexafluoride) with other gases included as an excess forcing projection. Three types of impact are calculated:

- economic impacts, which are impacts on marketed output and income, in sectors such as agriculture and energy use, that are directly included in GDP;
- noneconomic impacts, which are impacts on things like health and wilderness areas which are not directly included in GDP; and
- discontinuity impacts, which are the increased risks of climate catastrophes, such as the melting of the Greenland or West Antarctic ice sheet.

These three types of impacts are summed to calculate total impacts.

The Stern Review team modified a small number of inputs for their use of the model (Stern 2006). The version used in the Stern report differed by using purchasing power parity exchange rates throughout, a change which increases the weight of developing countries in the global totals. The Stern version also calculated the discount rates for each time period and region, using a Ramsey-type optimal growth function (Cline 2004). In Stern's notation, the discount rate r is the sum of pure time preference ρ, plus the product of the elasticity of marginal utility of consumption η and the growth rate of per capita consumption g for each region i and time period t:

$$(6.1) \qquad\qquad r_{i,t} = \rho + \eta g_{i,t}$$

In this equation, Stern set $\rho=0.1$ percent per year and $\eta=1$. The growth rate, and therefore the discount rate, varied with different runs of the Monte Carlo analysis; the average value of the discount rate was 1.4 percent per year, well below the discount rates used in many other analyses (although not unprecedented; see Cline (2004) and Ackerman and Finlayson (2006) for climate analyses with similar discount rates).

Previous applications of PAGE2002 typically treated pure time preference as a Monte Carlo variable, using a range of <1, 2, 3> for ρ (here, and throughout this chapter, the triangular brackets denote a triangular probability distribution with <minimum, most likely, maximum> parameter values). Stern's lower rate of pure time preference led to lower discount rates, and hence to higher present values for future damages. As a result, the Stern Review gave a mean estimate of the social cost of carbon (SCC) of $85 per ton of CO_2, or $312 per ton of carbon (Stern 2006), much higher than most previous estimates using PAGE2002, which have been in the range of $20 to $65 per ton of carbon (Hope 2005, 2006a).

In addition to the basic estimates, calibrated to the IPCC's 2001 scenarios, the Stern team developed a high climate sensitivity scenario. This incorporated a number of technical changes based on research since 2001, reflecting the risk that increasing concentrations of greenhouse gases may be changing the climate more rapidly than was previously believed. Stern's high climate sensitivity estimates generally showed damages about 40 percent greater than the comparable basic estimates. For simplicity, we will focus only on the basic estimates in this chapter.

Stern's US and Global Results from PAGE2002

The widely reported damage estimates from the Stern Review were expressed in terms of "balanced growth equivalents" – that is, the uniform reduction in growth throughout the two-century forecast period (to 2200) that would have the same present value as the estimated pattern of damages. This is a logical and informative measure, but it is relatively unfamiliar and cannot be directly compared to other models. For the sake of familiarity and comparability with other estimates, we will instead describe scenario results in terms of the annual damages in the year 2100, as a percentage of that year's GDP. Damages in 2100 will be generally lower than Stern's 200-year balanced growth equivalent, since PAGE estimates that damages will increase markedly after 2100. By comparing a future year's damages to the same year's GDP, we can avoid the difficult questions of discounting: regardless of discount rate, both numerator and denominator would be discounted by the same factor, so the ratio of damages to GDP would be unchanged.

The basic Stern Review damage estimates for 2100 are shown in Table 6.1. All figures are the mean results from a Monte Carlo analysis with 5000 runs, expressed as a percentage of world or regional GDP in 2100.

Table 6.1. Mean business-as-usual damages in 2100 – Stern Review version

	Annual damages as percent of GDP in 2100			
	Economic	Noneconomic	Catastrophic	Total
USA	–	0.3	0.1	0.4
Other OECD	–	0.8	0.2	1.0
Rest of World	0.8	1.7	0.4	3.0
World Total	0.6	1.4	0.3	2.2

Source: 5000 runs of the PAGE2002 model.
Note: "–" denotes less than 0.05%.

As Table 6.1 shows, Stern's estimates of damages at the end of the century were heavily concentrated in the developing countries. Total world damages, the indicator that gets the most attention, suggests noticeable losses. However, as late as 2100, projected economic damages in high-income countries, along with catastrophic damages everywhere, remain surprisingly close to zero. These results seem anomalous in the Stern Review – a report that described itself, and was widely taken by others, as a warning of the severity of impending climate damages.

If the results in Table 6.1 are accepted as reasonable forecasts, then the costs of a business-as-usual climate scenario are concentrated in near-term impacts on developing countries, in worsening worldwide conditions after 2100 (since Stern's calculations ran through 2200, and the low discount rate gave significant weight to the later damages), and to a lesser extent in the noneconomic, noncatastrophic damages in high-income countries. This is a possible but unsatisfying explanation: it appears inconsistent with the growing evidence that climate impacts are already being felt in the global North (used here as shorthand for high-income or OECD countries); and it could be read, in cynical terms, to support a parochial complacency in those countries. If serious impacts on the North are more than a century away, the narrowly self-interested Northern citizen might wonder, isn't this really someone else's problem?

Alternatively, it is possible that the Stern estimates understate the near-term economic impacts on the global North, and the risk of catastrophic change everywhere. A closer look at PAGE2002 and its parameters, in the next three sections, supports this alternative interpretation.

Adaptation Assumptions

The PAGE2002 defaults, adopted by the Stern Review, assume that substantial, nearly costless adaptation will occur; the reported damage estimates are for damages remaining after that adaptation takes place. Specifically, PAGE assumes that in developing countries, 50 percent of economic damages are eliminated by low-cost adaptation. In OECD countries, the assumption is even stronger: 100 percent of the economic damages resulting from the first 2 degrees of warming, and 90 percent of economic damages above 2 degrees, are eliminated. For noneconomic, noncatastrophic damages, adaptation is assumed to remove 25 percent of the impact everywhere. (No adaptation is assumed for catastrophic damages, which are discussed below.)

The adaptation assumptions sharply reduce reported damages everywhere, but have a much greater impact on OECD countries. It is hard to evaluate these assumptions: there undoubtedly will be some adaptation, particularly to the early stages of warming, and it seems plausible that richer countries will often be more successful in adaptation. Yet the experience of the European heat wave in 2003 and the impacts of Hurricane Katrina in the United States in 2005 might cast doubt on the assumption of 90–100 percent adaptation. Even in the richest countries, which have ample physical and economic resources for adaptation to many early impacts of climate change, there can be failures of planning, political will and implementation.

It seems more informative and transparent to report the model results for gross damages, under a "no adaptation" scenario. The PAGE results, comparable to Table 6.1 above but with no assumed adaptation, are shown in Table 6.2. The totals are larger, and economic damages in OECD countries have become relatively larger in comparison to other categories. Only the catastrophic damages remain unchanged.

Modeling the no-adaptation scenario is not meant to imply that this is a likely outcome; there will undoubtedly be successful adaptation to many aspects of climate damages. It is useful as a starting point, however, to see how much potential damage needs to be addressed by either adaptation or mitigation. That damage estimate can then be compared to the costs of adaptation and mitigation. In contrast, Stern's quantitative results are only presented as the

Table 6.2. Mean business-as-usual damages in 2100 – "no adaptation" scenario

	Annual damages as percent of GDP in 2100			
	Economic	Noneconomic	Catastrophic	Total
USA	0.3	0.4	0.1	0.8
Other OECD	0.7	1.0	0.2	1.9
Rest of World	1.6	2.3	0.4	4.3
World Total	1.2	1.8	0.3	3.4

Source: 5000 runs of the PAGE2002 model.

net effect after an assumed but unspecified high level of low-cost adaptation – a presentation that obscures the extensive need for adaptation expenditure.

Damage estimates for the no-adaptation scenario, in Table 6.2, remain smaller for the US than for other OECD countries; this results from a separate, intentional assumption. Compared to other rich countries, the United States has proportionally much more of its population, economic activity and capital stock in the interior of the country, rather than on the coast. Since sea-level rise and storm surges are among the most important early impacts of climate change, it is reasonable to adopt lower damage estimates for the United States than for Europe, Japan and other high-income countries.

Thresholds and Probabilities for Climate Catastrophes

PAGE assumes that a threshold temperature (measured in degrees above a recent base year) must be reached before catastrophic events become possible; once that threshold is crossed, the probability of catastrophe gradually rises along with the temperature. Two of the uncertain (Monte Carlo) parameters in PAGE are involved here. One is the threshold temperature, with minimum, most likely, and maximum values of <2, 5, 8> degrees Celsius in the Stern analysis. Much of the discussion of potential catastrophes, such as the loss of the Greenland or West Antarctic ice sheets, has suggested that they become possible or even likely at temperatures well below the PAGE model's "most likely" threshold of 5°C of warming; indeed, the narrative portions of the Stern Review make this suggestion. For this reason, the PAGE baseline assumption about threshold temperatures seems too conservative. We changed the threshold temperature to minimum, most likely, and maximum values of <2, 3, 4> degrees Celsius. Even this may still be conservative, in light of recent research suggesting non-zero probability of catastrophic outcomes at 2°C warming (Baer and Mastrandrea 2006; Meinshausen 2006).

A second parameter involved in this calculation is the rate at which the probability of catastrophe grows, as the temperature rises past the threshold. In the PAGE defaults, used by Stern, the probability of catastrophe increases by minimum, most likely, and maximum rates of <1, 10, 20> percentage points per degree Celsius above the threshold. This also seems unduly conservative, minimizing the risk of catastrophe until warming is far advanced. In our changes to the model, the probability of catastrophe grows at minimum, most likely, and maximum rates of <10, 20, 30> percentage points per degree Celsius above the threshold.

The Shape of the Damage Function

PAGE, like many economic models, assumes economic and noneconomic climate damages are a function of temperature, using a simple equation of the form:

$$(6.2) \qquad\qquad\qquad Damages = aT^N$$

Here, a is a constant, T is the temperature increase and N is the exponent governing how fast damages rise. If $N = 2$, then 4° is four times as bad as 2°; if $N = 3$, then 4° is eight times as bad, etc.

PAGE treats the exponent N as one of the uncertain parameters that is allowed to vary in the Monte Carlo analysis, with the minimum, most likely, and maximum values, respectively, set at <1, 1.3, 3>. There is essentially no evidence bearing directly on the value of this exponent, but the "most likely" value of 1.3 seems almost timid: it implies that 4° is only about 2.5 times as bad as 2°. In our variation, we set the minimum, most likely, and maximum values of the exponent at <1.5, 2.25, 3>. This alternative keeps the exponent within the same range used in the Stern Review, but weights the higher end of the range more heavily; it assumes that the exponent is most likely to be a little more than 2, the value used in many recent models.

The combination of our changes to the threshold for catastrophic events, and to the damage function exponent, more than doubles the projected damages from the no-adaptation scenario by 2100, as shown in Table 6.3. Comparing Tables 6.2 and 6.3, all categories show an increase in damages; the difference is greatest in the catastrophic risk category.

Table 6.3. Mean business-as-usual damages in 2100 – no adaptation, increased catastrophe risk and increased damage exponent

| | Annual damages as percent of GDP in 2100 | | | |
	Economic	Noneconomic	Catastrophic	Total
USA	0.4	0.5	0.6	1.5
Other OECD	0.9	1.3	1.6	3.8
Rest of World	2.0	2.9	3.2	8.2
World Total	1.6	2.3	2.6	6.4

Source: 5000 runs of the PAGE2002 model.

Worst-Case versus Average Damages

Although Stern emphasized and expanded the role of uncertainty in climate economics, another economist has argued that the problem goes even deeper. Martin Weitzman (2009) maintains that in complex, changing systems such as the global climate (or financial markets), we are inevitably forecasting the future based on limited information. As a result, we cannot learn enough to be confident about how bad, and how likely, the worst-case possibilities may be. If, for example, we had to estimate how fast the average temperature will increase based on 100 experimental observations, we could not say much about the 99th percentile – that is, one of the worst cases – of possible outcomes. Yet when faced with real, open-ended risks, people care a great deal about worst-case outcomes, out to the 99th percentile of possibilities and beyond. More formally, Weitzman proves that because the probabilities of key climate parameters are inferred from limited information, the resulting "fat-tailed" probability distributions imply that the expected value of harm – or equivalently, the value of reducing emissions and damages – can, in technical terms, become infinite. The message for climate change, according to Weitzman, is that we should worry less about calibrating the most likely outcomes, and more about insurance against worst-case catastrophes.

IPCC (2007b) discusses the important concept of "climate sensitivity," i.e., the expected temperature change from a doubling of atmospheric carbon dioxide; this is of immediate relevance because the world is likely to reach twice the pre-industrial level of carbon dioxide within this century. (If current emission trends do not change, that level could be reached in the first half of the century.) The IPCC's best estimate of climate sensitivity is an increase of 3°C as a result of a doubling of atmospheric carbon dioxide – well within the range of the ongoing debate over the impacts of predictable and expected damages. Weitzman argues, however, that the same IPCC reports imply that the 95th percentile value for climate sensitivity is 7°C, and the 99th percentile value is 10°C. Feedback mechanisms discussed in scientific literature suggest that the eventual temperature change could be even greater, perhaps a 95th percentile of 10°C and a 99th percentile of 20°C. Discussing a temperature increase of 10–20°, he says:

Such high temperatures have not been seen for hundreds of millions of years [...]
Because these hypothetical temperature changes would be geologically instantaneous, they would effectively destroy planet Earth as we know it. At a minimum such temperatures would trigger mass species extinctions and biosphere ecosystem disintegration matching or exceeding the immense planetary

die-offs associated in Earth's history with a handful of previous geo-environmental mega-catastrophes. (Weitzman 2009, 5)

A Monte Carlo analysis, in a model such as PAGE, allows at least a limited measurement of the worst-case risks emphasized by Weitzman. Since PAGE estimates are based on 5,000 runs of the model with varying parameters, it is easy to determine the 95th, 99th or any other percentile outcome.

As a partial step toward the focus on worst-case outcomes, we examined the upper end of what IPCC considers "likely" to occur. In the formal IPCC interpretation of the term, "likely" means a 66 percent probability of occurring, so the likely range of outcomes extends from the 17th to the 83rd percentile. Therefore, we took the 83rd percentile outcome from the PAGE runs to represent the worst of what is likely to occur. Table 6.4 presents 83rd

Table 6.4. Business-as-usual damages in 2100 – 83rd percentile estimates (no adaptation, increased catastrophe risk and increased damage exponent)

	Annual damages as percent of GDP in 2100			
	Economic	Noneconomic	Catastrophic	Total
USA	0.6	0.9	1.2	2.6
Other OECD	1.4	2.0	3.1	6.2
Rest of World	3.2	4.5	6.3	13.5
World Total	2.5	3.6	4.8	10.8

Source: 5000 runs of the PAGE2002 model.
Note: As the impacts are closely but not perfectly correlated, the 83rd percentile of the total damages is slightly less than the sum of the 83rd percentiles of the damages in the individual impact categories.

Table 6.5. Business-as-usual damages in 2100 – 95th percentile estimates (no adaptation, increased catastrophe risk and increased damage exponent)

	Annual damages as percent of GDP in 2100			
	Economic	Noneconomic	Catastrophic	Total
USA	1.1	1.5	2.0	4.3
Other OECD	2.4	3.4	5.0	9.9
Rest of World	5.4	7.9	10.1	21.5
World Total	4.2	6.1	8.0	16.8

Source: 5000 runs of the PAGE2002 model.
Note: As the impacts are closely but not perfectly correlated, the 95th percentile of the total column is slightly less than the sum of the 95th percentiles of the individual impact categories.

percentile outcomes, for the same scenario as Table 6.3 – the difference is that Table 6.3 presents the mean outcomes for the scenario. As Table 6.4 shows, even this limited movement toward worst-case outcomes has a substantial effect on the estimate of damages. Moving farther toward worst-case results would lead to bigger damages; Table 6.5 presents the 95th percentile estimates of damages, which are, in many categories, roughly 60 percent greater than the 83rd percentile damages in Table 6.4.

Conclusions

In our estimation, the Stern Review's version of PAGE2002, far from inflating damages, is more likely to have understated the potential costs of climate change for the United States and for the world. This is not only because of the revisions described in this chapter, but also because our research on US impacts suggests a much larger estimate of damages (Ackerman and Stanton 2008). The damages estimated in that study, 1.8 percent of US GDP by 2100, represent impacts projected in just four economic sectors under a business-as-usual scenario (the 83rd percentile of the IPCC's A2 scenario), with no significant mitigation of greenhouse gas emissions or adaptation to prevent damages. They do not include any valuation of externalities, or estimates of damages due to catastrophic risks.

These sectoral estimates are all subsets of PAGE's economic category of damages; they are most comparable to the PAGE results under the assumptions used in Table 6.4. As seen there, PAGE2002 projects annual economic damages from all sectors in the United States by 2100 equal to 0.6 percent of GDP at the 83rd percentile with no adaptation, increased risk of catastrophe and an increased damage function. In short, our disaggregated estimate for four sectors is three times the size of the comparable PAGE2002 estimate for all sectors. Thus the aggregate economic damages modeled in PAGE2002 would seem to represent an underestimate when compared to disaggregated damages projected for the United States on a sector-by-sector basis.

Because of the similarity in PAGE2002 parameter values chosen for the United States and for other nations, it is likely that the Stern Review results underestimate damages for all industrialized nations. As a consequence, projected total damages worldwide will be a much bigger share of global GDP under our assumptions than in the version reported by Stern. Indeed, the global damage calculation for 2100, combining economic, noneconomic and catastrophic risks, rises from 2.2 percent of GDP in the Stern version of PAGE (our Table 6.1) to 10.8 percent in our final version (Table 6.4).

Our revisions have a proportionally greater effect on damages in OECD countries: the estimated total damages in Table 6.4 are more than 6 times as great as in Table 6.1 for both the United States and other OECD, compared to 4.5 times as great for the rest of the world. Nonetheless, our modified PAGE2002 results still imply that damages are more than twice as large, relative to GDP, in developing nations as in the OECD: the costs of climate change – economic, noneconomic and catastrophic – will be far more severe in the places that have contributed the least to global emissions and that can least afford adaptation measures.

Chapter 7

CAN CLIMATE CHANGE SAVE LIVES? A COMMENT ON "ECONOMY-WIDE ESTIMATES OF THE IMPLICATIONS OF CLIMATE CHANGE: HUMAN HEALTH"

Frank Ackerman and Elizabeth A. Stanton

In a 2006 article published in the journal Ecological Economics, Francesco Bosello, Robert Rosom and Richard Tol make the remarkable prediction that one degree of global warming will, on balance, save more than 800,000 lives annually by 2050. They introduce enormous, controversial monetary valuations of mortality and morbidity, varying with income; they then focus primarily on modeling the much smaller, indirect economic effects of the changes in health outcomes. Their calculations, large and small, are driven by the huge projected reduction in mortality – an estimate that Bosello et al. fail to substantiate. They rely on research that identifies a simple empirical relationship between temperature and mortality, but ignores the countervailing effect of human adaptation to gradual changes in average temperature. While focusing on small changes in average temperatures, they ignore the important health impacts of extreme weather events. They extrapolate the effects of small changes in average temperature far beyond the level that is apparently supported by their principal sources, and introduce arbitrary assumptions that may bias the result toward finding net health benefits from warming.

Introduction

Could a little bit of global warming have wonderful consequences for human health? In their article, "Economy-wide Estimates of the Implications of Climate Change: Human Health," (2006, 579–91), Francesco Bosello, Roberto Roson and Richard Tol make the surprising prediction that the first stages of global warming will, on balance, save a large number of lives. As shown in their Table 1 (582), Bosello et al. estimate that in the year 2050 a global mean temperature 1.03°C higher than today's will result in 1,760,000 fewer deaths due to cardiovascular disease, only partially offset by 910,000 additional deaths due to malaria, diarrheal diseases and respiratory illness. The net effect is 850,000 avoided deaths, a huge change in worldwide mortality in a single year.

The estimate of reduced mortality is only the starting point for the ambitious set of calculations offered by Bosello et al. They seek to determine both the value of the direct welfare impacts of changes in mortality and morbidity due to climate change, and the indirect economic impacts of those changes in human health, including productivity losses and increased healthcare costs attributable to illness. The bulk of their analytical and modeling effort is applied to the relatively small indirect effects, with the direct welfare losses receiving much less attention. Nonetheless, the direct effects are enormous – and, if taken seriously, would have vast, controversial effects on the cost–benefit analysis of climate change.

In their discussion of the direct costs of mortality and morbidity, Bosello et al. write (585):

> Table 5 also shows the direct costs. Following Tol (2002a), we value a premature death at 200 times per capita income, and a year of life diseased at 80% of the annual income. Note that these estimates include the immaterial welfare losses of health impacts only; economic impacts are excluded. The direct costs, expressed as percent of GDP, are much larger than the economic impacts: The direct costs of risks of death and illness outweigh the indirect costs.

Because they find that the first degree of warming will reduce mortality and morbidity in most of the world, they estimate the direct effects as equivalent to a large increase in GDP: specifically, they predict values for direct health effects equivalent to an increase in GDP of roughly 9 to 14 percent in the United States, European Union, Eastern Europe and the former Soviet Union, Japan and much of the rest of Asia and more than 4 percent in China and India. Mortality and morbidity will increase elsewhere, with a value equivalent to a decrease in GDP of about 1 percent in the "energy exporting countries" and 3 percent in the rest of the developing world. (Bosello et al. 2006, Table 5, column 1.)

Since they have previously made it clear that they are calculating per capita income separately for eight regions of the world,[1] Bosello et al. are in effect valuing deaths quite differently, depending on where they occur. This is an idea that has had a troubled history. In the IPCC's Second Assessment Report, in 1995, economists calculating the monetary value of global warming damages decided to value deaths at $1,500,000 in rich countries, $300,000 in middle-income countries and $100,000 in low-income countries.

When these numbers came to light, governments of many countries were naturally outraged to find their citizens were "worth" only 1/15 as much as Europeans or North Americans. Much of the rest of the IPCC was outraged as well; last minute disclaimers were inserted into the Second Assessment Report, while the Third Assessment Report, issued in 2001, included a strong recommendation of alternate methodologies that made the value of lives independent of incomes (among many other accounts, see Ackerman and Heinzerling 2004, 73–74). The economists involved have continued to defend the income-based valuation of life, suggesting the use of equity weights in cost–benefit calculations to address income inequality (Fankhauser et al. 1997). However, a more common response was expressed by a researcher working in Brazil (Fearnside 1998, 83):

> Regardless of how much sense such a procedure may make to GDP-oriented economists, it is morally unacceptable to most of the world and needlessly damages efforts to build support for any global warming mitigation and adaptation strategies that may be proposed.

Although Bosello et al. do not include the direct cost estimates (i.e., the values of death) in their indirect-cost analysis, they have lent additional academic credibility to these huge, and unequal, hypothesized values for reduction in mortality. Even without such inequity, monetization of death and illness is a controversial and unsettled area, inevitably involving problematical hypotheses about the value of life and wellbeing (Ackerman and Heinzerling 2004).

For their detailed analysis, Bosello et al. use a computable general equilibrium (CGE) model to evaluate the effects of indirect health costs – losses of labor productivity, and health care expenditures – that are in the same direction as the direct costs (by region) but of a much smaller magnitude. The absolute value of these indirect cost impacts ranges from 0.014 to 0.101 percent of GDP, values that are well within the margin of error of any estimate of costs or benefits of climate change more than 40 years into the future.

Our concern in this note is not the magnitude of those small indirect effects, but rather the large underlying estimates of the reduction in human mortality resulting from climate change. Whether one accepts the direct cost estimates from Bosello et al., or other standards of evaluation, an annual reduction of 850,000 deaths is bound to loom large in the analysis of climate change.

The issue is important because of the large role of near- and medium-term events (which, in the multi-century scope of the climate problem, includes outcomes through 2050), both in political decision making about climate policy and in cost–benefit analyses. At a high discount rate, near- or medium-term benefits may outweigh enormous long-term damages when expressed in present value terms, creating a cost–benefit argument against vigorous emissions reduction efforts (Ackerman and Finlayson 2006). It is, therefore, crucial to be sure that any reported benefits of warming are reliable and well supported. This does not appear to be the case with the purported mortality reduction from the first degree of warming.

We have three criticisms of the analysis of mortality and temperature in Bosello et al.:

- They rely on research that identifies a simple empirical relationship between temperature and mortality, but ignores the countervailing effect of human adaptation to gradual changes in average temperature
- While focusing on small changes in average temperatures, they ignore the important health impacts of extreme weather events such as heat waves, droughts, floods and hurricanes
- They extrapolate this pattern far beyond the level that is apparently supported by their principal sources, and introduce an arbitrary assumption that may bias the result toward finding benefits from warming

The "Minimum-Mortality Temperature"

For estimates of cardiovascular and respiratory deaths, Bosello et al. rely on a simple empirical relationship between temperature and mortality: studies in many areas have found that there is a daily temperature that minimizes mortality; more deaths tend to occur when the temperature is either higher or lower. That is, a graph of mortality versus daily temperature is V-shaped, where the point of the V represents the minimum-mortality temperature.[2]

Bosello et al. represent at least a third generation in the studies of this relationship. In parts of their work, including the treatment of cardiovascular and respiratory mortality, they adapt the results of Tol (2002a), which in turn estimates worldwide impacts of temperature changes by extrapolating from research by Martens (1998).[3] A fundamental problem with this line of research can be seen in the original study by Martens.

Martens performed a meta-analysis of eight earlier studies of the effects of small changes in temperature on cardiovascular and respiratory mortality. These eight studies look at trends in mortality in a few areas around the world – most of them in cold climates – and report evidence of a "V-shaped" relationship between temperature and mortality. The point of this V – the minimum-mortality temperature – turns out to fall within the normal range of local temperatures, such that some months are generally below it and some above. In Martens's model, as temperatures warm, fewer days will be spent below the minimum-mortality temperature and more will be spent above it.

The left, or cold, side of the V is generally steeper than the right, or warm, side. That is, the reduction in mortality for 1° of warming in cold months is greater than the increase in mortality for 1° of warming in hot months. So as countries move 1° to the right across the V, the reductions in mortality in cold seasons will tend to outweigh the increases in warm seasons. This is the basis for the health benefit of warming in Martens and in those who have built upon his work.

A fundamental problem with this analysis is the implicit assumption that the position of the V, i.e., the minimum-mortality temperature, does not change. As Martens himself observes, people adapt to changing temperatures over time: "Acclimatisation may occur in several days, although complete acclimatisation may take up to several years" (Martens 1998, 338). Indeed, the minimum-mortality temperature is not a constant, but varies widely around the world. Martens mentions that it varies from 16.5°C in Amsterdam to as much as 29°C in some studies for Taiwan. A later study of cities in the eastern US found that the minimum-mortality temperature is 9°C higher in Miami than in Chicago (Curriero et al. 2002).

Although Martens discussed adaptation to temperature changes, and tempered his conclusions on that basis, Tol uses fixed-coefficient equations estimated directly from Martens's data (Tol 2002a, 60, Equations 3–7) and never mentions either "adaptation" or "acclimatization." Bosello et al., in turn, adopt the temperature-related mortality estimates from Tol (2002a), without significant modification, save for one possibility discussed below.

Yet adaptation does matter. Except in the very hottest parts of the world, it is reasonable to expect that people can adapt to gradual increases in average temperature. Since the minimum-mortality temperature varies widely around the world, and appears strongly correlated with average temperature, it seems likely that gradual warming will lead to gradual change in the minimum-mortality temperature as well. If this is the case, then rigid projections from Martens's data are mistaken, since there will be little or no mortality change from the first degree of warming based on the V-shaped relationship between temperature and death rates. To uphold projections based on the V-shaped relationship, in the manner of Martens and (particularly) his successors, it would at least be necessary to defend the hypothesis that the point of the V never moves, even as temperatures slowly rise. We have not found any such argument in the literature.

Extreme Weather

Models of climate change predict not only increases in average temperature, but also increased variability of weather conditions and more extreme weather events: more droughts and floods, more heat waves and more powerful storms (IPCC 2001a). According to one study, recent climate change has made extreme heat waves two to four times more likely, and over the next 40 years, these extreme heat events will become 100 times more likely (Epstein and Mills 2005).

With moderate changes in temperature and precipitation – such as the average changes forecast for the next few decades – there are good opportunities for human populations to adapt. When it comes to cardiovascular cold and heat stress, however, it isn't the average temperature that kills – it is temperature extremes. As our climate warms, the most important impact of temperature on mortality is unlikely to be avoided cold stress. Rather, human populations will adapt to new minimum-mortality temperatures, so that temperatures below the prevailing average will cause cold stress, while temperatures above the average will cause heat stress, especially in elderly or infirm people who have difficulty adjusting to rapid swings in temperature.

Average temperatures tell us nothing about the frequency of extreme divergences, hot or cold, from the local minimum-mortality temperature. Mounting evidence from climate scientists, however, indicates not only that recent temperatures have been more variable with more extremely hot temperatures, but also that the variability of temperatures and the frequency of heat waves is likely to accelerate in the coming decades (IPCC 2001a). While Bosello et al. (2006) exclude the impact of extreme weather, Martens's original study took care to acknowledge it: "[C]limate change is likely to increase the frequency or severity of heat waves [...] although this study focused on the long-term influence of climate changes upon health risk [...] research on heat wave-related mortality suggests an increase in predominantly cardio-respiratory mortality and illness" (Martens 1998, 342). It is, of course, notoriously difficult to predict the magnitude or precise rate of change of extreme weather events. But this does not mean that zero is a good estimate of the effects of extreme weather – as is implicitly assumed in a climate analysis that ignores such events.

No single weather event can be unambiguously linked to climate change, since there have always been climate fluctuations and occasional extremes. But climate change is increasing the frequency and intensity of extreme weather, causing a sharp upswing in weather-related deaths (Hales et al. 2003). As many as 50,000 people may have died in the 2003 heat wave in Europe (Brücker 2005). The United States suffered 1,800 deaths from Hurricane Katrina in 2005[4] and more than 700 fatalities from a 1995 heat wave in Chicago (Klinenberg 2002). The heat waves of summer 2006 killed at least 1,000 in the Netherlands and 200 in the United States.[5] Heat waves in India, in which temperatures sometimes reach 49°C, have killed more than a thousand people on several occasions in recent years (De et al. 2005).

Bosello et al. base their model on small changes in average temperature, not extreme weather events. Following Martens, they use average monthly temperatures instead of the daily temperature range, as employed by other researchers on this topic (Campbell-Lendrum et al. 2003, 142). Average monthly temperatures have little value in predicting whether or not the temperature on a given day will diverge very far from the minimum-mortality temperature and therefore cause cold or heat stress. It is the extremes in local temperature variation that are of concern in predicting changes in cardiovascular stress, not averages over the course of a month.

Unexplained Differences

Even if one accepts that the early stages of warming will lead to a reduction in mortality, based on the V-shaped relationship, the magnitude of the effect is quite different in Martens (1998), Tol (2002a) and Bosello et al. (2006) – and generally much larger in Bosello et al. than in the earlier studies. The problem is particularly severe for China and India, but affects the worldwide estimates of Bosello et al.

Martens does not produce worldwide estimates, but projects the effect on cardiovascular and respiratory mortality from a 1.2°C warming in 20 major cities located in 17 countries. Assuming that the cities are typical of the countries as a whole, he offers projections for the 17 countries. For China, where his projection is based on data for Beijing and Guangzhou, he estimates a mortality reduction of 4 per 100,000 population. For China's population of roughly 1.25 billion, this implies 50,000 avoided deaths from 1.2°C warming. Likewise, we calculate that his estimate implies roughly 60,000 avoided deaths in the US, and 10,000 avoided deaths in Japan.[6]

Tol extrapolates Martens's forecasts to the rest of the world, to obtain global estimates. As shown in Table 7.1, his estimates for changes to cardiovascular mortality from a degree of warming in OECD-America (excluding Mexico) and OECD-Pacific (excluding South Korea) are roughly in line with Martens's estimates for the United States and Japan, respectively. However, his projection for "centrally planned Asia," which is almost entirely China, is much higher than Martens's China estimate. Since Martens modeled a larger temperature change (1.2°C versus 1.0°C), Tol's China estimate is roughly twice as large as Martens's when adjusted to a comparable amount of warming.

The difference between Martens's and Tol's results might reflect Tol's surprising assumption that cardiovascular heat-related deaths occur only in urban areas, whereas cold-related deaths occur in both rural and urban areas (Tol 2002a, 60). The asymmetric treatment of rural areas has little effect on heavily urbanized societies such as the United States and Japan, but has

Table 7.1. Cardiovascular mortality changes from 1.0–1.2°C of warming

Martens	China	– 50,000
Tol	Centrally Planned Asia	– 80,000
Martens	US	– 60,000
Tol	US and Canada	– 50,000
Bosello et al.	US	– 170,000
Martens	Japan	– 10,000
Tol	Japan, Australia, NZ	– 10,000
Bosello et al.	Japan	– 60,000

Source: Martens 1998; Tol 2002; Bosello et al. 2006; Martens's estimates are our calculations from Martens's rates per 100,000 population.

a major impact on China with its huge rural population. The assumption of no heat-related cardiovascular deaths in rural areas is introduced by Tol without citation or justification, and appears to bias his results toward finding net benefits from warming.[7] Tol's assumption might be inspired by the more limited, well-known conclusion that the same regional temperature can be more painful in urban areas, due to urban "heat island" effects. While the negative effects of heat on health can be exacerbated in urban areas, it in no way follows that these effects are negligible in rural areas. The evidence on India's frequent heat waves should be studied carefully before assuming that rural death rates are so little affected by heat (De et al. 2005).

The estimates by Bosello et al. for the United States and Japan, also shown in Table 7.1, are sharply higher than those of either Martens or Tol. One difference is that Bosello et al. are modeling impacts in 2050, when the world's population will be larger and a greater proportion of the population will be elderly and, therefore, more susceptible to cold and heat stress. Tol, on the other hand, is modeling the effect of a static temperature increase on today's world. This is important to the results of these models because almost all temperature related mortality – 80 to 90 percent in most countries – is attributable to people 65 and over, and this group is expected to more than double in size by 2050 (Martens 1998; UN-DESA 2004).[8]

The difference between the estimates by Tol and Bosello et al. is explored further in Table 7.2, highlighting the puzzling nature of the estimates for China and India. Tol's "south and southeast Asia" region encompasses more than India, of course, but his two Asian regions, shown in the table, provide

Table 7.2. Change in mortality in China and India per degree of warming

		Cardiovascular	Respiratory	Total
Tol	2 Asian Regions	− 120,000	200,000	80,000
Tol (extrapolated to 2050)	2 Asian Regions	− 570,000	990,000	390,000
Bosello et al.	China and India	− 810,000	90,000	− 720,000

Source: Tol 2002; Bosello et al. 2006; extrapolation is our calculation as explained in text.

an approximate match to the Bosello et al. "China and India" region. For Tol, the two Asian regions together experience 130,000 fewer cardiovascular deaths per year, per degree of warming, offset by an increase of 200,000 in respiratory deaths. For Bosello et al., China and India experience 810,000 fewer cardiovascular deaths, but only 90,000 additional respiratory deaths. The coming demographic shift in India and China explains part, but not all, of the difference between the estimates by Tol and Bosello et al.: India and China's joint over-65 population is expected to quadruple, but Bosello et al. estimate cardiovascular mortality six times that of Tol. In addition, if a growing and aging population is meant to explain the difference between the results reported by Tol and Bosello et al., we would expect the change in respiratory mortality to be larger, not smaller, in Bosello et al. (see Table 7.2).

Using Martens's temperature-related change in deaths per 100,000 for the population under and over 65, we extrapolated to 2050 using the appropriate size and shares of the under- and over-65 population (see Table 7.3).[9] The estimated reduction in mortality using this method was 400,000 in India and China, 130,000 in the US and 30,000 in Japan – still much smaller than the Bosello et al. results.

One further innovation can be seen in the more recent study. Bosello et al. mention, in a single sentence unsupported by citation or evidence, that they assume there are no heat-related deaths in rural areas (583). This suggests that they have extended Tol's asymmetric treatment of rural areas to respiratory deaths – assuming that the rural population suffers only cold-related, but never heat-related, respiratory as well as cardiovascular deaths.[10] Since China and India include a large fraction of the world's rural population, the effects would show up most markedly in these countries, reducing the number of heat-related respiratory deaths included and increasing the estimates of avoided deaths reported by Bosello et al. As with Tol's more limited version of the same assumption, this introduces a bias toward finding net benefits of warming – and needs to be tested against empirical evidence on heat waves in countries such as India.

To summarize this intricate comparison, Tol appears to be consistent with Martens on developed country estimates, but has roughly doubled Martens's

Table 7.3. Changes in temperature-related mortality from 1.0–1.2°C of warming, with demographic transition

Martens (extrapolated to 2050)	China and India	– 400,000
Tol (extrapolated to 2050)	2 Asian Regions	+390,000
Bosello et al.	China and India	– 720,000
Martens (extrapolated to 2050)	US	– 130,000
Tol (extrapolated to 2050)	US and Canada	– 130,000
Bosello et al.	US	– 170,000
Martens (extrapolated to 2050)	Japan	– 30,000
Tol (extrapolated to 2050)	Japan, Australia, NZ	– 30,000
Bosello et al.	Japan	– 60,000

Source: Martens 1998; Tol 2002; Bosello et al. 2006; and our calculations as explained in text.

estimate for China, perhaps due to his unsupported assumption of no heat-related cardiovascular deaths in rural areas. Bosello et al. have increased Tol's estimates by a factor of almost four for cardiovascular deaths avoided by warming for most of the world, and by a factor of six in China and India, a difference that can only partially be explained by demographic transition. At the same time, they have sharply reduced Tol's estimate of the increased respiratory deaths in China and India due to warming, perhaps as a result of the combination of extending Tol's unsupported assumption about the absence of heat-related rural deaths to respiratory diseases and the Tol (1997) urbanization scenario. Quite apart from our skepticism about the validity of Martens's assumption of a constant minimum-mortality temperature discussed above, justification of the dramatic changes in the estimated impacts from one study to the next would require a fuller description of methodology on the part of Bosello et al.

Conclusions

The analysis presented by Bosello et al. predicts that the number of lives saved by climate change will be far greater than the number of lives lost, and uses this prediction to estimate direct and indirect economic impacts. Although the indirect economic impacts, modeled in detail by Bosello et al., are quite small, the underlying change in mortality is huge. The estimate that 1° of warming will result in 850,000 fewer net deaths in 2050 seems to rely heavily on three faulty assumptions. First, human populations are assumed to be unable to adapt to new climatic conditions, continuing to respond as they do today even as average temperatures gradually climb. Second, the focus on slow changes in average temperatures ignores the important issue of mortality and other impacts of extreme weather events related to climate change. Third, the incidence of increased heat-related cardiovascular and respiratory mortality is restricted to urban areas while decreases in cold-related cardiovascular mortality are assumed to occur in both urban and rural areas. Even with these assumptions, however, we could not reproduce the huge estimates made by Bosello et al. We urge them to produce a transparent explanation of the calculations behind their mortality estimate.

Like other predictions of benefits to be derived from climate change, estimates of reduced mortality from warming have an importance outside of the scholarly realm. Policy makers around the world respond to such predictions when making decisions regarding the type and extent of institutions created to combat climate change; predictions of large benefits from warming inevitably suggest that the problem is not so urgent to address. A model that accurately predicts the likely effects of climate change on mortality is essential to the formulation of climate and energy policies in countries around the world and to the future of international agreements regarding limits to the production of greenhouse gases. False optimism about climate impacts could have dangerous and long-lasting consequences.

Part III

THEORY AND METHODS OF INTEGRATED ASSESSMENT

Chapter 8

INSIDE THE INTEGRATED ASSESSMENT MODELS: FOUR ISSUES IN CLIMATE ECONOMICS

Elizabeth A. Stanton, Frank Ackerman and Sivan Kartha

Good climate policy requires the best possible understanding of how climatic change will impact human lives and livelihoods in both industrialized and developing counties. Our review of recent contributions to climate economics literature assesses 30 existing integrated assessment models in four key areas: the connection between model structure and the type of results produced; uncertainty in climate outcomes and projection of future damages; equity across time and space; and abatement costs and the endogeneity of technological change. Differences in treatment of these issues are substantial and directly affect model results and their implied policy prescriptions. Much can be learned about climate economics and modeling technique from the best practices in these areas; there is unfortunately no existing model that incorporates the best practices on all or most of the questions we examine.

Introduction

There is no shortage of models that join climate to economy with the goal of predicting the impacts of greenhouse gas emissions in the decades to come and offering policy advice on when, where and by how much to abate emissions. Some models are designed to offer a detailed portrayal of the climate, the process of economic growth or the feedback between these two systems; others focus on the long-run or the short-run, economic damages or environmental damages, carbon-based energy sectors or abatement technology. The best models produce results that inform and lend clarity to the climate policy debate. Some models surprisingly conclude – in direct contradiction to the urgency expressed in scientific literature – that rapid, comprehensive emissions abatement is both economically unsound and unnecessary. Some models seem to ignore (and implicitly endorse the continuation of) gross regional imbalances of both emissions and income.

Good climate policy requires the best possible understanding of how climatic change will impact human lives and livelihoods in industrialized countries and developing countries. No model gets it all right, but the current body of climate economics models and theories contains most of the ingredients for a credible model of climate and development in an unequal world.

Unfortunately, many climate economics models suffer from a lack of transparency, which affects both their policy relevance and their credibility. Building a model of the climate and the economy inevitably involves numerous judgment calls; debatable judgments and untestable hypotheses turn out to be of great importance in determining the policy recommendations of climate economics models and should be visible for debate. A good climate economics model would be transparent enough for policy relevance, but still sophisticated enough to get the most important characteristics of the climate and economy right.

Our review of recent contributions to climate economics literature assesses 30 existing integrated assessment models (IAMs) in four key areas:

1. Choice of model structure and the type of results produced
2. Uncertainty in climate outcomes and the projection of future damages
3. Equity across time and space
4. Abatement costs and the endogeneity of technological change

These models were chosen based on their prominence in climate economics literature over the last 10 years. Most of them have both climate and economic modules, and report results as damages in money values or as a share of GDP. A few models discussed here are better classified as physical impact IAMs, which report results in terms of physical damages.[1] In addition, a few models treat emissions as exogenous to the model structure.[2]

The next four sections of this review evaluate the body of existing climate economics models in terms of these key model characteristics, with illustrative examples of both problems and solutions taken from the literature. The concluding section summarizes our findings and their implications for the construction of climate economics models.

Choice of Model Structure

This review examines 30 climate economics models, all of which have been utilized to make contributions to IAM literature within the last 10 years.[3]

Table 8.1. Climate-economics models reviewed in this chapter

Model Category	Global	Regionally Disaggregated
Welfare Maximization	DICE-2007 ENTICE-BR DEMETER-1CCS *MIND*	RICE-2004 FEEM-RICE FUND MERGE CETA-M GRAPE AIM/Dynamic Global
General Equilibrium	JAM IGEM	IGSM/EPPA SMG WORLDSCAN ABARE-GTEM G-CUBED/MSG3 MS-MRT AIM IMACLIM-R WIAGEM
Partial Equilibrium		MiniCAM *GIM*
Simulation		PAGE-2002 ICAM-3 E3MG GIM
Cost Minimization	GET-LFL *MIND*	DNE21+ MESSAGE-MACRO

Note: Italics indicate that a model falls under more than one category.

These models fall into five broad categories, with some overlap: welfare optimization, general equilibrium, partial equilibrium, simulation and cost minimization (see Table 8.1).[1] Each of these structures has its own strengths and weaknesses, and each provides a different perspective on the decisions that are necessary for setting climate and development policy. In essence, each model structure asks a different question, and that question sets the context for the results it produces.

Differences in model structures

Welfare optimization models

Welfare optimization models tend to be fairly simple, which adds to their transparency. The production of goods and services causes both emissions and economic output, which can be used either for consumption or investment.

Greenhouse gas emissions affect the climate, causing damages that reduce production. Abatement reduces emissions but causes costs that reduce economic output. The models maximize the discounted present value of welfare (which grows with consumption, although at an ever-diminishing rate)[5] across all time periods by choosing how much emissions to abate in each time period, where abatement costs reduce economic output (see Figure 8.1). The process of discounting welfare (or "utility," which is treated as a synonym for welfare here and in many models) requires imputing speculative values to nonmarket "goods" like ecosystems or human lives, as well as assigning a current value to future costs and benefits. Dynamic optimization models – including all of the welfare optimization and cost minimization models reviewed here – solve for all time periods simultaneously, as if decisions could be made with perfect foresight.[6]

Our review of climate economics models includes four global welfare optimization models: DICE-2007 (Nordhaus 2008), ENTICE-BR (Popp 2006), DEMETER-1CCS (Gerlagh 2006) and MIND (Edenhofer et al. 2006a), and seven regionally disaggregated welfare maximization models: RICE-2004 (Yang and Nordhaus 2006), FEEM-RICE (Bosetti et al. 2006), FUND (Tol 1999), MERGE (Manne and Richels 2004), CETA-M (Peck and Teisberg 1999), GRAPE (Kurosawa 2004) and AIM/Dynamic Global (Masui et al. 2006).

General equilibrium models

General equilibrium models represent the economy as a set of linked economic sectors (markets for labor, capital, energy, etc.). These models are solved by finding a set of prices that have the effect of "clearing" all markets simultaneously (i.e., a set of prices that simultaneously equate demand and supply in every sector). General equilibrium models tend to use "recursive dynamics" – setting prices in each time period and then using this solution as the beginning point for the next period (thus assuming no foresight at all). Eleven general equilibrium models are reviewed in this study: JAM (Gerlagh 2008), IGEM (Jorgenson et al. 2004), IGSM/EPPA (Babiker et al. 2008), SMG (Edmonds et al. 2004), WORLDSCAN (Lejour et al. 2004), ABARE-GTEM (Pant 2007), G-CUBED/MSG3 (McKibbin and Wilcoxen 1999), MS-MRT (Bernstein et al. 1999), AIM (Kainuma et al. 1999), IMACLIM-R (Crassous et al. 2006) and WIAGEM (Kemfert 2001).

In dynamic versions of general equilibrium theory, multiple equilibria cannot always be ruled out (Ackerman 2002).[7] When multiple equilibria are present, general equilibrium models yield indeterminate results that may depend on details of the estimation procedure. For this reason, an assumption

Figure 8.1. Schematic representation of a welfare-optimizing IAM

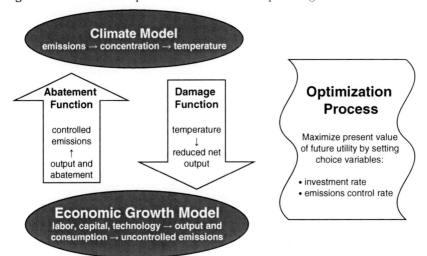

of constant or decreasing returns is often added to their production functions, an arbitrary theoretical restriction which is known to assure a single optimal result (Köhler et al. 2006). Because increasing returns to scale are important to accurate modeling of endogenous technological change, general equilibrium modelers must skirt between oversimplifying their representation of the energy sector and allowing unstable model results.

Partial equilibrium models

Partial equilibrium models – for example, MiniCAM (Clarke et al. 2007) and GIM (Mendelsohn and Williams 2004) – make use of a subset of the general equilibrium apparatus, focusing on a smaller number of economic sectors by holding prices in other sectors constant; this procedure also can help to avoid problems with increasing returns to scale.

Simulation models

Simulation models are based on off-line predictions about future emissions and climate conditions; climate outcomes are determined by an economic model of production, damages, consumption, investment and abatement costs. A predetermined set of emissions by time period dictates the amount of carbon that can be used in production and model output includes the cost of abatement and cost of damages. Simulation models cannot, in and of themselves, answer questions of what policy makers should do to maximize social welfare or minimize social costs. Instead, the simulation models reviewed in this study – PAGE2002 (Hope 2006a), ICAM-3 (Dowlatabadi 1998), E3MG (Barker et al. 2006) and GIM (Mendelsohn and Williams 2004) – estimate the costs of various likely future emission paths.

Cost minimization models

Cost minimization models are designed to identify the most cost-effective solution compatible with a particular objective. Some cost minimization models explicitly include a climate module, while others abstract from climate by representing only emissions, and not climatic change and damages. The four cost minimization models included in this review – GET-LFL (Hedenus et al. 2006), MIND (Edenhofer et al. 2006b), DNE21+ (Sano et al. 2006) and MESSAGE-MACRO (Rao et al. 2006) – have very complex "bottom-up" energy supply sectors, modeling technological choices based on detailed data about specific industries. Three of these models, excluding GET-LFL, combine a bottom-up energy supply sector with a top-down energy end-use sector, modeling technology from the vantage point of the macroeconomy.

Evaluation of model structures

The different types of model structures provide results that inform climate and development policy in very different ways. All five categories have strengths and weaknesses. Many of the best-known IAMs attempt to find the "optimal" climate policy, one that maximizes long-term human welfare. This calculation depends on several unknowable or controversial quantities, including the numerical measurement of human welfare, the physical magnitude and monetary value of all current and anticipated climate damages and the relative worth of future versus present benefits.

General equilibrium models can be extremely complex, combining very detailed climate models with intricate models of the economy; yet despite their detail, general equilibrium models' reliance on decreasing returns is a serious limitation to their usefulness in modeling endogenous technological change. When models are overly complex, both transparency and the plausibility of final results are compromised (this latter point is discussed in more detail below).[8] Partial equilibrium models circumvent the problem of increasing returns, at the cost of a loss of generality. In some cases, there appears to be a problem of spurious precision in overly elaborated models of the economy, with, for example, projections of long-term growth paths for dozens of economic subsectors.

Simulation models are well suited for representing uncertain parameters and for developing IAM results based on well-known scenarios of future emissions, but their policy usefulness is limited by a lack of feedback from their economic damages and abatement modules to emissions. Finally, cost minimization models address policy issues without requiring calculations of human welfare in money terms, but existing cost minimization models may suffer from the same tendency toward spurious precision exhibited in some general and partial equilibrium models.[9]

Uncertain Outcomes and Projections of Future Damages

IAMs inevitably rely on forecasts of future climate outcomes and the resulting economic damages, under conditions that are outside the range of human experience.[10] This aspect of the modeling effort raises two related issues: the treatment of scientific uncertainty about climate change and the functional relationships used to project future damages.

Scientific uncertainty in climate outcomes

There are inescapable scientific uncertainties surrounding climate science, for instance, in the climate sensitivity parameter (the temperature increase resulting from a doubling of CO_2 concentrations). As a result, low-probability, enormous-cost climate outcomes cannot be ruled out; the response to these extreme risks is often central to policy debate and would ideally be incorporated in economic models of climate change. Yet we found that most IAMs use central or average estimates to set parameter values, typically addressing uncertainty through a few sensitivity analyses of responses to selected changes in parameter values.[11] Those few models that express parameter values as distributions often use truncated distributions that inappropriately exclude or deemphasize low-probability, high-cost catastrophes.

Uncertainty is inescapable despite the ever-expanding body of climate research, because there are only a limited number of empirical observations relevant to questions such as estimation of the climate sensitivity parameter. As a result, the best estimates of the relevant probability distributions inevitably exhibit "fat tails," meaning that extreme outcomes are much more likely than a normal distribution would imply (Weitzman 2009). According to Weitzman, an economist who has raised this problem in recent debates, IPCC (2007d) data implies that an atmospheric concentration of 550 ppm of CO_2-equivalent would lead to a 98th percentile chance of 6°C increase in temperature, a point at which we "are located in the terra incognita of [...] a planet Earth reconfigured as science fiction [. . .where] mass species extinctions, radical alterations of natural environments, and other extreme outdoor consequences will have been triggered by a geologically-instantaneous temperature change that is significantly larger than what separates us now from past ice ages." (Weitzman 2007a, 716).[12]

In the face of such worst-case risks, it is misleading to look only at the most likely range of conditions. The future will happen only once. Suppose we knew that there were one hundred equally likely future scenarios, of which only one or a few would lead to truly catastrophic climate change. If we plan well for the most likely outcomes but instead one that we consider unlikely comes to pass, will we be comforted by our parsimonious rationality?

A thorough treatment of uncertainty through Monte Carlo analysis that varies multiple unknown parameters is seen in just a few IAMs. Even then it is difficult to fully explore the parameter space, especially given the fat-tailed distributions that characterize many key climate parameters and their poorly understood interactions.

One of the best-known models that incorporates Monte Carlo analysis is Hope's PAGE2002 (Hope 2006a), the model used in the Stern Review (Stern 2006). PAGE2002 includes triangular distributions for 31 uncertain parameters; Hope's standard analysis is based on 1,000 iterations of the model; as in other multivariate Monte Carlo analyses, he uses Latin Hypercube sampling[13] to select the uncertain parameters. This level of sensitivity analyses has a major impact on results. For the Stern Review, replacing the Monte Carlo analysis with a deterministic analysis using the modal parameter values decreases annual climate damages by an average of 7.6 percent of world output (Dietz et al. 2007).

The 31 uncertain parameters in PAGE2002 include two sets of seven regional parameters, but there are still 19 orthogonal (i.e., presumed unrelated or independent) parameters with independent distributions to be sampled for each iteration. This makes it essentially impossible for a Monte Carlo analysis to explore simultaneous worst cases in many or most of the parameters. To have, on average, at least one iteration with values from the worst quintile for all 19 parameters, it would be necessary to run the model an unimaginable 20 trillion times – a result of the so-called "curse of dimensionality" (Peck and Teisberg 1995).[14] Of course, parameters that are treated as orthogonal in the model could be interdependent in the real world. Greater interdependency among parameters would make seemingly rare extreme events (based on multiple worst-case parameter values) more likely. But as long as these parameters are represented as orthogonal in probabilistic IAMs, a high number of iterations will be necessary to assure even a single run with extreme values for multiple parameters. In PAGE2002, with 1,000 iterations, it is highly unlikely that there are any results for which more than a few parameters are assigned 95th percentile or worse values.

Only one other model among those reviewed has a built-in method of randomizing parameter values. Carnegie Mellon's ICAM is a stochastic simulation model that samples parameter values from probability distributions for 2,000 parameters for an unspecified number of iterations (Dowlatabadi 1998). An enormous number of iterations would be necessary to assure even one result with low-probability values for any large subset of these parameters. With any plausible number of iterations, the "curse of dimensionality" means that the primary choice being made by the Monte Carlo sampling is the selection of which parameters happen to have their worst cases influence the results of the analysis.

Several studies have added a Monte Carlo analysis onto other IAMs reviewed here. Nordhaus and Popp (1997) ran a Monte Carlo analysis on a modification of an earlier version of the DICE model – called PRICE – using eight uncertain parameters and 625 iterations, with five possible values for each of three parameters and a variation on Latin Hypercube sampling for the rest. Nordhaus also has run a Monte Carlo simulation using DICE-2007 (Nordhaus 2008) with eight parameters and 100 iterations. Kypreos (2008) added five stochastic parameters to MERGE and runs 2,500 iterations; Peck and Teisberg (1995) added one stochastic parameter to CETA-R with an unreported number of iterations; and Scott et al. (1999) added 15 stochastic parameters to MiniCAM with an unreported number of iterations. Webster et al. (1996) take a different approach to modeling uncertainty in ISGM/EPPA by using a collocation method that approximates the model's response as a polynomial function of the uncertain parameters.

None of the models reviewed here assume fat-tailed distributions and reliably sample the low-probability tails. Therefore, none of the models provide adequate representation of worst-case extreme outcomes, which are unfortunately not unlikely enough to ignore.

Projecting future damages

Most IAMs have two avenues of communication between their climate model and their economic model: a damage function and an abatement function (see Figure 8.1). The damage function translates the climate model's output of temperature – and sometimes other climate characteristics, such as sea-level rise – into changes to the economy, positive or negative.

Many models assume a simple form for this relationship between temperature and economic damage, such that damages rise in proportion to a power of temperature change:

(8.1) $$D = aT^b$$

Here D is the value of damages (in dollars or as a percent of output), T is the difference in temperature from that of an earlier period, and the exponent b determines the shape or steepness of the curve. Damages are calculated for multiple time periods, often at intervals of 5 or 10 years, over the course of as long as 600 years; annual damages for any given year are calculated by interpolation between adjacent estimates.[15] Implicitly, the steepness of the damage function at higher temperatures reflects the probability of catastrophe – a characteristic that can have a far more profound impact on model results than small income losses at low temperatures.

Our literature review revealed three concerns with damage functions in existing IAMs: the choice of exponents and other parameters for many damage functions are either arbitrary or under-explained; the form of the damage function constrains models' ability to portray discontinuities; and damages are commonly represented in terms of losses to income, not capital.[16]

Arbitrary exponent

DICE, like a number of other models, assumes that the exponent in the damage function is 2 – that is, damages are a quadratic function of temperature change.[17] The DICE-2007 damage function was assumed to be a quadratic function of temperature change with no damages at 0°C temperature increase, and damages equal to 1.8 percent of gross world output at 2.5°C; this implies, for example, that only 10.2 percent of world output is lost to climate damages at 6°C (Nordhaus 2007a).[18] Numerous subjective judgments, based on fragmentary evidence at best, are incorporated in the point estimate of 1.8 percent damages at 2.5°C (much of the calculation is unchanged from Nordhaus and Boyer (2000), which provides a detailed description). The assumption of a quadratic dependence of damage on temperature rise is even less grounded in any empirical evidence.

Our review of the literature uncovered no rationale, whether empirical or theoretical, for adopting a quadratic form for the damage function – although the practice is endemic in IAMs, especially in those that optimize welfare.[19] PAGE2002 (Hope 2006a) uses a damage function calibrated to match DICE, but makes the exponent an uncertain (Monte Carlo) parameter, with minimum, most likely, and maximum values of 1.0, 1.3 and 3.0, respectively. Sensitivity analyses of the Stern Review (Stern 2006) results, which were based on PAGE2002, show that fixing the exponent at 3 – assuming damages are a cubic function of temperature – increases average annual damages across the 200 year forecast horizon (above the Stern Review's business-as-usual baseline) by a remarkable 23 percent of world output (Dietz et al. 2007). Thus the equally arbitrary assumption that damages are a cubic, rather than quadratic, function of temperature would have a large effect on IAM results, and consequently on their policy implications.

Continuity

Damage functions are often defined to be continuous across the entire range of temperature rise, even though it is far from certain that climate change will in fact be gradual and continuous. Several climate feedback processes point to the possibility of an abrupt discontinuity at some uncertain temperature threshold or thresholds. However, only a few IAMs instead model damages as discontinuous, with temperature thresholds at which damages jump to much worse, catastrophic outcomes.

Two leading models incorporate some treatment of catastrophic change, while maintaining their continuous, deterministic damage functions. MERGE (Manne and Richels 2004) assumes all incomes fall to zero when the change in temperature reaches 17.7°C, which is the implication of the quadratic damage function in MERGE, fit to its assumption that rich countries would be willing to give up 2 percent of output to avoid 2.5°C of temperature rise. This formulation deduces an implicit level of catastrophic temperature increase, but maintains the damage function's continuity. DICE-2007 (Nordhaus 2007b) models catastrophe in the form of a specified (moderately large) loss of income, which is multiplied by a probability of occurrence (an increasing function of temperature), to produce an expected value of catastrophic losses. This expected value is combined with estimates of noncatastrophic losses, to create the DICE damage function; that is, it is included in the quadratic damage function discussed above.

In the PAGE2002 model (Hope 2006a), the probability of a catastrophe increases as temperature rises above some specified temperature threshold. The threshold at which catastrophe first becomes possible, the rate at which the probability increases as temperature rises above the threshold and the magnitude of the catastrophe when it occurs are all Monte Carlo parameters with ranges of possible values.

Income damages

Damages are commonly modeled in IAMs as losses to economic output, or gross domestic product (GDP), and therefore losses to income (GDP per capita) or consumption, leaving the productive capacity of the economy (the capital stock) and the level of productivity undiminished for future use. For example, noncatastrophic damages in the DICE-2007 model (Nordhaus 2007a) include impacts to agriculture, "other vulnerable markets," coastal property from sea-level rise, health, time-use and "human settlements and natural ecosystems," all of which are subtracted directly from total economic output. In reality, many of these categories are reductions to the capital stock and not directly to income, especially coastal property and human settlements damages. Others have multi-period effects on the marginal productivity of capital or labor, that is, the ability of technology to transform capital and labor into income; damages to agricultural resources and health are good examples of longer-term changes to productivity.

When damages are subtracted from output, the implication is that these are one-time costs that are taken from current consumption and investment, with no effects on capital, production or consumption in the next period – an unrealistic assumption even for the richest countries, as attested by the ongoing struggle to rebuild New Orleans infrastructure, still incomplete three years after Hurricane Katrina. FUND (Tol 1999) is unusual among welfare optimizing IAMs in that it models damages as one-time reductions to both consumption and investment, where damages have lingering "memory" effects determined by the rate of change of temperature increase.

Equity across Space and Time

Most climate economic models implicitly assume that little attention is needed to the problems of equity across time and space. In the area of intertemporal choice, most models have high discount rates that inflate the importance of the short-term costs of abatement relative to the long-term benefits of averted climate damage. Together with the common assumption that the world will grow richer over time, discounting gives greater weight to earlier, poorer generations relative to later, wealthier generations. Equity between regions of the world, in the present or at any moment in time, is intentionally excluded from most IAMs, even those that explicitly treat the regional distribution of impacts.

Equity across time

The impacts of climate change, and of greenhouse gas mitigation, will stretch centuries or even millennia into our future. Models that estimate welfare, income or costs over many years must somehow value gains and losses from different time periods. There are two leading approaches.

The early work of Ramsey (1928) provides the basis for the "prescriptive" approach, in which there are two components of the discount rate: the rate of pure time preference, or how human society feels about costs and benefits to future generations, regardless of the resources and opportunities that may exist in the future; and a wealth-based component – an elasticity applied to the rate of growth of real consumption – that reflects the diminishing marginal utility of income[20] over time as society becomes richer.

Algebraically, the discount rate, $r(t)$, combines these two elements: it is the rate of pure time preference, ρ, plus the product of the elasticity of marginal utility with respect to consumption per capita, η, and the growth rate of income or consumption per capita, $g(t)$.

$$(8.2) \qquad\qquad r(t) = \rho + \eta g(t)$$

Some models use the alternative, "descriptive" approach to discounting, where the market rate of interest or capital growth is taken to represent the discount rate.[21] These analyses typically either set the discount rate at 5 percent, or at an unspecified market rate of interest (e.g., Charles River Associates' MS-MRT (Bernstein et al. 1999), a general equilibrium model).

Because climate change is a long-term problem involving long time lags, climate economics models are extremely sensitive to relatively small changes in the assumed discount rate. There are longstanding debates on the subject, which are summarized well in the Stern Review (Stern 2006). Remarkably, the model descriptions for many IAMs do not state the discount rate or methodology they use, even when discussing discounting.

Choices about the discount rate inevitably reflect value judgments made by modelers. The selection of a value for the pure rate of time preference is a problem of ethics, not economic theory or scientific fact. Pure time preference of zero would imply that (holding real incomes constant) benefits and costs to future generations are just as important as the gains and losses that we experience today. The higher the rate of pure time preference, the less we value harm to future generations from climate change and the less we value the future benefits of current actions to avert climate change. Pure rates of time preference found in this literature review range from 0.1 percent in the Stern Review's PAGE2002 analysis (Hope 2006a) to 3 percent in RICE-2004 (Yang and Nordhaus 2006).

Only a few model descriptions directly state their elasticity of marginal utility of consumption, although the use of this elasticity, implying that marginal utility declines as consumption grows, is common to many IAMs. In DICE-2007 (Nordhaus 2008), the elasticity of the marginal utility of consumption is set at 2, and the discount rate declines from 4.7 percent in 2005 down to 3.5 percent in 2395. In the Stern Review's version of PAGE2002 (Hope 2006a), the elasticity of the marginal utility of consumption is set at 1, and the discount rate averages 1.4 percent.

A higher elasticity of marginal utility of consumption reflects a greater emphasis on equity: the larger the elasticity, the greater the value to social welfare of an increase in consumption for a poorer person, versus a richer one.[22] However, in a global model – lacking regional disaggregation – there is only one utility function for the world as a whole. The practical upshot of this is that the diminishing marginal utility of income is applicable only in comparisons across time (e.g., the present generation versus the future) and not in comparisons across different regions or socioeconomic characteristics (e.g., Africa versus North America today, or at any given point in time).

The four cost minimization models included in this literature review – GET-LFL (Hedenus et al. 2006), MIND (Edenhofer et al. 2006a), DNE21+ (Sano et al. 2006) and MESSAGE-MACRO (Rao et al. 2006) – all report a 5 percent discount rate.[23] The ethical issues involved in discounting abatement costs are somewhat more straightforward than those involved in discounting welfare. Abatement technologies have well-defined monetary prices, and thus are more firmly situated within the theoretical framework for which discounting was developed. Many abatement costs would occur in the next few decades – over spans of time, which could fit within the lifetime and personal decisions of a single individual. To pay for $1,000 worth of abatement 50 years from now, for example, one can invest $230 today in a low-risk bond with 3 percent annual interest. On the other hand, welfare optimization models must inevitably assign subjective, contestable values to the losses and gains to future generations that are difficult to monetize, such as the loss of human life or the destruction of ecosystems. No investment today can adequately compensate for a loss of life or irreversible environmental damage; and even if an agreeable valuation were established, there is no existing or easily imagined mechanism for compensating victims of climate change several hundred years in the future.

Equity across space

IAMs that optimize welfare for the world as a whole – modeled as one aggregate region – maximize the result of a single utility function by making abatement and investment choices that determine the emissions of greenhouse gases; emissions then determine climate outcomes and damages, one of the inputs into utility. This utility function is a diminishing function of per capita consumption. The IAM chooses emission levels for all time periods simultaneously – when more emissions are allowed, future periods lose consumption to climate damages; when emissions are lowered, abatement costs decrease current consumption.

The model's optimizing protocol (or more picturesquely, the putative social planner) balances damages against abatement costs with the goal of maximizing utility – not income or consumption. Because utility is modeled with diminishing returns to consumption, the value to society of a given cost or benefit depends on the per capita income level at the time when it occurs. A change to income in a rich time period is given a lower weight than an identical change to income in a poor time period (even if the rate of pure time preference is zero). If, as usual, per capita income and consumption are projected to keep growing, the future will be richer than the present.[21] Under that assumption, the richer future matters less, in comparison to the relatively poorer present.

Regional welfare optimizing IAMs apply the same logic, but with separate utility functions for each region. The model is solved by choosing abatement levels that maximize the sum of utility in all regions. Seemingly innocuous, the disaggregation of global IAMs into component regions raises a gnarly problem for modelers: with identical, diminishing marginal returns to income in every region, the model could increase utility by moving income toward the poorest regions. This could be done by reallocating responsibility for regional damage and abatement costs, or inducing transfers between regions for the purpose of fostering technical change, funding adaptation or purchasing emission allowances or any other channel available in the model for inter-regional transfers.

Modelers have typically taken this tendency toward equalization of income as evidence of the need for a technical fix. In order to model climate economics without any distracting rush toward global equality, many models apply the little-known technique of "Negishi weights" (Negishi 1972). Stripped of its complexity, the Negishi procedure assigns larger weight to the welfare of richer regions, thereby eliminating the global welfare gain from income redistribution.[25]

In more detail, the technical fix involves establishing a set of weights for the regional utility functions. The model is run first with no trade or financial transfers between regions; the regional pattern of per capita income and marginal product of capital from that autarkic (no-trade) run is then used to set the so-called Negishi weights, for each time period, that equalize the marginal product of capital[26] across all regions. Since the marginal product of capital is higher in lower-income regions, the Negishi weights give greater importance to utility in higher-income areas. In a second iteration, the normal climate economics model, with transfers possible between regions, is restored, and the Negishi weights are hardwired into the model's utility function. The result, according to the model descriptions, is that the models act as if the marginal product of capital were equal in all regions and, therefore, no transfers are necessary to assuage the redistributive imperative of diminishing marginal returns.[27] The (usually) unspoken implication is that the models are acting as if human welfare is more valuable in the richer parts of the world.

Describing the use of Negishi weights as a mere technical fix obscures a fundamental assumption about equity. Negishi weights cause models to maximize welfare as if every region already had the same income per capita – suppressing the obvious reality of vastly different regional levels of welfare, which the models would otherwise highlight and seek to alleviate (Keller et al. 2003; Manne 1999; Nordhaus and Yang 1996).

In IAMs that do not optimize welfare, Negishi weights are not used and inter-regional effects can, therefore, remain more transparent. For example, in PAGE2002 (Hope 2006a) – a simulation model that reports regional estimates – no radical equalization of per capita income across regions occurs, but utility is not being maximized, and the simulations do not claim to represent optimal policy outcomes.[28]

By including discounting over time as well as Negishi weights, welfare optimizing IAMs accept the diminishing marginal utility of income for intergenerational choices, but reject the same principle in the contemporary, inter-regional context. Some justification is required if different rules are to be applied in optimizing welfare across space than those used when optimizing welfare across time. At the very least, a climate economics model's ethical implications should be transparent to the end users of its analyses. While ethical concerns surrounding discounting have achieved some attention in policy circles, the highly technical but ethically crucial Negishi weights are virtually unknown outside the rarified habitat of modelers and welfare economists. The Negishi procedure conceals one strong, controversial assumption about welfare maximization, namely that existing regional inequalities are not legitimate grounds for shifting costs to wealthier regions, but inequalities across time are legitimate grounds for shifting costs to wealthier generations. Other assumptions, needless to say, could be considered.

Abatement Costs and the Endogeneity of Technological Change

The analysis of abatement costs and technological change is crucial to any projection of future climate policies. An unrealistic picture of fixed, predictable technological change, independent of public policy, is often assumed in IAMs – as is the treatment of investment in abatement as a pure loss. These choices are mathematically convenient, but prevent analysis of policies to promote and accelerate the creation of new, low-carbon technologies. This oversimplification supports the questionable conclusion that the best policy is to avoid immediate, proactive abatement, and wait for automatic technical progress to reduce future abatement costs.

Choices in modeling abatement technology

There have been rapid advances in recent years in the area of modeling endogenous technological change. A review by the Innovation Modeling Comparison Project (Edenhofer et al. 2006b; Grubb et al. 2006; Kohler et al. 2006) offers a thorough description of the most recent attempts to model endogeneity and induced technological innovation – an effort that we will not attempt to reproduce here. Instead, this section briefly discusses three choices that all IAM modelers must make with regard to their representation of abatement technology: how to model increasing returns; how much technological detail to model; and how to model macroeconomic feedback.

Many models, especially general equilibrium models, assume technologies are characterized by decreasing returns to scale (meaning that doubling all inputs yields less than twice as much output), a provision which ensures that there is only one, unique equilibrium result. The assumption of decreasing returns may be realistic for resource-based industries such as agriculture or mining, but it is clearly inappropriate to many new, knowledge-based technologies – and indeed, it is inappropriate to many branches of old as well as new manufacturing, where bigger is better for efficiency, up to a point. Some industries exhibit not only increasing returns in production, but also "network economies" in consumption – the more people that are using a communications network or a computer operating system, the more valuable that network or operating system is to the next user.

The problem for modeling is that increasing returns and network economies introduce path dependence and multiple equilibria into the set of possible solutions. Small events and early policy choices may decide which of the possible paths or output mixes the model will identify as "the solution." An inferior computer operating system, energy technology or other choice may become "locked in" – the established standard is so widely used and so low-priced because it is produced on such a large scale, that there is no way for individual market choices to lead to a switch to a technologically superior alternative. Modeling increasing returns, path dependence and multiple equilibria can bring IAMs closer to a realistic portrayal of the structure and nature of emissions abatement and economic development options, but at the expense of making models more difficult to construct and model results more difficult to interpret.

Knowledge spillovers are also related to increasing returns. Some of the returns to research and development are externalities, that is, they impact on third parties – other companies, industries or countries. Because of the public goods character of knowledge, its returns cannot be completely appropriated by private investors. Without public incentives for research and development, private firms will tend to under-invest in knowledge, with the result that the total amount of research and development that occurs is less than would be socially optimal. Increasing returns are modeled either as a stock of knowledge capital that becomes an argument in the production function, or as learning curves that lower technological costs as cumulative investments in physical capital or research and development grow.

A second choice that IAM modelers must make is how much technological detail to include. This encompasses not only whether to model increasing returns but also how many regions, industries, fuels, abatement technologies or end uses to include in a model. A more detailed technology sector can improve model accuracy but there are limits to the returns from adding detail – at some point, data requirements, spurious precision and loss of transparency begin to detract from a model's usefulness. On the other hand, a failure to model sufficient technological diversity can skew model results. Abatement options such as renewable energy resources, energy efficiency technologies and behavioral shifts serve to limit abatement costs; models without adequate range of abatement options can exaggerate the cost of abatement and therefore recommend less abatement effort than a more complete model would.

The final modeling choice is how to portray macroeconomic feedback from abatement to economic productivity. A common approach is to treat abatement costs as a pure loss of income, a practice that is challenged by new models of endogenous technological change, but still employed in a number of IAMs, such as DICE-2007 (Nordhaus 2008). Two concerns seem of particular importance. Modeling abatement costs as a dead-weight loss implies that there are no "good costs" – that all money spent on abatement is giving up something valuable and thereby diminishing human welfare. But many costs do not fit this pattern: money spent wisely can provide jobs or otherwise raise income, and can build newer, more efficient capital. A related issue is the decision to model abatement costs as losses to income. Abatement costs more closely resemble additions to capital, rather than subtractions from income. (A similar argument can be made regarding many kinds of damage costs: see the earlier section on projecting future damages.)

Cost minimization models

Many of the IAMs making the most successful inroads into modeling endogenous technological change are cost minimization models. All four of the cost minimization models reviewed in this study – GET-FL (Hedenus et al. 2006), DNE21+ (Sano et al. 2006), MIND (Edenhofer et al. 2006a) and MESSAGE-MACRO (Rao et al. 2006) – include learning curves for specific technologies and a detailed rendering of alternative abatement technologies.

GET-FL, DNE21+, MIND and MESSAGE-MACRO are all energy systems models that include greenhouse gas emissions but not climate change damages. These models include various carbon-free abatement technologies, carbon capture and storage and spillovers within clusters of technologies. GET-FL has learning curves for energy conversion and investment costs. DNE21+ has learning curves for several kinds of renewable energy sources and a capital structure for renewables that is organized in vintages. Both MIND and MESSAGE-MACRO combine an energy system model with a macroeconomic model. MIND has learning curves for renewable energy and resource extraction research; development investments in labor productivity; trade-offs between different types of research and development investment; and a vintaged capital structure for renewables and carbon capture and storage technologies. MESSAGE-MACRO models interdependencies from resource extraction, imports and exports, conversion, transport and distribution to end-use services; declining costs in extraction and production; and learning curves for several energy technologies (Edenhofer et al. 2006b; Kohler et al. 2006).

These energy system models demonstrate the potential for representing induced innovation and endogeneity in technological change. Unfortunately, the very fact of their incredible detail of energy resources, technologies and end uses leads to a separate problem of unmanageably large and effectively opaque results in the most complex IAMs. (For example, the RITE Institute's DNE21+ models historical vintages, eight primary energy sources and four end-use energy sectors, along with five carbon capture and storage methods, several energy conversion technologies and separate learning curves for technologies such as wind, photovoltaics and fuel cells.) A model is constructed at the level of detail achievable from present day energy sector data, providing accuracy in the base year calculations. Then the model is extended into the future based on unknowable and untestable projections, running the risk of turning historical accuracy into spurious precision in future forecasts. A high level of specificity about the future of the energy sector cannot be sustained over the number of years or decades necessary to analyze the slow, but inexorable, advance of climate change.

Conclusions

The best-known climate economics models weigh the costs of allowing climate change to continue against the costs of stopping or slowing it, and thus recommend a "best" course of action: one that, given the assumptions of the model, would cause the least harm. The results of such models are, of course, only as good as their underlying structures and parameter values.

Analysis of climate change, in economics as well as in science, inescapably involves extrapolation into the future. To understand and respond to the expected changes, it is essential to forecast what will happen at greenhouse gas concentrations and temperature levels that are outside the range of human experience, under regimes of technological progress and institutional evolution that have not yet even been envisioned. While some progress has been made toward a consensus about climate science modeling, there is much less agreement about the economic and societal laws and patterns that will govern future development.

IAMs seek to represent both the impacts of changing temperature, sea level and weather on human livelihoods, and the effects of public policy decisions and economic growth on greenhouse gas emissions. IAMs strive not only to predict future economic conditions but also to portray how we value the lives, livelihoods and natural ecosystems of future generations – how human society feels about those who will inherit that future. The results of economic models depend on theories about future economic growth and technological change, and on ethical and political judgments.

Model results are driven by conjectures and assumptions that do not rest on empirical data and often cannot be tested against data until after the fact. To the extent that climate policy relies on the recommendations of IAMs, it is built on what looks like a "black box" to all but a handful of researchers. Better-informed climate policy decisions might be possible if the effects of controversial economic assumptions and judgments were visible and were subjected to sensitivity analyses.

Our review of the literature has led to several concrete lessons for model development:

- Many value-laden technical assumptions are crucial to policy implications and should be visible for debate. Existing models often bury assumptions deep in computer code and parameter choices, discouraging discussion.
- Crucial scientific uncertainties – such as the value of the climate sensitivity parameter and the threshold for irreversible catastrophe – must be addressed in the model structure. Most IAMs use central or average estimates, and thereby ignore catastrophic risk.
- Modeling climate economics requires forecasts of damages at temperatures outside historical experience; there is no reason to assume a simple quadratic (or other low-order polynomial) damage function.
- Today's actions affect the climate and economy of future generations, thus linking current and future welfare. Many models effectively break this link by using high discount rates, inflating the importance of near-term abatement costs while trivializing long-term benefits of mitigation.

- Climate choices occur in an unequal world and inevitably affect opportunities for development. Most regionally disaggregated models use a technical device ("Negishi welfare weights") that freezes the current income distribution, constraining models to ignore questions of inter-regional equality.
- Measures to induce or accelerate technological change will be crucial for a successful climate policy; a realistic model must allow endogenous technical change and increasing returns. Many IAMs assume decreasing returns and/or exogenous technological progress and treat abatement costs as an unproductive loss of income, not an investment in energy-conserving capital.

Climate economics models have improved over the years, including expanded treatment of externalities, technological innovation and regional disaggregation. But there is still tremendous scope for further improvement, including more extensive sensitivity analyses and more rigorous examination of risk and uncertainty. Fundamentally subjective judgments, especially those that embody deeply value-laden assumptions, can be made more explicit.

What difference would it make to change these features of climate economics modeling? In the absence of a better model, we can only speculate about the results. Our guess is that the modifications we have proposed would make a climate economics model more consistent with the broad outlines of climate science models, portraying the growing seriousness of the problem, the ominous risks of catastrophe and the need for immediate action.

Chapter 9

LIMITATIONS OF INTEGRATED ASSESSMENT MODELS OF CLIMATE CHANGE

Frank Ackerman, Stephen J. DeCanio, Richard B. Howarth and Kristen Sheeran

The integrated assessment models (IAMs) that economists use to analyze the expected costs and benefits of climate policies frequently suggest that the "optimal" policy is to go slowly and to do relatively little in the near term to reduce greenhouse gas emissions. We trace this finding to the contestable assumptions and limitations of IAMs. For example, they typically discount future impacts from climate change at relatively high rates. This practice may be appropriate for short-term financial decisions, but its extension to intergenerational environmental issues rests on several empirically and philosophically controversial hypotheses. IAMs also assign monetary values to the benefits of climate mitigation on the basis of incomplete information and sometimes speculative judgments concerning the monetary worth of human lives and ecosystems, while downplaying scientific uncertainty about the extent of expected damages. In addition, IAMs may exaggerate mitigation costs by failing to reflect the socially determined, path dependent nature of technical change and ignoring the potential savings from reduced energy utilization and other opportunities for innovation. A better approach to climate policy, drawing from recent research on the economics of uncertainty, would reframe the problem as buying insurance against catastrophic, low-probability events. Policy decisions should be based on a judgment concerning the maximum tolerable increase in temperature and / or carbon dioxide levels given the state of scientific understanding. The appropriate role for economists would then be to determine the least-cost global strategy to achieve that target. While this remains a demanding and complex problem, it is far more tractable and epistemically defensible than the cost–benefit comparisons attempted by most IAMs.

Introduction

The scientific consensus on climate change is clear and unambiguous; climate change is an observable phenomenon with the potential for catastrophic impacts (IPCC 2007a). The large-scale computer models that helped build this consensus have acquired a good reputation in the scientific community. The leading general circulation models (GCMs) demonstrate ever more detailed and extensive descriptions of the physical processes of climate change, which are testable either directly, or indirectly through "backcasting" of historical climate data. These models are grounded in physical laws that are well established, both theoretically and empirically, although significant uncertainty surrounds key parameters such as the climate sensitivity.

Economists also employ multi-equation computer models in their approach to climate change. These models, known as integrated assessment models (IAMs), build on the results of GCMs to assess the benefits and costs of climate policy options. Economists use IAMs to identify the "optimal" policy response, the option that maximizes the difference between benefits and costs (i.e., net benefits). As the debate over climate policy shifts from scientific uncertainty to economic feasibility, the results of IAMs grow in importance. Interpreting IAMs properly is critical for scientists and others who support a proactive response to the climate problem.

The results of most IAMs are surprising. While many scientists advocate more stringent emissions targets aimed at stabilizing atmospheric greenhouse gas (GHG) concentrations during this century, recent IAMs suggest a cautious approach that involves only modest early action to limit emissions with the limits gradually becoming more stringent over time (Kelly and Kolstad 1999; Tol 2002a; Manne 2004; Mendelsohn 2004; Nordhaus 2007c). For example, the optimal emissions reduction rate according to Nordhaus's most recent version of the widely cited DICE model is only 14 percent compared to a "business-as-usual" or no-control emission scenario in 2015, rising to 25 percent by 2050 and 43 percent by 2100 (Nordhaus 2007c). Other IAMs have estimated a positive net benefit from climate change in Organization for Economic Co-operation and Development (OECD) countries (while acknowledging net losses in poor countries), leading researchers such as Tol to conclude that "climate change and greenhouse gas abatement policy is essentially a problem of justice" (Tol 2002b). On the other hand, it has been estimated that the recently considered suite of Congressional proposals to limit carbon emissions to 50–80 percent below 1990 levels by 2050 would impose large welfare losses on the US economy.[1]

How can we reconcile the apparent disconnect between science, which provides an objective characterization of the potentially catastrophic implications of climate change, and economics, which claims that aggressively mitigating climate change is too costly? We maintain that IAMs enjoy an epistemic status different from their natural science counterparts, and that economic models mix descriptive analysis and value judgments in ways that deserve close and critical scrutiny. To build their models, economists have had to embrace assumptions that reflect longstanding practices within economics but that nonetheless are associated with well-known conceptual problems. Alternative models, built on different assumptions that are equally as plausible as those embedded in commonly cited IAMs, would lead to qualitatively different results (Cline 1992; Stern 2006; Ackerman and Finlayson 2006).

Scientific understanding of the climate system is continuously improving. For example, the review article by Hall and Behl (2006) highlights the consequences of climate instability and rapid large-scale shifts in global climate for the economic analysis of climate change. Lenton et al. (2008) identify and catalogue potential "tipping elements" in the climate system. In addition, a variety of decision making frameworks extending beyond the conventional utility-maximizing economic component of IAMs have been identified (Toth et al. 2001). These include "tolerable windows" and "safe landing" approaches, "robust decision-making" and "cost-effectiveness analysis," among others. A recent conference was devoted to the implications of "avoiding dangerous anthropogenic interference with the climate system" as a guide to policy-making (Schellnhuber et al. 2006). Our objective in this chapter is not to provide a comprehensive review of the most recent developments in climate science[2] or an all-encompassing treatment of decision making with regard to climate. Rather, our critique focuses on the conceptual economic framework of the most common utility-maximizing IAMs and on the specific details of how these models' standard economic approach is arguably deficient: the discounted utility framework, which attaches less weight to future outcomes; the characterization and monetization of the benefits of mitigation; and the projection of mitigation costs, which rests on assumptions about the pace and nature of technical change. We address these issues in the following three sections and conclude with recommendations for an alternative approach to the economics of climate change that reflects recent advances in the economics of uncertainty.

The Discounted Utility Framework

IAMs, like the economic theory from which they are derived, start from a particular understanding of human nature and preferences and seek to identify the choices that will maximize the satisfaction of those desires. Climate outcomes enter the analysis as factors that increase or decrease human satisfaction. The "optimal" target is not a safe or predetermined climate stabilization level, but rather the maximum subjective satisfaction.

Echoing nineteenth century utilitarian moral philosophy, economists refer to satisfaction as "utility" and assume it to be a scalar variable – in short, an ideal objective for maximization. This stylized psychological model, as it has been elaborated in economics, requires careful estimation and comparison of benefits and costs. To compare utilities across generations, economists invoke assumptions about how much additional weight present outcomes deserve over future outcomes. But when economists resort to this technique of discounting the future, the present value of the harms caused by future climate change can easily shrink to the point where it is hardly "worth" doing anything today in order to prevent them.

The basic construct of the typical IAM involves a social welfare function that stretches into the distant future (far enough ahead to experience significant climate change). Frequently, IAMs assume a single representative agent in each generation, or equivalently, that all members of a generation are identical in both consumption and preferences. With slight variations between models, the generic framework is to maximize

$$(9.1) \qquad W = \int_{0}^{\infty} e^{-\rho t}\, U\big[c(t)\big]\, dt$$

where W is social welfare, ρ is the "rate of pure time preference," $c(t)$ is consumption at time t and $U[\bullet]$ is the utility function specifying how much utility is derived from a particular level of consumption. Economists have studied this problem since the time of Ramsey (1928), and the methods they have developed to solve it are now standard elements of the conventional IAM framework. Although this framework dominates the economics of climate change, economists have proposed a number of alternatives (e.g., Howarth and Norgaard 1992; Chichilnisky et al. 1995; Howarth 1998; DeCanio 2003b; Bella 2006).

Equation 9.1 and the techniques required to maximize W embody a large set of questionable assumptions. First note that with $\rho > 0$, a given amount of utility occurring further in the future is worth less than the same amount of utility today. This implies that the wellbeing of this generation matters more than that of its children, who in turn matter more than their children. Thus $e^{-\rho t}$ may be interpreted as the relative weighting given to the utility or wellbeing of various generations. If a generation is 35 years in duration and $\rho = 0.05$, the weight given to a unit of utility at the end of the second generation is only 3 percent of the weight given to the same unit of utility today. Numerous economists and philosophers since Ramsey have argued that weighing all generations equally, $\rho = 0$, is the only ethically defensible practice (for modern treatments, see Cline 1992 and Broome 1994); yet IAMs continue to assume $\rho > 0$. This is at least in part a mathematical necessity: with $\rho = 0$, the integral in Equation 9.1 does not converge if future utility is constant or growing (or merely declining sufficiently gradually) (Dasgupta and Heal 1979).

Second, implicit in the formulation of a social welfare function is the aggregation of preferences across different individuals. In Equation 9.1, this aggregation depends only on the total consumption of goods and not on the distribution of that consumption. Whatever method for aggregation is used, it necessarily involves strong and value-laden assumptions.[3] This is an inescapable consequence of the discounted utility framework. Because the framework requires that preferences be compared and added within and across generations, it forces economists to make normative decisions regarding the comparison of individual utilities and discount rates. Though a social welfare function can be solved mathematically to yield the "optimal" solution, the solution is dependent on the values and biases that are unavoidably embedded in the model and its parameterization.

Third, it is worth noting that the discounted utility characterization of behavior for *individuals* that underlies this formulation of the social policy problem is not well supported by the evidence (Frederick et al. 2002). The optimizing psychological and behavioral assumptions adopted by economic modelers do not have the status of laws of nature. They are matters of convenience and convention, not deep structural features of human action (Laitner et al. 2000; Kahneman and Tversky 2000).

The formulation of Equation 9.1 does not include uncertainty about either the consequences of climate change or about the future growth of the economy. This omission is serious, for it is at odds with empirical observations and has strong implications for the treatment of discounting. In this context, it is significant that a recent National Research Council report lists "realistic and credible treatment of uncertainties" as one of its 11 elements of effective assessments (Committee on Analysis of Global Change Assessments 2007). The problems caused by uncertainty can be illustrated by an even simpler version of the decision problem represented by Equation 9.1. Our discussion closely follows Cochrane (2005), Mehra (2003) and Howarth (2003, 2009), but the theory is entirely generic. To keep things simple, instead of the infinite horizon intertemporal welfare function, suppose the social decision is based on maximizing a two-period utility function of the following form:

(9.2) $$U\left[c_t, c_{t+1}\right] = u\left(c_t\right) + \frac{1}{1+\rho} E\left[u\left(c_{t+1}\right)\right]$$

where $1/(1 + \rho)$ is the "discount factor" corresponding to $e^{-\rho t}$ in Equation 9.1, $E[\cdot]$ represents the expected value of the argument as of time t, and c_t and c_{t+1} are consumption at times t and $t + 1$ respectively. Then if agents are able at time t to purchase an asset (i.e., make an investment) that has an (uncertain) payoff x_{t+1} in the future, the basic rule for the pricing of that asset will be:

$$(9.3) \qquad p_t = E\left[\frac{1}{1+\rho} \frac{u'(c_{t+1})}{u'(c_t)} x_{t+1} \right]$$

This is simply the first-order condition for the solution to the problem of maximizing U in Equation 9.2. The issues of concern to us can be illustrated without loss of generality by making the common simplifying assumption that u has the form of the "constant relative risk aversion" type, namely

$$(9.4) \qquad u(c) = \frac{c^{1-\eta} - 1}{1-\eta}$$

where the parameter η is the "coefficient of relative risk aversion." The marginal utility of consumption is given by $u'[c] = c^{-\eta}$, which is decreasing in c provided η is positive. In the absence of uncertainty, it is easy to show that Equations 9.3 and 9.4 yield a formula for the market interest or discount rate given by:

$$(9.5) \qquad 1+r = (1+g)^\eta (1+\rho) \Rightarrow r \approx \rho + \eta g$$

where g is the rate of growth of consumption, with the approximation holding for small ρ and g. By analogy with short-term financial calculations, it is typically asserted that future incomes and consumption should be discounted at the interest rate r (in contrast to utility, which is discounted at the rate ρ). That is, $\$Y$ at a time N years from now has a present value of only $\$Ye^{-rN}$ for continuous time models, or $\$Y(1 + r)^{-N}$ for annual calculations in discrete-time models. With r greater than zero, this becomes the basis for the reduced importance of distant-future outcomes in economic calculations.

This shrinkage of future values is not an inevitable consequence of Equation 9.5. It has been noted before by Tol (1994), Amano (1997) and Dasgupta et al. (1999) that if environmental damage is sufficiently great so as to reduce consumption in the future, then g may be negative and the discount rate will actually be *less* than the pure rate of time preference. A sufficiently negative g could even make r negative in this situation. In addition, Equation 9.5 needs modification if the economy consists of multiple goods with different growth rates of consumption. If we define the economy to include environmental services, the proper discount rate for evaluating investments in environmental protection will be considerably lower than r, and possibly even negative, as long as the elasticity of substitution in demand between produced goods and environmental services is low and the produced goods sector grows faster than the environmental services sector (which may be constant or even declining) (Hoel and Sterner 2007).

When uncertainty enters the picture, Equation 9.5 is no longer valid. In the real world, multiple interest rates and a variety of assets that reflect varying degrees of risk are observed. There is no single "market" discount rate that embodies the return on investment. The importance of this simple empirical fact for climate policy analysis has been pointed out by Howarth (2003), and a number of economists have begun to explore the consequences of uncertainty for discounting (e.g., Newell and Pizer 2003; Ludwig et al. 2005; Howarth 2009; Howarth and Norgaard 2007; Sandsmark and Vennemo 2007; Pesaran et al. 2007). In particular, the discount rate (or expected return) attached to a particular investment has to take into account the covariance between the asset's return and overall consumption. One version of this general relationship is:

(9.6)
$$E\left[r^{i}\right] = r^{f} - \frac{cov\left[u'\left(c_{t+1}\right), r_{t+1}^{i}\right]}{E\left[u'\left(c_{t+1}\right)\right]}$$

where $E[r^i]$ is the expected market discount rate for asset of type or risk class i and r^f is the risk-free discount rate. Equation 9.6 requires some interpretation, because $E[r^i]$ moves in the opposite direction as the price of asset i, and the marginal utility of consumption u' decreases as consumption increases. Cochrane (2005, 13–14) puts it this way:

> Investors do not like uncertainty about consumption. If you buy an asset whose payoff covaries positively with consumption, one that pays off well when you are already feeling wealthy, and pays off badly when you are already feeling poor, that asset will make your consumption stream more volatile. You will require a low price to induce you to buy such an asset. If you buy an asset whose payoff covaries negatively with consumption, it helps to smooth consumption and so is more valuable than its expected payoff might indicate. Insurance is an extreme example. Insurance pays off exactly when wealth and consumption would otherwise be low—you get a check when your house burns down. For this reason, you are happy to hold insurance, even though you expect to lose money—even though the price of insurance is greater than its expected payoff discounted at the risk-free rate.[4]

In the particular case in which (c_{t+1}/c_t) is lognormally distributed, with $E[ln(c_{t+1}/c_t)] = g$ and $Var[ln(c_{t+1}/c_t)] = \sigma^2$, the risk-free rate can be expressed in terms of the underlying parameters as[5]

$$(9.7) \qquad\qquad r^f = \rho + \eta g - \frac{1}{2}\eta^2\sigma^2$$

where the third term on the right side of the equation is attributable to *precautionary savings*. Examination of Equations 9.6 and 9.7 therefore shows quite clearly that "the" discount rate under uncertainty is quite different from the "Ramsey rule" discount rate given by Equation 9.5. Even if the rate of growth of consumption is positive on average, considerations of precautionary saving and insurance can lower the discount rate appropriate for valuing climate protection investments (Howarth 2009).

Uncertainty about the underlying structure of the interaction between climate change and the economy creates additional problems for the discounted utility framework. In a series of path-breaking papers, Weitzman (2007a, 2007b, 2009) has shown that climate catastrophes, with low but unknown probabilities and very high damages, dominate discounting considerations in formulating a rational policy. This fundamental challenge to the standard IAM approach will be discussed in the concluding section.

Finally, it should be noted that there are serious empirical problems with all of the discounting formulas exemplified by Equations 9.5 –9.7. Plausible and/or historical values of the parameters of these equations (the coefficient of relative risk aversion, the growth rate and variance of consumption, the covariance between returns and the marginal utility of consumption and the subjective rate of time preference) do *not* yield discount rates that match the rates which are observed in the market. These anomalies go by names such as "the equity premium puzzle" and "the risk-free rate puzzle," and they show up strongly not only in data for the US, but also in data for other countries with well-developed asset markets (Campbell 2003; Mehra and Prescott 2003). Despite an enormous amount of effort by the best economists to resolve these paradoxes (literally hundreds of scholarly papers have been published on these puzzles), there is no professional consensus on how they might be resolved. These paradoxes present the same kind of challenge to the conventional economic theory of discounting as the Michelson–Morley experiment presented to Newtonian physics. It is surely dubious for climate policy analysis to rely exclusively on a model that faces unexplained empirical challenges to its fundamental theory.

As Mehra and Prescott (who originally discovered the equity premium puzzle 1985) comment,

> The puzzle cannot be dismissed lightly, since much of our economic intuition is based on the very class of models that fall short so dramatically when confronted with financial data. It underscores the failure of paradigms central to financial and economic modeling to capture the characteristic that appears to make stocks comparatively so risky. Hence the viability of using this class of models for any quantitative assessment, say, for instance, to gauge the welfare implications of alternative stabilization policies, is thrown open to question (Mehra and Prescott 2003, 911).

Mehra and Prescott were referring to policies for macroeconomic stabilization, but their admonition applies equally to the use of IAMs to guide climate policy.

Predicting the Unpredictable and Pricing the Priceless

IAMs analyze the costs and benefits of climate mitigation. Cost–benefit analysis assumes that costs and benefits can be expressed in monetary terms with a reasonable degree of confidence. At least in principle, the costs of environmental protection consist of well-defined monetary expenditures (although there are significant problems in the standard approach to projecting mitigation costs, as discussed in the next section). The benefits of environmental protection, however, are generally more difficult to quantify. In the case of climate change, economists confront a double problem; the benefits of mitigation are intrinsically unpredictable and unpriceable.

The unpredictability of climate outcomes reflects, in part, what we do not know, because the effects of climate change are quite likely to be nonmarginal displacements that put us outside the realm of historical human experience. Unpredictability is reflected in what we *do* know as well. We know that the Earth's climate is a strongly nonlinear system that may be characterized by threshold effects and chaotic dynamics. Under such conditions, forecasts are necessarily indeterminate; it becomes appropriate to say that within a broad range of possible outcomes, anything can happen. IAMs, for the most part, do not incorporate this approach to uncertainty, but instead adopt best guesses about likely outcomes (Kelly and Kolstad 1999; Tol 2002a; Manne 2004; Mendelsohn 2004; Nordhaus 2007c). The Stern Review (Stern 2006) represents an advance over standard practice in this respect, employing a Monte Carlo analysis to estimate the effects of uncertainty in many climate parameters. As a result, the Stern Review finds a substantially greater benefit from mitigation than if it had simply used "best guesses."

But underneath one layer of assumptions lies another. Even if we assume precision in predicting climate impacts, the problem of assigning meaningful monetary values to human life, health and natural ecosystems still remains. This problem affects all cost–benefit analysis. Because a numerical answer is required, environmental economists have long been in the business of constructing surrogate prices for seemingly priceless values. The results are not impressive. Should we estimate the value of human life on the basis of the small wage differentials between more and less dangerous jobs, as Clinton administration analysts assumed? Or, should we rely on responses to long questionnaires asking people how much they would pay to avoid small risks of death under abstract hypothetical scenarios, as the Bush administration did?[6] Should we value ecosystems according to what people living nearby report they are willing to pay to preserve their scenic vistas or their favorite large animals? A noneconomist could be forgiven for assuming that these are rhetorical questions. Yet these approaches are regularly applied in policy analyses to estimate monetary values for health and environmental benefits (Diamond and Hausman 1994; Hanemann 1994; Portney 1994).

Should the value of a human life depend on individual or national income levels? Should nature located in a rich country be worth more than if it is located in a poor country? Remarkably, economists often answer "yes" to both of these disturbing questions. Values of human life differentiated by national income made a brief and unwelcome appearance in the IPCC's *Second Assessment Report* (1996) but appeared to be banished by the time of the *Third Assessment Report* (2001). Similar values, however, continue to appear in the economics literature, making their way into IAMs (Tol 2002b; Bosello et al. 2006), where the lives of citizens of rich countries are often assumed to be worth much more than those of their poorer counterparts.

Income bias is inherent to the process of valuation. When asked how much they are willing to pay to protect some small part of the natural world (a technique called contingent valuation), individuals' responses cannot help but reflect how much they are actually able to afford. While this survey method may provide plausible information about subjective values for local amenities, such as parks that neighborhoods will pay for, it is of little use in a complex, interdependent world where essential ecosystem services are not always visible or local and where incomes and information are very unequally distributed.

Indeed, one of the anomalies of the IAMs is the frequency with which economists have discovered benefits from near-term warming. Even if benefits are thought to disappear after a few degrees, or a few decades, a high discount rate ensures that the years of benefits loom large in present value terms when compared to the more remote and heavily discounted later years of damages.

For example, Nordhaus long maintained that there is a substantial subjective willingness to pay for warmer weather on the part of people in cold, rich countries. He observes that US households spend more on outdoor recreation in the summer than in the winter and, on the basis of that slim empirical foundation, concludes that subjective enjoyment of the climate worldwide would be maximized at a year-round average temperature of 20°C (Nordhaus and Boyer 2000). This is well above the current global average; it is approximately the temperature of Houston and New Orleans in the US, or Tripoli in Libya. There are many people who live in areas hotter than Houston, but they are generally much poorer than the people who live in areas colder than Houston. Thus if willingness to pay is indeed limited by ability to pay, there is a large net global willingness to pay for warming. In the 2000 version of DICE, this factor outweighed all damages and implied net benefits from warming until the middle of this century (Nordhaus and Boyer 2000). However, that oddity of the earlier DICE has been criticized (Ackerman and Finlayson 2006) and the latest DICE (of 2007), while still including and monetizing subjective gains for warming up to 20°C along with other costs and benefits, no longer allows any region to have overall net benefits from warming (Nordhaus 2007b).

A more quantifiable, but equally contestable, benefit from warming involves the impacts of warming on agriculture. Early studies of climate impacts suggested substantial agricultural gains from warming, as a result of longer growing seasons in high latitudes and the effects of CO_2 fertilization on many crops. Mendelsohn et al. (2000) and Tol (2002a) incorporated large estimated agricultural gains from early stages of warming. Successive studies, however, have steadily reduced the estimated benefits. Outdoor experiments have shown smaller benefits from CO_2 fertilization than earlier experiments conducted in greenhouses (IPCC 2007d). Recent research predicts that the negative effects of ground-level of ozone, which is produced by the same fossil fuel combustion processes that emit CO_2, may offset the impacts of a longer growing season and CO_2 fertilization and lead to a small net decrease in agricultural productivity in the US (Reilly et al. 2007). Another recent study finds that the market value of nonirrigated farmland in the US is highly correlated with climate variables. The optimum value occurs at roughly the current US average temperature with somewhat more than the current US average rainfall. This study's projections of climate change to the end of the century imply substantial losses in farm value, due primarily to crop damage from the increase in the number of days above 34°C (Schlenker et al. 2006).

As these examples of potential benefits suggest, there is a significant degree of subjective judgment involved in estimating the value of climate damages; but IAMs are completely dependent on the shape of their assumed damage functions.

It is conventional to assume that damages are a quadratic function of temperature increases, based, perhaps, on the common notion that damages should rise faster than temperature. But why a quadratic function in particular? The Stern Review (Stern 2006) made the exponent on the damage function a Monte Carlo parameter, ranging from 1 to 3 (damages ranged from a linear to a cubic function of temperature). Even though Stern's modal estimate was only 1.3, the cases with a higher exponent had a large effect on the outcome. In later sensitivity analyses in response to critics, the Stern Review researchers showed that if the assumed damages were a cubic function of temperature, the result was an enormous increase in the estimate of climate damages, changing their prediction by more than 20 percent of world output (Dietz et al. 2007).

In short, unlike the scientific modeling involved in GCMs, the results of IAMs are tied to subjective judgments about the shape of the damage function as we move into temperature regimes that are unknown in human or recent planetary history.

Technology Forecasts: Not So Bright

IAMs simulate the macroeconomic impacts of climate policies designed to achieve particular emissions trajectories. IAMs typically estimate costs as an annual percentage loss in GDP. IAMs cannot forecast job losses – the issue most politicians demand clarity on – because supply equals demand in every market (including the labor market) by design. The IPCC's *Fourth Assessment Report* summarizes the range of cost estimates for a low stabilization target (445–535 ppm-CO_2 equivalent) and finds that for all available studies, costs do not exceed 3 percent of global GDP in the medium term (i.e., 2030). For higher stabilization targets, estimates range from 2–2.5 percent of GDP (IPCC 2007c). Is 3 percent of global GDP worth sacrificing to avoid the damages of climate change? In the US, losing 3 percent of GDP in 2007 would mean reverting to the per capita income Americans enjoyed in 2006. In dollar terms, it is equivalent to spending $350 billion per year or $1,170 per capita. Whether we think $350 billion per year is too high a price to pay to avoid climate change depends on the severity of the climate damages we anticipate. Given the problems inherent in IAM estimates of climate damages, it is impossible to conclude from IAMs that 3 percent of GDP is, or is not, worth spending.

What we do know is that there is good reason to believe that IAMs overestimate the costs of achieving stabilization targets. Estimating mitigation costs in dollar terms is more straightforward, in principle, than measuring mitigation benefits. The adoption of energy-efficient equipment, appliances, industrial processes and automobiles, as well as more widespread use of combined heat and power technologies, wind energy systems, solar panels and other measures for reducing emissions all involve purchases of marketed goods and services whose attendant cash flows can be easily counted. The evolution of these technologies is uncertain, however, particularly over the long time periods involved in climate modeling. Forecasts of mitigation costs, therefore, depend on assumptions about the pace of development of new (and existing) technologies and their costs.

IAMs typically adopt conservative assumptions about the pace of technical change, abstracting away from the potential for learning-by-doing and the positive role public policy can play in steering investment choices and promoting technical change. Most IAMs assume a predictable annual rate of productivity improvement in energy use, and/or a predictable rate of decrease in emissions per unit of output. Thus a paradoxical result emerges from the models' overly mechanistic structure. Because climate change is a long-term crisis, and predictable, inexorable technological change will make it easier and cheaper to reduce emissions in the future, it seems better to wait before addressing the problem of climate change. Hence, most IAMs advocate a cautious approach that involves only modest early action to limit emissions with gradually increasing limits over time. Alternative models that assume endogenous technical change reach different conclusions and frequently recommend more aggressive carbon abatement policies, with results varying according to how the models are specified (e.g., Goulder and Schneider 1999; Gerlagh 2007; for recent surveys of this literature, see the special issue of *Resource and Energy Economics* edited by Carraro et al. 2003; Edenhofer et al. 2006b, and the special issue of *The Energy Journal* (2006) in which it appears; and Gillingham et al. 2007).

Furthermore, most IAMs exclude the possibility for "no-regrets" options – investments that could reduce emissions without imposing significant opportunity costs. These options do exist, largely in the area of improved energy efficiency (IPCC 1996; Interlaboratory Working Group 2000; Lovins 2005; Elliott et al. 2006; Shipley and Elliott 2006; Laitner et al. 2006; McKinsey Global Institute 2007). IAMs ignore these opportunities because they assume that the economy functions on its production possibilities frontier. This means that businesses and consumers behave with perfect rationality to achieve their objectives and are successful in optimizing their behaviors. It is increasingly well understood in economics literature, however, that businesses do not exploit every opportunity for profit. There are many opportunities to increase efficiency, reduce costs and improve productivity that are not taken up due to organizational and institutional constraints (DeCanio et al. 2000, 2001). Incomplete information about technologies, societal norms, difficulty in capitalizing on energy efficient investments and distorted market prices for energy are all well-known examples of barriers to the adoption of more energy efficient measures. Well-designed climate policy can play a decisive role in removing these barriers. If technical change is socially determined and its results are path dependent, we can only arrive in the future with new energy technology choices available if we start conscious, carefully planned development of those technologies today. Waiting for the *deus ex machina* of technical change, the misleading option suggested by IAMs, will ensure that we face fewer options in the future at significantly higher costs.[7]

There are more satisfying ways of mapping cost-effective technologies into climate models that yield different impacts. The costs of climate policy depend heavily on how technology and its benefits over time are characterized (Worrell et al. 2003). For example, Krause et al. (2002, 2003) include the efficiency improving possibilities documented in the "5-lab study" (Interlaboratory Working Group 2000) to arrive at least-cost estimates of the economic costs of emissions reduction. Policy assessments typically include savings on energy bills and lower compliance costs, such as the benefits of new energy technologies, but overlook the potential for "non-energy" benefits, such as lower maintenance costs, increased production yields, safer work conditions, positive spill-over effects and economies of scale and scope. These benefits increase the return on energy-related investments; if recognized, firms and consumers may become more willing to adopt or invest in them (Finman and Laitner 2001). These benefits may, in some cases, exceed the associated energy bill savings (Worrell et al. 2003).

The productivity enhancing effects of investing in these technologies can help offset any drag on the economy imposed by higher fossil fuel prices. New technologies can stimulate new investment, save consumers money, stimulate productive research and development with spill over benefits for other sectors and positive multiplier effects and help to reduce energy imports and increase technology exports. Massive public investment in military technology since World War II led to the widespread adoption of jet aircraft, semi-conductors and the Internet by the private sector and is partly responsible for the technological advantage the US holds globally. In the early 1980s, US companies led the world in wind energy technologies. Today, we import those technologies (Goodstein 2007). As the rest of the world moves forward with climate policy, the US risks losing its technological advantage unless it charts (and funds) a careful and deliberate new technology path.

Insurance, Precaution and the Contribution of Climate Economics

In the three preceding sections, we argued that most IAMs rely on an analytical framework that privileges immediate, individual consumption over future-oriented concerns; that the benefits, or avoided damages, from climate mitigation are both unpredictable in detail and intrinsically nonmonetizable; and that the conventional economic view of technology misrepresents the dynamic, socially determined nature of technical change. Not much is left, therefore, of the standard economic approach and its ambitions to perform a complete cost–benefit analysis of climate policy options. In light of these criticisms, how should we think about policy options and the economics of climate change?

It should be emphasized that the optimal control approach to climate policy embodied in Equation 9.1 above is not the only one proposed in the literature. For example, the early growth literature proposed the notion of the "Golden Rule" steady state growth path (Solow 1970). In this simple model with the savings rate as the only policy variable, optimal growth is the path yielding the highest level of consumption per capita among all *sustainable* growth paths. Sustainable growth, in this context, is a path that does not sacrifice the consumption of future generations by consuming society's capital (including natural capital) for the benefit of the present generation. In such a model, the market rate of interest is equal to the rate of growth of consumption.

If the "willingness to pay" on the part of future generations to avert environmental destruction is proportional to income, then the effective discount rate on the Golden Rule growth path is zero (DeCanio 2003b). The notion of the Golden Rule growth path has been generalized to "Green Golden Rule" growth, with different implications for the discount rate depending on the assumptions made about the interaction between the environment and the market economy (Chichilnisky et al. 1995; Bella 2006).

A present generation that cares nothing about the fate of future generations will do nothing to preserve the stability of the Earth's climate, and no economic calculations can show otherwise. But whether and how much people care about the future can be represented in various ways – through the rate of subjective time preference in optimal growth models, through the weighting of different generations' welfare in overlapping generations models (Howarth and Norgaard 1992; Howarth 1996), through thought experiments in which the generations are able to transact with one another (DeCanio and Niemann 2006) – and the results, not unexpectedly, will reflect the depth and strength of the intergenerational ties. The upshot of these alternative ways of characterizing the intergenerational decision making problem is that the *normative assumptions that are made about how future generations are treated are as important as the technical details.* Not having happened yet, the future is unobservable; moreover, there are no reliable, universally accepted economic laws that shape our understanding of the future in the way that the laws of natural science do for the physical reality of climate change. When it comes to economics, there is no escape from value-laden assumptions about the future. Furthermore, consciousness and intergenerational concern are influenced by social and political discourse. In the case of climate policy where fundamental values and ethical principles are at stake, it is an abdication of responsibility for economists to act as if peoples' preferences are simply given and fixed.

One of the most interesting new areas of economic theory as applied to climate involves the analysis of uncertainty. If the probabilities of a range of possible outcomes were known, as in casino games or homework exercises in statistics classes, then there would be no need for a new theory; it would be a straightforward matter to calculate the expected value of climate outcomes and economic consequences. However, this is a poor model for many of the most important climate problems. When probability distributions themselves are unknown, the problem of uncertainty is much more difficult to address. The combination of unknown probability distributions and potentially disastrous outcomes provides a strong motivation for precautionary policy, as insurance against those disasters. As noted in a recent review of scientific knowledge about potential "tipping elements" of earth systems, "[s]ociety may be lulled into a false sense of security by smooth projections of global change [...] present knowledge suggests that a variety of tipping elements could reach their critical point within this century under anthropogenic climate change" (Lenton et al. 2008; see also Committee on Abrupt Climate Change 2002). Uncertainty about the climate sensitivity, the key parameter in assessing the probability for ranges of potential equilibrium global temperature changes, is intrinsically resistant to improvements in scientific understanding of particular climate processes (Roe and Baker 2007).

Several economists working at the theoretical frontier have proposed new ways of dealing with these kinds of deep uncertainties (e.g., Gjerde et al. 1999; Chichilnisky 2000; Hall and Behl 2006; Dasgupta 2008; Weitzman 2007a, 2007b, 2009). For example, Martin Weitzman has developed a model applicable to financial markets as well as climate change. People learn about the world through repeated experiences, but if the relevant structure of the world is changing rapidly or greatly enough, only the most recent experiences can be relied on, and everyone is effectively engaged in Bayesian estimation from a finite sample. In this circumstance, the best available estimate of the true probability distribution has fat tails. Because people are risk-averse, the attempt to avoid the disturbing possibility of very large losses dominates policy decisions. The result, Weitzman argues, is that fine-tuning the estimates of the most likely level of climate damages is irrelevant; what matters is how bad and how likely the worst extremes of the possible outcomes are. There is little doubt that the 95th percentile, or 98th percentile, of possible adverse climate outcomes over the next century (to pick two arbitrary points out in the tail of the distribution) would look like the devastation of the planet in a science fiction dystopia, not like a matter for carefully weighing costs and benefits.

Intuitively, this is the same logic that motivates the purchase of insurance, a precautionary decision that people make all the time. The most likely number of house fires that you will experience next year, or even in your lifetime, is zero. Very few homeowners find this a compelling reason to go without fire insurance. Similarly, healthy young adults often buy life insurance to protect their children's future in the worst possible case. Residential fires, and deaths of healthy young adults, have annual probabilities measured in the tenths of 1 percent. In other words, people routinely insure themselves against personal catastrophes that are much less likely than worst-case climate catastrophes for the planet.[8]

How would this perspective change our approach to climate economics and policy choices? Economics would find itself in a humbler role, no longer charged with determining the optimal policy. Instead, a discussion of scientific information about catastrophic possibilities and consequences would presumably lead to the choice of maximum safe targets, expressed in terms of allowable increases in temperature and CO_2 levels. Once safe targets have been established, there remain the extremely complex and intellectually challenging tasks – for which the tools of economics are both appropriate and powerful – of determining the least-cost global strategy for achieving those targets, designing policies that effectively and with confidence meet the targets[9] and sharing responsibility for the costs and implementation of that strategy.

This cost-effectiveness task, despite its daunting difficulty, is more limited than the cost–benefit analysis attempted by IAMs – and the reduced scope avoids many of the problems we have discussed. Discounting is less of an issue, because the costs of mitigation and adaptation, while still spread out in time, generally occur much sooner than the full range of anticipated damages. Precise estimation and monetization of benefits is no longer necessary, because cost-effectiveness analysis takes the benefits side as fixed (or, in the language of economics, assigns an infinite shadow price to the constraint of meeting the chosen target – another way of saying that cost calculations are not allowed to override the prior choice of a safe standard).

There are two take-home messages here. The first is that policy makers and scientists should be skeptical of efforts by economists to specify optimal policy paths using the current generation of IAMs. These models do not embody the state of the art in the economic theory of uncertainty, and the foundations of the IAMs are much shakier than the general circulation models that represent our best current understanding of physical climate processes. Not only do the IAMs entail an implicit philosophical stance that is highly contestable, but they also suffer from technical deficiencies that are widely recognized within economics. Second, economists do have useful insights for climate policy. While economics itself is insufficient to determine the urgency for precautionary action in the face of low-probability climate catastrophes, or make judgments about intergenerational and intragenerational justice, it does point the way toward achieving climate stabilization in a cost-effective manner. IAMs cannot, however, be looked to as the ultimate arbiter of climate policy choices.

Chapter 10

NEGISHI WELFARE WEIGHTS IN INTEGRATED ASSESSMENT MODELS: THE MATHEMATICS OF GLOBAL INEQUALITY

Elizabeth A. Stanton

In a global climate policy debate fraught with differing understandings of right and wrong, the importance of making transparent the ethical assumptions used in climate economics models cannot be overestimated. Negishi weighting is a key ethical assumption in climate economics models, but it is virtually unknown to most model users. Negishi weights freeze the current distribution of income between world regions; without this constraint, IAMs that maximize global welfare would recommend an equalization of income across regions as part of their policy advice. With Negishi weights in place, these models instead recommend a course of action that would be optimal only in a world in which global income redistribution cannot and will not take place. This chapter describes the Negishi procedure and its origin in theoretical and applied welfare economics, and discusses the policy implications of the presentation and use of Negishi-weighted model results, as well as some alternatives to Negishi weighting in climate economics models.

Introduction

Climate change and global income inequality are intimately and inextricably interrelated. Regional income per capita is well correlated with past and present greenhouse gas emissions. Damages from climate change are expected to be far worse in developing countries, many of which have special geographic vulnerabilities (such as tropical climates or low-lying islands) and most of which can ill afford the adaptation measures necessary to fend off climate impacts. International climate negotiations hinge on finding a compromise between philosophical differences of developed and developing countries on the meaning of equity: what determines each country's responsibility in reducing emissions? What determines each country's responsibility in paying for emissions reductions and adaptation measures at home and abroad?

Climate economics models play an important role in this policy debate by quantifying the value of climate damages and abatement costs under various mitigation scenarios. Many of these integrated assessment models (IAMs) offer policy advice in the form of an optimal scenario: a recommended course of action telling us how much emissions should be abated in what time periods to achieve the greatest human wellbeing[1] across the centuries. In a policy debate fraught with differing understandings of right and wrong, the importance of making transparent the ethical assumptions used in these models cannot be overestimated.

Like any economic models, IAMs are not value-free – many of the assumptions that go into building climate economics models are based on moral judgments, and not on scientific facts. The choice of a discount rate is, perhaps, the best-known example. The optimal course of action recommended by an IAM can only be understood in the context of the discount rate employed – the higher the discount rate, the lower the value that we place on the wellbeing of future generations (Stern 2006).

Negishi weighting is another key ethical assumption at work in climate economics models, but one that is virtually unknown to most model users. Negishi weights freeze the current distribution of income between world regions; without this constraint, IAMs that maximize global welfare would recommend an equalization of income across regions as part of their policy advice. With Negishi weights in place, these models instead recommend a course of action that would be optimal only in a world in which global income redistribution cannot and will not take place.

The next sections of this chapter describe the Negishi procedure and its origin in theoretical and applied welfare economics. The final section discusses the policy implications of the presentation and use of Negishi-weighted model results, as well as some alternatives to Negishi weighting in climate economics models.

Negishi Weighting in Climate Economics Models

In welfare-optimizing climate economics models, production results in both emissions and consumption: emissions affect the climate, causing damages that reduce production and, as a result, consumption. These models maximize the discounted present value of welfare (which grows with consumption, although at an ever-diminishing rate[2]) across all time periods. They accomplish this by choosing how much to abate emissions in each time period, where abatement costs reduce production and consumption. Examples of welfare-optimizing IAMs include both global (single-region) models – DICE-2007 (Nordhaus 2008), ENTICE-BR (Popp 2006), DEMETER-1CCS (Gerlagh 2006) and MIND (Edenhofer et al. 2006a) – and regionally disaggregated models – RICE-2004 (Yang and Nordhaus 2006), FEEM-RICE (Bosetti et al. 2006), FUND (Tol 1999), MERGE (Manne and Richels 2004), CETA-M (Peck and Teisberg 1999), GRAPE (Kurosawa 2004) and AIM/Dynamic Global (Masui et al. 2006).[3]

Global welfare-optimizing IAMs

Some of the IAMs that are solved by optimizing welfare treat the world as one homogenous region. A social welfare function for the world as a whole, summed across all time periods, is maximized by adjusting the shares of global output that are spent on emissions abatement – avoiding future damages – or recycled as investment in productive enterprises, thereby increasing consumption. Models choose unique abatement spending and investment values for every time period simultaneously, as if there were perfect foresight. Social welfare is measured as the individual utility of a representative agent, which is a function of average per capita consumption, multiplied by the population. If little is spent on abatement in a given period, emissions are higher and future climate damages are higher, reducing future consumption levels. In time periods when abatement spending is prioritized over regular investment, emissions are lower, but so too is current-day consumption.

Welfare-optimizing IAMs maximize utility, not income or consumption. All individuals are assumed to have identical utility functions, which are modeled with diminishing marginal returns to utility from changes in consumption. Each new unit of additional consumption provides a little less utility than the last unit, so that as consumption rises, so too does utility, but at a diminishing rate. Consumption's contribution to utility depends on the individual's income, and a new dollar of consumption means more to the poor than to the rich. In a global welfare-optimizing IAM, there is only one individual – the world as a whole – but there are many time periods. In these models, a new dollar of consumption contributes more to social welfare in a poorer time period than in a richer one.

When diminishing marginal returns to utility from consumption are combined with the standard assumption that per capita income will grow over time, the result is that in these IAMs, a new dollar of consumption contributes more to social welfare in the (relatively poorer) present than it does in the (relatively richer) future. If the worst climate damages are to be averted, far-reaching emissions abatement measures must take place in the next few decades. If abatement measures do not take place, then large-scale climate damages will occur closer to the end of this century, and extending from there into the future. As a generalization, abatement costs reduce current consumption for our "poorer" generation, while climate damages reduce future consumption for a "richer" generation. The same reduction to consumption, whether from current abatement costs or future damages, does not have the same impact on social welfare when measured according to these assumptions. If returns to utility from consumption are diminishing on the margin, and income per capita is expected to grow over time, today's $1 million abatement cost is assigned a much bigger reduction to social welfare than $1 million in future climate damages.

The degree to which the marginal utility of income diminishes as income grows is one of two components to the discount rate in a "Ramsey" model. Frank Ramsey's (1928) widely used "prescriptive" approach to discounting[1] distinguishes between:

- the rate of pure time preference, or how human society feels about costs and benefits to future generations regardless of the resources and opportunities that may exist in the future; and
- an income-based component – an elasticity applied to the rate of growth of real consumption – that reflects the diminishing marginal utility of consumption over time as society becomes richer.

The discount rate, $r(t)$, combines these two elements: the rate of pure time preference, ρ, plus the product of the elasticity of marginal utility with respect to consumption per capita, η, and the growth rate of consumption per capita, $g(t)$.

$$(10.1) \qquad\qquad r(t) = \rho + \eta\, g(t)$$

Choices about the discount rate inevitably reflect value judgments made by modelers. The selection of a value for the pure rate of time preference is determined by a modeler's ethical viewpoint, not economic theory or scientific fact. It is one thing to observe an individual's time preference over his or her own lifetime, and quite another to use this time preference as part of weighting the importance of costs and benefits to different individuals or generations (see Ackerman et al. 2009a). A pure time preference of zero would imply that, holding real incomes constant, benefits and costs to future generations are just as important as the gains and losses that we experience today. The higher the rate of pure time preference, the less we value harm to future generations from climate change, and the less we value the benefits that we can confer on future generations by averting climate change.

The degree to which the marginal utility of consumption diminishes is controlled by the elasticity of marginal utility with respect to consumption per capita, η; by convention, this is a function of per capita consumption and the marginal utility of consumption.

$$(10.2) \qquad \eta = \frac{-c \, / \, u'(c)}{\delta c \, / \, \delta u'(c)}$$

Both the rate at which the marginal utility of consumption falls and the inputs to the production function that determine the projected growth in per capita income are chosen by the modeler. In most IAMs, per capita income is assumed to grow at something like its long-term historical trend (the rate typically diminishes over time and may be lower for regions with higher incomes in a regionally disaggregated model); of course, projecting future growth requires accurate forecasting of both global output and the change in global population over time – neither of which can be known with much confidence over the next 50 years, much less over the multi-century time scale of many climate economics models.

The existence of a diminishing marginal utility of consumption is a standard assumption in economic analysis. There is, however, no standard value, or even a range of standard values, for the degree to which utility diminishes as consumption grows. There is no standard value because conventional economic theory maintains that utility cannot be measured (the history of this theoretical notion and its obvious contradiction in applied economic models that measure utility, such as IAMs, are discussed in a subsequent section).

Regionally disaggregated IAMs

In models with more than one region, the IAM maximizes the sum of regional utilities. Without Negishi weights, IAMs treat gains in consumption as having a greater contribution to welfare in a poor region than in a rich region. Because of the diminishing marginal utility of consumption, the welfare contribution of an abatement or damage cost depends on the per capita income in the region where it occurs. An unconstrained model will allocate income gains to poorer regions (where each dollar has the biggest impact on welfare) and will allocate income losses to richer regions (where each dollar has the smallest impact on welfare). The result is an equalization of incomes across all regions – a radical redistribution of world income. From scholarly articles describing two leading models:

> *For RICE:* Under the utilitarian weights, regions have different shadow prices of capitals. The social planner can improve the global welfare by moving capitals

from low price [richer] places to high price [poorer] places [...] However, there are no conventional capital flow channels in our setting. The capital from [the richest region] "inundates" the small scale inter-connections of technological transfers. Such flows are redistributions under the pretext of technological transfers. [...] reasonable and correct magnitude and directions of technological transfers can only be modeled by using the Negishi social welfare weights (Yang and Nordhaus 2006, 731, 738).

For MERGE: A fixed set of Negishi weights defines a so-called Negishi welfare problem, the solving of which corresponds to the maximizing of the global welfare function. MERGE updates iteratively the Negishi weights in solving sequentially the corresponding Negishi welfare problems. The steps to update the Negishi weights are performed until a Pareto-optimal equilibrium solution is found (Kypreos 2005, 2,723).

Many models discuss Negishi weighting in terms of equalizing the shadow price (or marginal price) of capital instead of using the more transparent language of equalizing the marginal utility of consumption. Because both terms are proportional to the labor–capital ratio, these two goals – equalizing the shadow price of capital or the marginal utility of consumption – have an identical impact on the regional contribution to social welfare of additional consumption.[5]

Modelers have viewed the tendency toward equalization of incomes across regions as a problem, where the solution is to constrain the model to view the marginal utility of income as being the same in every region (in any given time period). A set of "Negishi weights" is included in the regional utility functions such that the weighted contribution to social welfare of one dollar of additional consumption is the same in all regions. Higher weights are assigned to welfare in richer countries, while welfare in poorer countries receives lower weights. This procedure obviates the IAMs' equalization of income, preventing any redistribution of income from taking place. The course of action recommended by a Negishi-weighted model takes the current income distribution among regions of the world as immutable.

In essence, climate economists using Negishi-weighted models are trying to have it both ways by embracing the diminishing marginal utility of income when it appears convenient (for intergenerational distribution) but suppressing it when it inconveniently calls for change (in inter-regional distribution). Modelers' choice to ignore equity concerns results in a lack of transparency in how costs and benefits to different people or generations are weighted in IAMs; it also renders opaque a set of technical assumptions that anyone without an advanced degree in economics would find ethically dubious.

Negishi weighting explained

Takashi Negishi (1972), writing after the Arrow and Debreu (1954) proofs of the existence and optimality of general equilibrium, offered a simpler but closely related proof. His social welfare function is a weighted sum of individual utilities, with constant weights that add up to one across the population.[6] Negishi demonstrated that maximizing this social welfare function also maximizes individual utility – that is, everyone is at the maximum level of utility allowed by their initial endowments – if and only if the weights are equal to the inverse of individuals' marginal utility of income at that maximum.

From this proof Negishi offered a procedure for constructing the optimal equilibrium point for a given set of endowments (i.e., for a given *status quo ante* distribution of income and wealth): (1) make an arbitrary starting guess at the weights; (2) calculate how far off the budget constraint each individual is; (3) adjust the weights to bring everyone closer to their budget lines; (4) repeat until the process converges. (For a detailed accounting of this procedure, see Rutherford (1999) on sequential joint maximization.) The Negishi weighting procedure results in a Pareto-optimal allocation that is compatible with the given initial endowments, essentially freezing the distribution of income and suppressing any tendency for global utility calculations to call for equalizing incomes.[7] In the words of modelers using this approach,[8]

> The Negishi weights are an instrument to account for regional disparities in economic development. They equalize the marginal utility of consumption in each region for each period in order to prevent large capital flows between regions [...] although [...] such capital flows would greatly improve social welfare, without the Negishi weights the problem of climate change would be drowned by the vastly larger problem of underdevelopment (Keller et al. 2003:7).
>
> In order to apply this approach, Negishi weights must be determined for each of the regions. These are chosen so that each region's outlays do not exceed the value of its wealth. In equilibrium, the weight must equal each region's share of the world's wealth [...] The Negishi weights may be interpreted as each region's dollar voting rights in the allocation of the world's resources (Manne 1999, 393, 394).

In less technical language, if consumption is assumed to have diminishing returns to utility, the only way to achieve the Negishi result – such that a dollar has the same impact on utility regardless of the region's income per capita – is to weigh the welfare of richer regions more heavily than that of poorer regions. In climate economics models, the Negishi procedure works like this: first, the regionally disaggregated welfare optimizing IAM is run without weights and without any possibility of trade or transfers between regions (an autarkic run).

Then for each time period, a set of weights is created that when multiplied by the marginal utility of consumption gives an equal product across all regions (that is, the weights are the inverse of each region's marginal utility of consumption). These weights are then included as fixed values to each region's utility function by time period, and the model is run a second time with these fixed weights in place. In the Negishi-weighted model, every region has the same effective marginal utility of income (in any one time period), which means that a dollar gained or lost is treated just the same regardless of the region. Dollars in different time periods, however, are still treated differently; not only is the future discounted, but in addition, the Negishi weights need not be constant over time.

In short, in Negishi-weighted models human welfare is more valuable in richer regions, and redistribution of income among world regions is suppressed, maintaining the existing income distribution. According to model descriptions, these assumptions have a large impact on the optimal results or course of action recommended by the model. When such important modeling choices are dryly described in technical terms – equalizing the shadow price of capital – and not in terms of the equity implication and the full meaning of the final results, something is lost.

The dysfunctional relationship between maximizing social welfare, diminishing marginal returns to consumption and reducing income inequality has a long history in the field of economics, both theoretical and applied. Only by viewing Negishi weights in this historical context is it possible to reconcile modelers' conflicting assumptions and to understand the ethical precepts that are at work inside the black box of economic modeling.

Equity weighting in IAMs

It is important to note that a few IAMs explicitly include equity weights that enhance regional differences in income or wealth in a way that causes greater weight to be placed on poorer regions. The PAGE model (used in the Stern Report (2006), although without these weights[9]) has been modified to include equity weights (Hope 2008). The FUND model includes equity weights, and its lead author has written extensively on the inclusion of such weights in IAMs (Kemfert and Tol 2002; Tol 2001; Anthoff and Tol 2007). In addition to PAGE and FUND – both of which are well-known regionally disaggregated models – Azar (1999) and Baer and Templet (2001) each present a simple climate economics model with equity weights for the purpose of analyzing the impact that these weights could have on policy decisions. Alternative approaches to regional weighting in IAMs are discussed in the final section of this chapter.

Theoretical Welfare Economics: A Short Intellectual History

In conventional, or neoclassical, economics "utility" is a term that has come to mean an individual's mental state of satisfaction, with the proviso that levels of satisfaction or utility cannot be compared across individuals. It is a concept that is simultaneously too broad and too narrow. Almost anything can be seen to have and give utility, albeit with diminishing returns. At the same time, the standard theoretical treatment of the "utility" concept suffers from severe limitations. In the absence of interpersonal comparability, the utility of individuals cannot be aggregated in order to consider social welfare, nor can it be compared in order to consider distribution. While a theory of wellbeing that can address neither aggregate social welfare nor inequality seems of little practical or conceptual use, this modern definition of utility has nonetheless been the dominant measure of human welfare used in much of economic theory since the 1930s.

A prescription for income redistribution

Jeremy Bentham's (1970 [1789], ch.1) *Introduction to the Principles of Morals* was not the first, but may be the best remembered discussion of the philosophy of Utilitarianism, in which human behavior is described as motivated by pleasure and pain – their net satisfaction being "utility." Society's wellbeing was the sum of these utilities, such that an ethical course of action was that which led to "the greatest happiness for the greatest number." In theory, utility could be summed across individuals to determine "social welfare," but utilitarianism did not offer any practical way to actually measure either individual or societal wellbeing.

The most direct antecedents of today's neoclassical economists were called the Material or Marginalist Welfare School; writing roughly a century after Bentham, these theorists preserved the basic precepts of Utilitarianism, but used new mathematical tools to make their arguments. At the center of their economic theory were two related ideas: first, that the goal of individuals was to maximize utility, and, second, that utility was concave, or diminishing on the margin.[10] Following the work of Arthur Cecil Pigou, the marginalists restricted their analysis to the necessities of life, using money as a "measuring stick." Focusing on the most material aspects of welfare led to the insight that additional income was more useful to the poor than the rich. Many of the marginalists were explicitly in favor of income redistribution because it would lead to more material wants being satisfied. As economics' most famous author of undergraduate textbooks, Paul Samuelson (1956, 12), noted:

> Because Marshall, Edgeworth, Walras, Wicksell, Böhm-Bawerk, and the others thought that men were much alike and subject to interpersonally summable diminishing marginal utility, they all tended to regard existing capitalistic society

as too unequal in its income distribution. They felt that only after there takes place a redistribution of the initial wealth could one regard the dollars voted in the market place as being of ethically equal weight; only then would the invisible hand of perfectly competitive markets lead to the social optimum.

In summary, the economic thought of the early twentieth century assumed that: 1) individual utilities could be summed together as a measure of social welfare; 2) maximizing total social welfare was viewed as a societal objective; and 3) diminishing marginal utility of income gave a strong formal justification for income redistribution. This conclusion was a problem for twentieth century marginalists, and it's a problem for twenty-first century climate modelers. Regionally disaggregated welfare optimizing IAMs – which attempt to maximize social welfare measured as the sum of regional welfares and assume a diminishing marginal utility of income – solve the "problem" of fundamental income redistribution by using Negishi weights.

The ordinalist revolution

In 1932, British economist Lionel Robbins called for the rejection of all interpersonal comparisons of utility, arguing that cardinal measurement and interpersonal comparisons could never capture the unobservable utility or satisfaction of others; therefore, in his view, it could not be demonstrated or assumed that the marginal utility of income for the poor is greater than the marginal utility of income for the rich (Robbins 1984 [1932]). The success of Robbins's rejection of cardinal measures of utility led to the so-called "Ordinalist Revolution" in economics, and the birth of neoclassical economics as we know it today. According to ordinalist theory – well preserved in modern microeconomics – utility can only be classified according to an ordinal numbering system, not a cardinal one: that is, utility can be compared only in terms of a rank ordering of preferences and never in terms of any absolute scale.

Robbins noticed that if one were to combine the utilitarian concept of social welfare (defined as the sum of individual welfares) with another important marginalist assumption, the diminishing marginal utility of income, the logical outcome is a very subversive result: social welfare reaches its maximum when income is distributed equally across the population. If income were unequally distributed and welfare were concave in income, you could always increase social welfare by redistributing some income from the rich to the poor. Ian Little (1955, 11–15) elaborated on Robbins's critique, arguing that individual satisfactions cannot be summed up, that satisfaction is never comparable among different individuals and that the field of welfare economics up until that time had been – to its detriment – entirely normative.

The utilitarian definition of social welfare was gradually replaced in welfare economics by the idea of "Pareto optimality." In the concept of Pareto optimality, individual welfare is still utility, but social welfare is defined by the absence or presence of Pareto optimality (a situation in which no one can be made better off without making someone else worse off). This is a somewhat empty concept of social welfare, since a wide array of situations can be Pareto optimal, and the only real opportunities for "Pareto improvements" – when someone is made better off while no one is made worse off – occur when there are unclaimed or wasted resources.[11] In *On Ethics and Economics*, Nobel Laureate Amartya Sen (1987, 33–34) calls this redefinition of social wellbeing the "narrowing" of welfare economics: "In the small box to which welfare economics got confined, with Pareto optimality as the only criterion of judgment, and self-seeking behavior as the only basis of economic choice, the scope for saying something interesting in welfare economics became exceedingly small."

A Pareto optimal outcome can be achieved on the basis of any initial allocation of income, however equal or unequal.[12] Negishi weighting accepts the current distribution of income and the Pareto optimal outcome that arises from it. One of the most important conceptual limitations of neoclassical economics is its treatment of the distribution of endowments – who owns what – as "given" (or as off-limits to economic analysis), a practice that damages this approach's effectiveness in applied analysis, whether of modern day issues such as climate change and the global distribution of income, or of countless historical issues with distributional consequences. Outside of the narrow confines of mainstream economic thought, the distribution of a global atmospheric commons, or of income and wealth among the countries of the world and the residents of those countries, is very much on the table: in international negotiations regarding climate and development; in the diplomatic agendas of the nations of the Global South; and in the studies of environment and development law, policy and philosophy (Botzen et al. 2008; Heyward 2007; Klinsky and Dowlatabadi 2009; Ott et al. 2008).

The innovations of Robbins, Little and Pareto avoid advocacy of income redistribution by 1) rejecting the summability of individual utilities into an aggregate social welfare, and 2) rejecting the objective of maximizing total social welfare in favor of the more restrictive aim of changes that leave some better off while leaving none worse off ("Pareto improvement"). Negishi's method can be thought of as a mathematical elaboration of the idea of Pareto improvement, since the solution to his system is that each region attains the maximum utility or welfare consistent with a given initial allocation of resources. Since the Negishi solution is a Pareto optimal outcome, no further Pareto improvement is possible – by this definition, social welfare cannot be improved by income redistribution.

Applied welfare economics and welfare optimizing IAMs

Pareto optimality is the core of theoretical neoclassical welfare economics. The applied economics of social welfare takes the form of cost–benefit analysis (CBA) – of which welfare optimizing climate economics models form a subset. CBA is a common tool for making decisions about whether a project will improve social welfare (and therefore should be carried out) or will reduce social welfare (and should not be carried out). According to CBA, if the value of the future stream of costs and benefits of a project is positive, we should carry out the project, but if the value is negative we should not carry out the project. Abstracting from the vexing question of discount rates, this means that any addition to the size of the "economic pie" is good, regardless of the distribution of costs and benefits (a definition that allows changes that improve the welfare of some while diminishing that of others to qualify as social welfare improvements).

Connecting CBA back to ordinalist welfare economics takes a blind eye and a few, difficult to justify, conceptual leaps. The compensation test, introduced by Nicholas Kaldor (1939) and John Hicks (1940), is a method for determining whether or not there has been a *potential* Pareto improvement such that those who receive net benefits (the winners) could in principle compensate those who bear net costs (the losers) and still be better off. When benefits net of costs are positive, if one group gets all of the benefits but has to pay back everyone who suffers costs, the first group could potentially pay all of the losers and still have a positive benefit left for itself. Of course, this fails to bring solace to the losers unless they are compensated in practice. As Sen (2000, 947) put it:

> If compensations are actually paid, then of course we do not need the comparison criterion since the actual outcome already includes the paid compensations and can be judged without reference to compensation tests […] On the other hand if compensations are not paid, it is not at all clear in what sense it can be said that this is a social improvement […] The compensation tests are either redundant or unconvincing.

The criterion of potential Pareto improvement (or the compensation test) runs sharply counter to that of Pareto optimality, since it embraces changes that make some better off while making others worse off. In this respect, it is very similar to Utilitarian social welfare as the sum of all individual welfares, but with one key difference: money is summed rather than utility. Thus in applied welfare economics, interpersonal comparability reenters through the back door (income is summed), but the diminishing marginal utility of income drops out of sight (income is treated as equivalent to utility).

Negishi-weighted models have an inherent contradiction – the diminishing marginal utility of consumption is in play intertemporally, but not inter-regionally. Any model that includes diminishing marginal returns to social welfare from consumption and maximizes the sum of multiple utility functions (whether by time period or by region) invites redistribution to equalize incomes. Across time periods, if the future is assumed to be richer than the past, this redistribution takes the form of prioritizing increases to the consumption of the present generation. Across regions, this redistribution would take the form of prioritizing increases to consumption for poorer regions. In these models, the prioritization of current consumption is permitted, but the prioritization of increased consumption in poor regions is suppressed by the Negishi weights.

Policy Implications and Alternatives

The presentation of Negishi-weighted results without a clear explanation of their equity implications introduces an unknown and unexamined political bias into the policy debate. IAM results are taken as impartial truth, instead of as one position in the current ethical debate regarding who should pay for worldwide emissions reductions and adaptation measures (Baer et al. 2007, 2008).

Welfare-optimizing climate economics models ignore equity in three ways. First, welfare-optimizing IAMs abstract over groups, winners and losers to focus on a global result. Even regionally disaggregated welfare-optimizing IAMs employ this logic: their decision rule maximizes the sum of regions' social welfare. Second, welfare-optimizing IAMs commonly employ a very high discount rate, which has the effect of prioritizing short-term savings (avoided abatement costs) over long-term savings (avoided climate damages). Third, welfare-optimizing IAMs differ from many other forms of cost–benefit analysis in that they optimize a cardinal measure of utility, modeled with diminishing returns, instead of optimizing dollars. This means that any regionally disaggregated welfare-optimizing IAM includes both a social welfare function defined as the sum of regional welfares and measured in cardinal units, and the principle of diminishing marginal returns – exactly the theoretical combination against which Robbins and Little cautioned. Negishi weights counteract the model's resultant preference for equalizing incomes across regions, thereby making the implicit assumption that utility in richer regions is more important to global social welfare than utility in poorer regions.

Regionally disaggregated welfare-optimizing climate economics models – such as RICE and MERGE – use Negishi weights to prioritize the wellbeing of rich regions over that of poor regions. In the absence of these weights, the models would recommend equalization of income on a global scale as part of the optimal course of action to maximize social welfare. With the weights, the models return a result that has policy relevance only if decision makers agree that income redistribution is impossible, forbidden or otherwise impractical.

Clearly, global income redistribution is neither impossible nor forbidden in reality. Richer countries' development assistance to poorer countries in the form of grants, loans, technical assistance and debt forgiveness is income redistribution, however modest the scale. Equalizing incomes around the world may seem impractical or politically infeasible – the rich having a certain attachment to their higher incomes and greater wealth – but subjective practicality is a poor criterion for the inclusion of a policy mechanism in a climate economics model. IAMs commonly recommend a scale of abatement measures that is beyond the horizon of today's technology, and warn of climate damages that are outside the bounds of the historical record.

Technical model descriptions that explain the Negishi process most often use the language of an equalization of the shadow price of capital across regions. It is not uncommon for model results to be presented devoid of any context regarding their modeling assumptions, including any explanation of the Negishi weighting process. It is extremely likely that many, if not most, end users of these model results – policy makers, NGOs, the public – are unaware that a model's recommended course of action is "optimal" only given the assumptions that rich countries' welfare is prioritized over that of poor countries, and income redistribution cannot take place.

There are four broad solutions to the opacity of Negishi weighting in welfare optimizing IAMs and the bias that this weighting lends to results: continue weighting but make the impact on model results transparent; discontinue weighting, thereby allowing income to be redistributed; optimize money instead of utility; or use other kinds of IAMs that avoid the pitfalls of welfare optimization.

1. *Continue weighting, but make the impact on model results transparent*: Negishi weighting may be useful in avoiding a result – global income redistribution – that would seem politically infeasible in the Global North. As with any modeling assumptions that have important impacts on results and policy advice (for example, the choice of the discount rate or the rate at which new technology is adopted), end users need to be made aware of the context in which a result is said to be "optimal."[13]

2. *Discontinue weighting, thereby allowing income to be redistributed*: Just as Negishi-weighted results (coupled with full disclosure regarding modeling assumptions) may seem more politically feasible in the Global North, unweighted results that treat income redistribution as a key component of a viable climate policy may have a greater political trenchancy in the

Global South. Presenting paired model results, with and without Negishi weights, would give policy makers the most complete understanding of the interaction of climate damages, climate abatement and the global distribution of income.

3. *Optimize money instead of utility*: Maximizing the sum of regional gross incomes, modeled without any diminishing returns, is a plausible decision rule for global climate policy; this is the strict cost–benefit analysis approach, which has become almost ubiquitous in environmental decision making. This approach eliminates diminishing returns to income gains both in richer regions and in richer time periods – a more consistent application of the theoretical principles embodied in the Negishi weighting process. If policy makers wish to consider a weighting of income gains by regional income per capita, it would be computationally simple to add a transparent mechanism for equity weighting that could be ratcheted up or down as a policy lever.

4. *Use other kinds of IAMs that avoid the pitfalls of welfare optimization*: In IAMs that do not optimize welfare, assumptions regarding the inter-regional effects of diminishing marginal utility of income are not negated by Negishi weights. In the Stern Review's PAGE model (Hope 2006) – a simulation model – for example, the elasticity of the marginal utility of income is set at 1 (such that utility is the natural logarithm of per capita income), but no radical equalization of per capita income across regions occurs because utility is not maximized. In IAMs that do not optimize welfare (and, therefore, do not use Negishi welfare weights), inter-regional equity has the potential to be an active, and central, model parameter.

Any one or a combination of these solutions would be a vast improvement to the current status quo. Achieving a successful climate policy will be one of the greatest challenges of the twenty-first century, and it is already apparent that equity concerns will be at the center of global climate negotiations (Edmonds et al. 2008; Kok et al. 2008; Ott et al. 2008). In order to achieve greater political relevance, all climate economics models must make explicit their equity assumptions.

Part IV

APPLICATIONS OF INTEGRATED ASSESSMENT MODELS

Chapter 11

CLIMATE RISKS AND CARBON PRICES: REVISING THE SOCIAL COST OF CARBON

Frank Ackerman and Elizabeth A. Stanton

The social cost of carbon – or marginal damage caused by an additional ton of carbon dioxide emissions – has been estimated by a US government working group at $21/tCO$_2$ in 2010. That calculation, however, omits many of the biggest risks associated with climate change, and downplays the impact of current emissions on future generations. Our reanalysis explores the effects of uncertainty about climate sensitivity, the shape of the damage function and the discount rate. We show that the social cost of carbon is uncertain across a broad range, and could be much higher than $21/tCO$_2$. In our case combining high climate sensitivity, high damages and a low discount rate, the social cost of carbon could be almost $900/tCO$_2$ in 2010, rising to $1,500/tCO$_2$ in 2050.

The most ambitious scenarios for eliminating carbon dioxide emissions as rapidly as technologically feasible (reaching zero or negative net global emissions by the end of this century) require spending up to $150 to $500 per ton of reductions of carbon dioxide emissions by 2050. Using a reasonable set of alternative assumptions, therefore, the damages from a ton of carbon dioxide emissions in 2050 could exceed the cost of reducing emissions at the maximum technically feasible rate. Once this is the case, the exact value of the social cost of carbon loses importance. The clear policy prescription is to reduce emissions as rapidly as possible, and cost-effectiveness analysis offers better insights for climate policy than cost–benefit analysis.

Introduction

With the US Environmental Protection Agency's recent historic step toward regulation of greenhouse gas emissions, cost–benefit analyses of proposed American regulations can now include an estimate of damages caused by greenhouse gas emissions – or conversely, the benefits of reducing those emissions.

It is, however, a very small step: the "social cost of carbon" (SCC), i.e., the damage per metric ton of carbon dioxide (tCO_2), is estimated at \$21 for 2010, in 2007 dollars (Interagency Working Group 2010). Equivalent to \$0.21 per gallon of gasoline,[1] such a low cost seems to suggest that only modest, inexpensive measures are needed to address climate risks.[2]

The analysis by the federal Interagency Working Group is significant for its role in setting US climate policy, and for its recognition that policy should be based on global, rather than domestic, impacts (unlike most national environmental policies). It is also noteworthy as a rare instance where economic theories and analyses have been newly introduced into the public policy debate.[3] Thus it is important to examine the uses of climate economics in the Working Group analysis, particularly the treatment of the crucial uncertainties that characterize the field. This paper presents an examination and reanalysis of the SCC, finding that four major uncertainties in the economics of climate change could imply much larger estimates. In each case, the Working Group has chosen the option that minimizes estimates of climate risks and damages.

We begin with a discussion of the choice of models and scenarios for the SCC calculation. Our reanalysis relies on the Dynamic Integrated model of Climate and the Economy (DICE), one of the models used in the Interagency Working Group analysis that produced the \$21/tCO_2 estimate. We use the Working Group's modified version of DICE, the same five scenarios on which they based their calculations, and the same framework of Monte Carlo analysis.

We then introduce four major areas of uncertainties that affect the calculation: the sensitivity of the climate to greenhouse gases; the level of damages expected at low temperatures; the level of damages expected at high temperatures; and the discount rate. We recalculate the SCC based on combinations of high and low alternatives for each of these factors, yielding an array of 16 values, both for 2010 and for 2050.

Some of the resultant values for the SCC are extremely high; the highest ones are close to \$900/tCO_2 in 2010 and \$1,500 in 2050. In contrast, a review of scenarios that reach zero or negative net global emissions within this century finds that they often imply carbon prices, and marginal abatement costs, of \$150 to \$500/tCO_2 by 2050. Many of our alternative SCC values are within or above this range – and still would be, even if recalculated on a low-emissions scenario.

We conclude with a discussion of the meaning of very high SCC estimates. Once the SCC reaches or exceeds the cost of bringing net emissions to zero, its exact value becomes less important; if the SCC were twice as large, it would have the same policy implications. At such high SCC values, cost–benefit analysis of individual policies provides no useful information; what is needed instead is a cost-effectiveness analysis of the least-cost, most efficient pathway to reach zero or negative net emissions.

Choice of Models

The Interagency Working Group used three well-known models of climate economics: DICE, Policy Analysis of the Greenhouse Effect (PAGE) and Framework for Uncertainty, Negotiation and Distribution (FUND).[4] They ran each of the models on the same five scenarios, in Monte Carlo mode, examining the effects of a range of values for climate sensitivity and (in PAGE and FUND) many other uncertainties. Under their "central case" – the mean value at a 3 percent discount rate – the value of the SCC, averaged across the five scenarios, was $28/tCO$_2$ in DICE, $30 in PAGE and $6 in FUND, for a three-model average of $21.

Our reanalysis uses only the DICE model, which is the easiest of the three to modify for our purposes. As suggested by the Working Group's central case results, it is likely that FUND would have produced lower estimates than those reported below, while PAGE would have produced higher estimates. Regarding the latter, PAGE has an explicit treatment of potential climate catastrophes, using a Monte Carlo analysis that allows variation in the size of catastrophes, the temperature threshold at which they become possible and the likelihood of catastrophe once the threshold has been passed. DICE, in contrast, includes the certainty equivalent or expected value of catastrophe in its damage function. As a result, PAGE estimates a higher SCC than DICE at lower discount rates or higher climate sensitivity.[5] Our analysis includes both lower discount rates and higher climate sensitivity, so our SCC estimates would have been higher if we had used PAGE.

Choice of Scenarios

The Working Group analysis rejects the widely used Intergovernmental Panel on Climate Change (IPCC) climate scenarios, and instead uses scenarios from four other models: the business-as-usual scenarios from IMAGE, MERGE, MESSAGE and MiniCAM, and a 550 ppm stabilization scenario.

It is difficult to interpret the inclusion of the 550 ppm scenario. Does it imply a guess that, under business-as-usual conditions, there is a 20 percent chance that the world will reach agreement on stabilization at that level? No explanation is offered. Moreover, the 550 ppm scenario is not even a single, internally consistent scenario; rather, its GDP, population and emissions trajectories are averages of the values in the 550 ppm scenarios from the other four models (see Interagency Working Group 2010, 16).

Figure 11.1. Comparing EMF and IPCC CO_2 emission scenarios

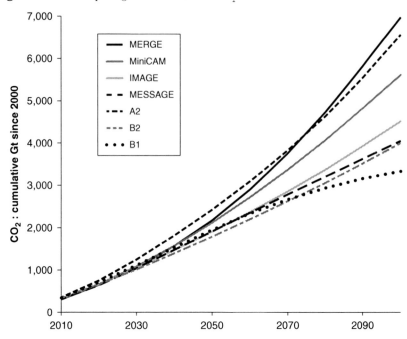

Nonetheless, inclusion of the 550 ppm scenario makes little difference in practice. Excluding it would cause only a $1 increase to the $21/t$CO_2$ SCC average estimate from DICE, FUND and PAGE, or the $28 estimate from DICE alone. For the ensemble of 16 SCC estimates in our analysis, presented below, exclusion of the 550 ppm scenario would cause an average increase of less than 4 percent; all of our estimates would change by less than 17 percent in either direction.

The four business-as-usual scenarios used by the Working Group were adopted from an Energy Modeling Forum (EMF) model comparison exercise (Clarke et al. 2009). For those who are not familiar with EMF, it may be helpful to contrast the selected EMF scenarios with the IPCC's SRES scenarios.[6] Figure 11.1 and Figure 11.2 compare the cumulative carbon dioxide emissions and current methane emissions from the four EMF scenarios and three IPCC scenarios, A2, B2 and B1.[7] As Figure 11.1 shows, carbon dioxide emissions in the four EMF scenarios (solid lines) are close to the B1 and B2 scenarios for the first half of this century, spreading out to roughly span the interval from A2 to B2 by 2100.

For methane emissions, Figure 11.2 shows that three of the four EMF scenarios start out well below the level of the B1 and B2 scenarios; by 2100, all

Figure 11.2. Comparing EMF and IPCC methane emission scenarios

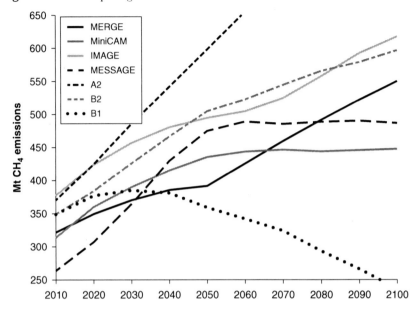

four are roughly at or below the level of B2. In short the emissions trajectories of the EMF scenarios are broadly within, but toward the lower end of, the spectrum of IPCC SRES scenarios, perhaps closest to B2.

All else being equal, lower emissions usually imply lower temperatures, lower damages and therefore a lower estimate of the SCC (a discussion of countervailing factors is included later in this chapter). Use of a scenario in which emissions grow more rapidly, such as A2, would likely have led to higher values for the SCC.

For the sake of comparability with the Working Group results, we have adopted the same five scenarios in our analysis of uncertainties. Kopp and Mignone (2011) provide a more detailed evaluation of the Working Group's emission scenarios as part of a discussion of the full set of assumptions used in the Working Group's analysis.

Four Uncertainties

This section explores four major uncertainties that affect the SCC calculation: the value of the climate sensitivity parameter; the level of climate damages expected at low temperatures; the level of damages at high temperatures; and the discount rate. The next section presents multiple estimates of the SCC, based on alternatives for each of these uncertainties.

Climate sensitivity

The climate sensitivity parameter is the long-term temperature increase expected from a doubling of the concentration of carbon dioxide in the atmosphere. This crucial parameter, which measures the pace of global warming, remains uncertain, and there are reasons to believe that significant uncertainty about climate sensitivity is inescapable (Roe and Baker 2007).

On this topic, the Working Group analysis is impressively thorough. They discuss the scientific evidence on likely values of climate sensitivity, and adopt a probability distribution which assumes a two-thirds probability that climate sensitivity is between 2.0°C and 4.5°C. The minimum is zero and the maximum is 10°C; the distribution has a median of 3.0°C and a 95th percentile of 7.14°C. They then perform a Monte Carlo analysis, repeatedly selecting a climate sensitivity value from this probability distribution. In PAGE and FUND, there are numerous other Monte Carlo variables, representing other uncertainties; in DICE, normally a deterministic model, climate sensitivity is the only Monte Carlo variable in the Working Group analysis.

The Working Group reports, but does not emphasize, the 95th percentile results. For DICE in particular, those results are a measure of the potential impact of uncertainty about climate sensitivity. Results for DICE, and for the three-model average used by the Working Group, are presented in Table 11.1.

We follow the Working Group in calculating average and 95th percentile SCC results over 10,000 iterations, using the same probability distribution for climate sensitivity as the Working Group, in each of the five climate scenarios for each of the variations described below. In DICE, the average and 95th percentile results may correspond to climate sensitivity somewhat below 3.0°C and 7.14°C, respectively, since actual climate sensitivity in DICE (and several other integrated assessment models) is lower than the reported values. DICE uses a default climate sensitivity of 3.0°C, but actually responds to a doubling of atmospheric carbon dioxide with a long-run temperature increase of 2.77°C (van Vuuren et al. 2011a).

Table 11.1. SCC estimates 2010 and 2050, 3 percent discount rate

Emissions Year	Result	DICE	3-Model Average
2010	Average	$28	$21
2010	95th Percentile	$56	$65
2050	Average	$64	$45
2050	95th Percentile	$123	$136

Sources: DICE 2050 – our calculations.
All other: Working Group report 2010.

Damage function estimates

Like climate sensitivity, the relationship between temperature increases and economic damage is uncertain. The Working Group says little about the estimates of economic damages from climate change, except to call for additional research. Kopp et al. (2011) modify the Working Group's version of the DICE model by including uncertainty in the damage function and varying the level of risk aversion in the discount rate. We take a simpler approach: the damage function remains a certainty equivalent, but we explore alternative functional forms and parameter values.

DICE assumes that as temperatures rise, an increasing fraction of output is lost to climate damages. We will use D for damages as a fraction of the GDP that would be produced in the absence of climate change; $R = 1 - D$ for the net output ratio, or output net of climate damages as a fraction of output in the absence of climate change; and T for global average temperature increase in °C above 1900. The DICE damage function is:

(11.1) $R = 1 / (1 + .00284\ T^2)$

or equivalently,

(11.2) $R = 1 / [1 + (T / 18.8)^2]$

The DICE net output ratio can be viewed as combining two separate estimates: first, for low temperatures, William Nordhaus, the creator of DICE, estimates that damages are 1.7 percent of output at 2.5°C (Nordhaus 2007); second, at high temperatures, it is assumed by default that the quadratic relationship of damages to temperature in (11.1) or (11.2) continues to apply. Separate research addresses the low-temperature and high-temperature estimates, suggesting alternatives to each.

The DICE low-temperature damage estimate is based on an evaluation of several categories of climate damages at 2.5°C (Nordhaus 2008; Nordhaus and Boyer 2000). In a review and critique of the Nordhaus estimates as applied to the United States, Michael Hanemann develops alternative estimates for damages at 2.5°C, which are, in total, 2.4 times the Nordhaus value (Hanemann 2008).[8] If the same relationship applies worldwide, then a reasonable alternative at low temperatures is to keep the form of Equation 11.1 or 11.2, but recalibrate damages to 4.2 percent of output at 2.5°C. This yields the equation:

(11.3) $R = 1 / [1 + (T / 12.0)^2]$

Neither the Nordhaus nor the Hanemann 2.5°C estimate provides a basis for projecting damages at much higher temperatures.[9] It has become conventional to extrapolate the same quadratic relationship to higher temperatures, but there is no economic or scientific basis for that convention. The extrapolation implies that damages grow at a leisurely pace, especially in the Nordhaus version: from Equations 11.2 and 11.3, it is easy to see that half of world output is not lost to climate damages until temperatures reach almost 19°C according to DICE, or 12°C in the Hanemann variant.

In a discussion of damage functions and catastrophic risks, Martin Weitzman argues that even if the Nordhaus estimate is appropriate for low-temperature damages, the increasingly ominous scientific evidence about climate risks implies much greater losses at higher temperatures (Weitzman 2010). He suggests that damages should be modeled as 50 percent of output at 6°C and 99 percent at 12°C, as better representations of the current understanding of climate risks; the latter temperature can be taken as representing the end of modern economic life, if not human life in general. In support of this disastrous projection for 12°C of warming, Weitzman cites recent research showing that at that temperature, areas where half the world's population now lives would experience conditions, at least once a year, that human physiology cannot tolerate, resulting in death from heat stroke within a few hours (Sherwood and Huber 2010).

Weitzman creates a damage function that matches the DICE estimate at low temperatures, but rises to his suggested values at 6°C and 12°C. He modifies Equation 11.2 by adding a higher power of T to the denominator:[10]

$$(11.4) \qquad R = 1 \ / \ [1 + (T \ / \ 20.2)^2 + (T \ / \ 6.08)^{6.76}]$$

When T is small, the quadratic term in Equation 11.4 is more important, providing a close match to the original DICE damage function; when T is large, the higher-power term is more important, allowing the damage function to match Weitzman's values for higher temperatures.

The same method can be applied to the Hanemann low-temperature estimate in Equation 11.3; calibrating to Hanemann's value at 2.5°C, and Weitzman's values at 6°C and 12°C, we obtain:

$$(11.5) \qquad R = 1 \ / \ [1 + (T \ / \ 12.2)^2 + (T \ / \ 6.24)^{7.02}]$$

Equations 11.2, 11.3, 11.4 and 11.5 incorporate all combinations of two low-temperature alternatives (Nordhaus and Hanemann), and two high-temperature alternatives (Nordhaus and Weitzman). Using their initials, these can be labeled as the N–N, H–N, N–W and H–W

Figure 11.3. Damages as a share of GDP in four damage functions

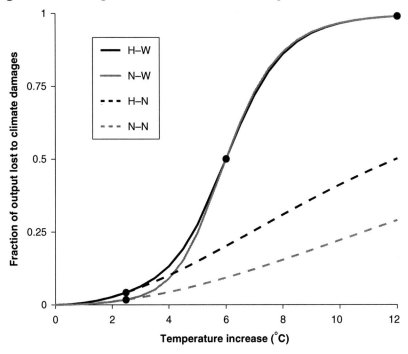

damages functions, respectively. They are displayed in Figure 11.3 (the graph presents damages as a share of GDP, i.e., $D = 1 - R$), with large dots indicating the points used for calibration. Below 3°C, the low-temperature alternatives are dominant, and the high-temperature alternatives make no visible difference; at 6°C and above, the high-temperature alternatives determine the shape of the damage function. In particular, the two damage functions with the Weitzman high-temperature assumption are nearly identical above 6°C.[11]

Discount rates

The Working Group's analysis of the SCC is based on projected costs and benefits extending 300 years into the future, as is our reanalysis. Across such spans of time, the discount rate is crucial to the bottom-line evaluation: the lower the discount rate, the more important the outcomes in later years will be. It seems safe to say that there is ongoing controversy and a lack of consensus on the appropriate discount rate to use in climate economics.

The Working Group discusses the discount rate at length, justifying their choice of a fixed rate of 3 percent. This is one of the discount rates normally

Figure 11.4. Estimates of the SCC in 2010

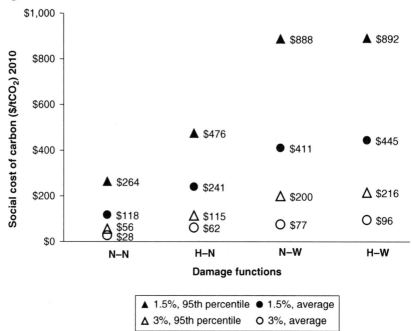

recommended for use in US government policy analyses. It can be supported within either of the two frameworks used to determine the discount rate, the descriptive and prescriptive approaches (Arrow et al. 1996). The descriptive approach calls for use of an appropriate market interest rate; the Working Group estimates the real risk-free rate of return, after tax, at 2.7 percent. The prescriptive approach deduces the discount rate from first principles, as the sum of "pure time preference" (the discount rate that would apply if per capita consumption were constant) plus a multiple of the rate of growth of per capita consumption. The Working Group concludes that "arguments made under the prescriptive approach can be used to justify discount rates between roughly 1.4 and 3.1 percent" (Interagency Working Group 2010, 23), and expresses skepticism about the lower end of that range.

Both descriptive and prescriptive arguments can be made for discount rates below 3 percent. The long-term average risk-free rate is often estimated to be lower than 2.7 percent.[12] In addition, if climate mitigation, like insurance, is most valuable in circumstances that reduce incomes, then the discount rate should be lower than the risk-free rate of return. Using the prescriptive approach, the Stern Review spells out in detail the arguments for a low discount rate, on grounds of intergenerational equity (Stern 2006).

Figure 11.5. Estimates of the SCC in 2050

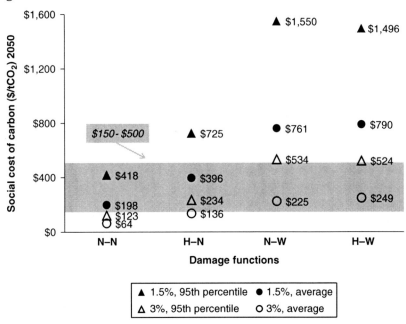

Stern's recommended formula for the discount rate is 0.1 percent plus the rate of growth of per capita consumption; this implies an average of 1.4 percent per year, in the Stern Review's model.

To explore the effect of discount rates on the SCC, we use two rates, 3 percent and 1.5 percent per year – approximating the range that the Working Group identified as supportable under the prescriptive approach (as quoted above). Our lower rate is close to the Stern Review's rate; moreover, it is the average rate that would result from applying Stern's formula, 0.1 percent plus the rate of growth of per capita consumption, to the first 200 years of the Working Group's four business-as-usual scenarios.[13]

Results

The previous section identified two alternatives for each of four major factors influencing the SCC:

- Average versus 95th percentile climate sensitivity
- Nordhaus versus Hanemann damage estimates at low temperatures
- Nordhaus versus Weitzman damage estimates at high temperatures
- 3.0 versus 1.5 percent fixed discount rate

We calculated the SCC under each combination of these alternatives, making no other changes to the Working Group's version of DICE.[14] This involved rerunning the Monte Carlo analysis, with 10,000 iterations sampling the same probability distribution for climate sensitivity used by the Working Group, for each of the four damage functions shown in Figure 11.3, the 1.5 and 3.0 percent discount rates and the five EMF climate scenarios. The results are shown in Figure 11.4 for 2010, and Figure 11.5 for 2050. Circles represent average climate sensitivity, and triangles 95th percentile; solid symbols represent 1.5 percent discount rates, and outlined symbols 3 percent. Results for the four damage functions are shown in four columns on the graphs, as marked.

The SCC is generally higher for later years, since GDP, as well as atmospheric concentrations of greenhouse gases, and temperatures, will be higher at that time – implying that the incremental damage from another ton of carbon dioxide emissions will be greater as well. So it is not surprising that the SCC estimates for 2050 are much higher than the corresponding figures for 2010.

In both graphs, the N–N (original DICE) damage function leads to lower estimates than any of the alternatives. If Hanemann is right about low-temperature damages, then the SCC in 2050 is above $100/tCO_2$ at a 3 percent discount rate, or about $400 at 1.5 percent. If Weitzman is right about high-temperature damages, the mid-century SCC is above $200 at a 3 percent discount rate, or above $700 at 1.5 percent. At either discount rate, the estimates with Weitzman high-temperature damages and 95th percentile climate sensitivity are almost four times higher than the N–N (original DICE) 95th percentile values, and seven to eight times higher than the N–N average values.

Abatement Costs

In a cost–benefit analysis of climate policy, the costs of doing nothing about climate change – i.e., the SCC – should be compared to the costs of doing something to mitigate it – i.e., the cost of reducing emissions. In several ambitious scenarios for drastic reduction in global emissions, the marginal cost per ton of abatement is lower than many of the SCC estimates presented above.

An inter-model comparison project, run by researchers at the Postdam Institute for Climate Change Research (PIK) in Germany, compared scenarios from five models that stabilize carbon dioxide concentrations at 400 ppm by 2100.[15] Because carbon dioxide remains in the atmosphere for decades or centuries, and we are already at 390 ppm, these scenarios have to achieve negative net global emissions before 2100, through measures such as reforestation and biomass burning with carbon capture and sequestration (CCS). In general, the 400 ppm scenarios strain the limits of plausible rates of technological and socioeconomic change. Their carbon prices reach $150–$500/tCO$_2$ by 2050, with an average of $260.[16]

A similar, though slightly more pessimistic, scenario from the International Energy Agency (IEA), stabilizes the atmosphere at 450 ppm of CO$_2$. This scenario – IEA's "BLUE Map" – again strains the limits of possible technical change, and is meant to represent the maximum feasible pace of abatement. The marginal abatement cost in 2050 is between $175 and $500/tCO$_2$, depending on the degree of technological optimism or pessimism in cost forecasts (International Energy Agency 2008, 2010).

A more optimistic variant on this theme, from McKinsey & Company, projects rapid abatement leading to eventual stabilization at 400 ppm CO$_2$-equivalent; atmospheric concentration peaks at 480 ppm CO$_2$-e in the 2060s before declining. McKinsey estimates the marginal abatement cost of this scenario at $90–$150/tCO$_2$-e in 2030 (McKinsey & Company 2009).

The British government assigns values to carbon emissions for use in long-term policy appraisals. Its estimates are based on marginal abatement costs under scenarios that are consistent with staying under 2°C of warming – which, in practice, is close to the maximum technically feasible pace of abatement. Their estimated carbon value for 2050 is £200 ± £100/t CO$_2$-e (U.K. Department of Energy & Climate Change 2009). At mid-2011 exchange rates, £100–£300 is equivalent to about $165–$495.

Comparing these abatement cost estimates to our SCC calculations, the low-stabilization trajectory scenarios compared by PIK, the IEA BLUE Map and the UK government carbon values all imply abatement costs of roughly $150 to $500/tCO$_2$ by 2050 – the region shaded in gray in Figure 11.5. Only three of our 16 SCC estimates for 2050 are below this range; all three assume Nordhaus (lower) high-temperature damages and a 3 percent discount rate. Eight of our estimates are within or barely above this range, and five are well above it. All of the top five assume a 1.5 percent discount rate, and four of the five assume Weitzman high-temperature damages.

The McKinsey estimate of the marginal cost for rapid abatement, $90–$150/tCO$_2$ in 2030, is a range that has already been reached or exceeded by most of our SCC estimates for 2010. Four of the eight estimates for 2010 at a 3 percent discount rate, and all eight of the estimates for 2010 at 1.5 percent, are at or above the McKinsey marginal abatement cost estimate for 2030.

In short, if either low-temperature or high-temperature damages are worse than DICE assumes, then the SCC is roughly at the marginal abatement cost for a maximal abatement scenario at a 3 percent discount rate, or well above that level at a 1.5 percent discount rate. Even with the original DICE damage function, the SCC estimates at a 1.5 percent discount rate are roughly comparable to the marginal cost of a maximal abatement path.

Sensitivity Analysis: SCC Estimates with Low Emissions

It would be possible to raise the objection that the comparison presented here is inappropriate: we compare the SCC, estimated on relatively high emissions scenarios, to marginal abatement costs of ambitious mitigation scenarios with much lower emissions. If the SCC were re-estimated on a rapid abatement trajectory, where marginal abatement costs reach $150 to $500/$tCO_2$ by 2050, would the SCC still equal or exceed this range?

To test this possibility, we replaced the CO_2 emissions and non-CO2 forcings in all five DICE scenarios with the corresponding data for the IPCC's new RCP2.6 scenario (also called RCP3-PD).[17] RCP2.6 is designed to represent the emission reductions required to reach the widely discussed target of keeping temperature increases under 2°C; it projects more than 95 percent reduction in annual emissions of all greenhouse gases by 2100, and implies marginal abatement costs of around $160 per ton of CO_2 in 2050 (van Vuuren et al. 2011b).

Our use of the RCP2.6 emissions and forcings is a sensitivity analysis, not a complete implementation of the RCP2.6 scenario assumptions. Specifically, we left GDP and population projections unchanged in all five of the Working Group's DICE scenarios, and assumed constant annual emissions and forcings after 2100. Nonetheless, recalculation of our results with RCP2.6 emissions and forcings provides a good test of the sensitivity of SCC estimates to emissions trajectories. The results for 2050 with RCP 2.6 emissions are shown in Figure 11.6, which can be compared to Figure 11.5, our 2050 results with the Working Group emissions trajectories.

The estimates with the N–N (original DICE) damage function are relatively little changed; they are only 2 to 14 percent smaller with the drastically lower RCP2.6 emissions, compared to the Working Group scenarios. This is consistent with the findings of Hope (2006b), who demonstrates that the SCC is insensitive to variations in emissions trajectories in the PAGE model. Hope's explanation is that two opposite effects are roughly equal in importance. On the one hand, radiative forcings, and therefore temperatures, are proportional to the logarithm of atmospheric concentrations of greenhouse gases; this implies that at lower concentrations, a given increase in emissions causes a greater increase in temperature. On the other hand, damages increase more than linearly with temperature; this implies that at higher concentrations and temperatures, a given increase in temperature causes a greater increase in damages.

Figure 11.6. Estimates of the SCC in 2050 with RCP2.6 emissions

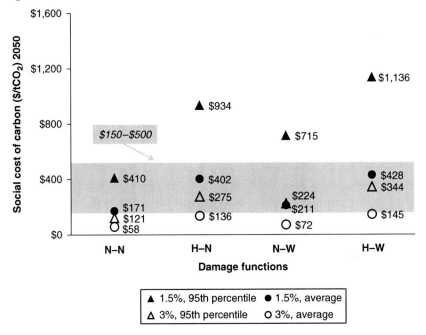

While these two effects will always work in opposite directions, the near equality in their magnitude found by Hope (2006b) appears to depend on the assumed shape of the damage function. Our N–N damage function may be the closest, among our four options, to the PAGE damage function used in that analysis.

Our results with the H–N damage function are, counterintuitively, unchanged or higher with RCP2.6 emissions (Figure 11.6) than with the Working Group scenarios (Figure 11.5). This reflects a small anomaly in the data. While RCP2.6 emissions become sharply lower by late in this century, and remain very low thereafter, they do not start out below the Working Group scenarios. Under RCP2.6, CO_2 emissions are close to the average of the five Working Group scenarios for the first three decades; and RCP2.6 non-CO_2 forcings are well above the Working Group scenario average for the first five decades.[18] The H–N damage function uses our higher assumption about low-temperature damages, which would result from early emissions, but our lower assumption about high-temperature damages, which result primarily from later emissions. Thus its results are the most affected by the initial years when the RCP2.6 trajectory is at or above the Working Group scenario average.

Conversely, the N–W damage function is less sensitive to low-temperature damages and early emissions, but more sensitive to high-temperature damages and later emissions. The RCP2.6 reduction in later emissions has the greatest effect here, with all four N–W SCC estimates in Figure 11.6 at less than half of the corresponding levels in Figure 11.5. The H–W damage function is, in this respect, an intermediate case; the H–W SCC estimates are reduced by roughly one-quarter to one-half under RCP2.6, compared to the Working Group emissions.

The bottom line is that even with the rapid emission reductions projected under RCP2.6, our SCC estimates are at or above the estimated marginal abatement cost for a maximal abatement strategy ($150–$500/tCO_2) in 11 of the 16 cases, as seen in Figure 11.6. The worst cases, involving 95th percentile climate sensitivity, a 1.5 percent discount rate and any damage function except N–N, are all above $700/t$CO_2$. At the other extreme, the only cases with SCC below $100/t$CO_2$ at mid-century are the two estimates using average climate sensitivity, a 3 percent discount rate and the Nordhaus estimate of low-temperature damages.

Conclusions

We began by reviewing the US government's estimate of the SCC, developed for use in cost–benefit analysis of regulatory proposals. We have ended with alternate estimates that are not just minor revisions to the published figure of $21 per ton, but are higher, in most cases, by an order of magnitude or more. These estimates appear to be well outside the bounds of realistic short-term policy options, in the United States or elsewhere. How should these ultra-high SCC values be interpreted?

The SCC represents the marginal cost of climate damages, or the cost of doing nothing about climate change. In a cost–benefit framework, it should be compared to the marginal cost of climate protection. We have compared our SCC estimates to the marginal abatement cost on several versions of a maximum feasible abatement scenario, which would lead to zero or negative net global emissions before the end of this century. In the federal Working Group's analysis, the SCC is well below the abatement cost for these scenarios. We found that under many alternate sets of assumptions, the SCC is roughly equal to or greater than the cost of maximum feasible abatement. This remains true even when the SCC is re-estimated using a rapid reduction emissions trajectory.

Once the SCC is high enough to justify maximum feasible abatement in cost–benefit terms, then cost–benefit analysis becomes functionally equivalent to a precautionary approach to carbon emissions. All that remains for economic analysis of climate policy is to determine the cost-minimizing strategy for eliminating emissions as quickly as possible. This occurs because the marginal damages from emissions have become so large; the uncertainties explored in our analysis, regarding damages and climate sensitivity, imply that the marginal damage curve could turn nearly vertical at some point, representing a catastrophic or discontinuous change.

The factors driving this result are uncertainties, not known facts. We cannot know in advance how large climate damages, or climate sensitivity, will turn out to be. The argument is analogous to the case for buying insurance: it is the prudent choice, not because we are sure that catastrophe will occur, but because we cannot be sufficiently sure that it will not occur. By the time we know what climate sensitivity and high-temperature damages turn out to be, it will be much too late to do anything about it. The analysis here demonstrates that plausible values for key uncertainties imply catastrophically large values of the SCC.

This result can be generalized to other environmental issues: when there is a credible risk that the marginal damage curve for an externality turns vertical at some threshold (representing discontinuous, extremely large damages), then the shadow price of the externality, such as the SCC, can become so large that cost–benefit analysis turns into cost-effectiveness analysis of the least-cost strategy for staying safely below the threshold.

Our results offer a new way to make sense of the puzzling finding by Martin Weitzman: his "dismal theorem" establishes that under certain assumptions, the marginal benefit of emission reduction could literally be infinite (Weitzman 2009). The SCC, which measures the marginal benefit of emission reduction, is not an observable price in any actual market. Rather, it is a shadow price, deduced from an analysis of climate dynamics and economic impacts. Its only meaning is as a guide to welfare calculations; we can obtain a more accurate understanding of the welfare consequences of policy choices by incorporating that shadow price for emissions.

Once the shadow price is high enough so that maximum feasible abatement is a welfare improvement, there is no additional meaning to an even higher price. Doubling or tripling the SCC beyond that level would have exactly the same implications for market behavior and policy choices: it would still be optimal to eliminate emissions as rapidly as possible. In this sense, it bears some resemblance to infinity, which is unaffected by doubling or tripling.[19] Our highest SCC estimates are clearly not infinite – but they may be close enough to infinity for all practical purposes.

What's left, finally, of the economic arguments for gradualism in climate policy, which seem to be endorsed by the Working Group's $21/tCO$_2$ SCC? To support this approach, given our results, one would have to endorse the

Working Group's view of most or all of the key assumptions and uncertainties explored in our analysis: the original DICE damage function, a discount rate of 3 percent and average rather than 95th percentile climate sensitivity. Changes in these assumptions quickly push the SCC up into the $150–$500 range by midcentury, justifying the maximum feasible pace of abatement; changes in all of these assumptions yield an SCC well above that range. At such levels, cost–benefit analysis provides a result that is identical to a precautionary approach supporting immediate, large-scale action to reduce emissions and avoid dangerous levels of climate change.

Chapter 12

EPSTEIN–ZIN UTILITY IN DICE: IS RISK AVERSION IRRELEVANT TO CLIMATE POLICY?

Frank Ackerman, Elizabeth A. Stanton and Ramón Bueno

Climate change involves uncertain probabilities of catastrophic risks, and very long-term consequences of current actions. Climate economics, therefore, is centrally concerned with the treatment of risk and time. Yet conventional assumptions about utility and optimal economic growth create a perverse connection between risk aversion and time preference, such that more aversion to current risks implies less concern for future outcomes, and vice versa. The same conflation of risk aversion and time preference leads to the equity premium puzzle in finance. A promising response to the equity premium puzzle, the recursive utility of Epstein and Zin, allows separation of risk aversion and time preference – at the cost of considerable analytic complexity. We introduce an accessible implementation of Epstein–Zin utility into the DICE model of climate economics, creating a hybrid "EZ–DICE" model. Using Epstein–Zin parameters from finance literature and climate uncertainty parameters from science literature, we find that the optimal climate policy in EZ–DICE calls for rapid abatement of carbon emissions; it is similar to standard DICE results with the discount rate set to equal the risk-free rate of return. EZ–DICE solutions are sensitive to the intertemporal elasticity of substitution, but remarkably insensitive to risk aversion. Insensitivity to risk aversion may reflect the difficulty of modeling catastrophic risks within DICE. Implicit in DICE are strong assumptions about the cost of climate stabilization and the certainty and speed of success; under these assumptions, risk aversion would in fact be unimportant. A more realistic analysis will require a subtler treatment of catastrophic climate risk.

Introduction: The Need for a New Utility Function

Economic analysis of climate change is often framed in cost–benefit terms. On the one hand, spending money now on reducing emissions means that less is available for current consumption and ordinary investment. On the other hand, not spending money now on reducing emissions means that less will be available for future consumption and investment as climate damages increase. An optimal economic growth path can be calculated, subject to these two constraints; among other results, it includes an optimal climate policy, or pace of emission reduction.

This much is standard economic methodology, equally applicable to many different problems. Climate change, however, is unique both in the magnitude of the uncertain risks it poses, and the long time spans, often exceeding a century, between physical causes and effects. The attempt to stretch standard methods to cover such extremes of risk and time reveals a hole in the theoretical fabric.

The growth model commonly used in climate economics (and elsewhere) can be traced back to Ramsey (1928), who demonstrated that along an optimal growth path, the discount rate for consumption equals the productivity of capital. Later analysis (Cass 1965; Koopmans 1965) formalized this conclusion in what is now known as the "Ramsey equation":

$$(12.1) \qquad r = \delta + \eta g$$

Here r is the discount rate for consumption, δ is the rate of pure time preference (or equivalently, the discount rate for utility), η is the elasticity of the marginal utility of consumption (or equivalently, the inverse of the intertemporal elasticity of substitution) and g is the rate of growth of per capita consumption, which is assumed to be known with certainty.[1] Informally, growth means that future generations will be richer and the marginal utility of increasing their consumption will be lower, so their consumption is discounted relative to ours today. The larger the value of η, the more we are focused on our own, relatively lower-income circumstances, rather than on our wealthier descendants.

The model is developed in an expected utility framework. Although many utility functions could be used, it is mathematically convenient to adopt the constant relative risk aversion (CRRA) function. Under this assumption, the utility obtained from current consumption, c, is[2]

$$(12.2) \qquad u(c) = \frac{c^{1-\eta} - 1}{1 - \eta}$$

Here η, the same parameter as in Equation 12.1, is the coefficient of relative risk aversion; it determines the curvature of the utility function. The larger the value of η, the more we are focused on avoiding risks of losses rather than gambling for uncertain gains.

While these two interpretations of η might appear to parallel each other – larger η means greater aversion to lower consumption in each case – they are actually on a collision course. Expressing more aversion to climate risks, via larger η in Equation 12.2, implies a higher discount rate and greater disinterest in the future in Equation 12.1. Economists are thus apparently condemned to choose between a low discount rate, reflecting heightened concern for future generations but a very low level of current risk aversion (as in Cline 1992; Stern 2006), or a high discount rate, reflecting more aversion to current risks at the expense of greater indifference to future generations (as in Nordhaus 2008 and many others). There is no natural way to model a combination of strong risk aversion and strong future orientation.[3] A similar problem can be seen in survey research, which finds that the same people express attitudes toward risk and toward time preference that imply very different values of η (Atkinson et al. 2009).

Indeed, the expected utility framework in general may be an obstacle to a realistic analysis of risk aversion. Within such a framework, the assumptions of plausible levels of risk aversion toward large risks and non-zero aversion toward small risks have been shown to be incompatible (Rabin 2000).

Epstein–Zin Utility

Similar problems arise in other areas of economics. The same expected utility framework, including the same conflation of risk aversion and time preference, is unable to explain why rates of return are so high on equity and so low on risk-free assets (Mehra and Prescott 1985). More than 25 years of discussion of this "equity premium puzzle" has not yet produced a consensus on the solution, but has given rise to a number of possible explanations (DeLong and Magin 2009). Many of them involve new theories of investor behavior, challenging or expanding the traditional understanding of economic rationality.

One of the most promising responses to the equity premium puzzle is the recursive utility model of Epstein and Zin (1989, 1991). They propose a utility function with an additional degree of freedom, allowing separate calibration of risk aversion and time preference. Epstein–Zin utility at time t, or U_t, depends both on current consumption, c_t, and on the certainty equivalent at time t of future utility, $\mu_t(U_{t+1})$:

$$(12.3) \qquad u_t = \left[(1 - \beta) c_t^\rho + \beta \left(\mu_t \left[U_{t+1} \right] \right)^\rho \right]^{1/\rho}$$

Here β is the discount factor for utility;[1] the rate of pure time preference is $\delta = (1 - \beta)/\beta$. Time preference is also affected by ρ; the intertemporal elasticity of substitution (IES) is $\psi = 1/(1 - \rho)$. The certainty equivalent of future utility is specified as:

$$(12.4) \qquad \mu_t\left(U_{t+1}\right) = \left(E_t\left[U_{t+1}^{\alpha}\right]\right)^{1/\alpha}$$

Here E_t is the expected value operator at time t. Risk aversion is measured by α; the coefficient of relative risk aversion is $\gamma = 1 - \alpha$. In the special case where $\rho = \alpha$, (12.3) becomes equivalent to the present value (over the unlimited future) of (12.2), with $\eta = \gamma = 1/\psi$. However, this special case appears unrealistic, since both risk aversion (γ) and the IES (ψ) must be greater than one to fit observed financial market patterns (Bansal and Yaron 2004); matching such patterns is possible with (12.3) but not with (12.2).

There have been a few applications of Epstein–Zin utility to climate economics; the first may be by Ha-Duong and Treich (2004), using a simplified four-period model. Traeger and several colleagues are exploring the theoretical implications of Epstein–Zin utility for climate analysis, with applications to a model derived from the well-known DICE model (Crost and Traeger 2010; Jensen and Traeger 2011).[5] In DICE and similar models, the constraints of the expected utility framework lead to the paradoxical result that a higher coefficient of relative risk aversion can lead to reduced abatement efforts; Kaufman (2012), using a simplified DICE-like model, shows that Epstein–Zin utility eliminates this paradox.

The existing studies that apply Epstein–Zin utility to climate economics demonstrate the importance of this approach. They show that it leads to optimal solutions and policy recommendations that are significantly different from the conventional approach based on the Ramsey equation and the expected utility framework. The paradoxes that result from the traditional entanglement of risk aversion and time preference are neatly resolved.

This accomplishment, however, comes at a great analytical cost. The applications of Epstein–Zin utility to date have required a level of mathematical sophistication and complexity well beyond the norm for integrated assessment literature, yet have analyzed only very simplified climate models – often using ad hoc models based on or resembling DICE, but with substantial simplifications of its structure (Crost and Traeger 2010; Kaufman 2012). Even with the best mathematical techniques, there are inherent obstacles to direct application of Epstein–Zin utility to a model such as DICE.

The problem results from the recursive nature of Epstein–Zin utility. The separation of risk aversion and time preference in Equation 12.3 makes current utility depend not only on current consumption, but also on expectations about the next period's utility, which in turn depends on the following period, and so on into the indefinite future. Thus utility is defined only on the complete branching tree of possible futures growing out of the present moment. The DICE model analyzes futures over 60 time periods (decades); for use in this chapter we have truncated it at 40 periods. If one binary choice is made in each of 40 time periods, the tree of possible futures has 2^{40}, or roughly a trillion branches. To calculate Epstein–Zin utility in the first period, it would be necessary to follow every one of those trillion branches to its endpoint.

One response to this problem is to model very few time periods, thereby losing the long-term modeling of climate and economic dynamics found in integrated assessment models (Ha-Duong and Treich 2004; Kaufman 2012). Another approach is taken by Crost and Traeger (2010), who analyze a model based on DICE over an infinite time horizon, using the Bellman equation to reduce the recursive dynamic programming problem to a single-period problem. This is only a limited success, however: in order to obtain an approximate numerical solution to the Bellman equation, it was necessary to replace the DICE treatment of the carbon cycle and climate dynamics with a much simpler and physically less realistic alternative (Crost and Traeger 2010, 6).

The EZ–DICE Model

Our goal is to demonstrate the applicability of Epstein–Zin utility to a model at the level of complexity of DICE – which, it should be remembered, is among the simplest of the integrated assessment models. The existing Epstein–Zin climate analyses have retained the full theoretical treatment of uncertainty but applied it to a stylized simplification of a climate model; we adopt the opposite strategy, retaining the full structure of DICE but combining it with a stylized simplification of uncertainty. Specifically, we achieve a drastic pruning of the tree of future consequences by modeling only one form of uncertainty, regarding the climate sensitivity parameter.

Climate sensitivity is the long-term global average temperature increase caused by a doubling of the atmospheric concentration of carbon dioxide. It is a crucial determinant of the expected pace of climate change. Although it remains uncertain, perhaps inescapably so, there is an emerging near-consensus on how to model its probability distribution (Roe and Baker 2007). The true value of climate sensitivity will, of course, eventually become known or knowable in retrospect, when it may well be too late to do anything about climate change.

We introduce the following form of uncertainty into the DICE model: climate sensitivity, at the outset, adopts one of five possible values. At first, only the probabilities of these five values are known. The actual value becomes known at a specific date in the future. Our interest is in the optimal decisions made under uncertainty, in the years before the true value of climate sensitivity is discovered.

The date for the resolution of uncertainty should, on general principles, be in the later years of this century. If it is much less than 50 years into the future, then the prior period of decision making under uncertainty becomes too short for useful analysis. If, on the other hand, it is more than a century from now, then climate outcomes are all but determined prior to the resolution of uncertainty – and, with a century of additional data, it seems unlikely that climate sensitivity would remain completely uncertain.[6]

For the numerical results presented here, we chose the midpoint of the second half of the century – 2075, or 70 years after the model's base year – for the resolution of uncertainty. Experiments with the model (not presented here) showed that other dates in the second half of this century would yield qualitatively similar results. An additional result of the specific choice of 2075 is explained below.

To implement this picture of uncertainty, we run the DICE model simultaneously for five possible states of nature, differing only in climate sensitivity. The five states are constrained to make identical investment and abatement choices for the first 70 years, since it is not yet known which state prevails; in all other respects, the five states are independent of each other. The solutions to DICE in all five states, both before and after the discovery of true climate sensitivity in 2075, are chosen to maximize first-period Epstein–Zin utility:

$$(12.5) \qquad U_1 = \left[(1 - \beta)c_1^\rho + \beta\left(\mu_1\left[U_2\right]\right)^\rho \right]^{1/\rho}$$

Here the first-period certainty equivalent value of next-period utility, $\mu_1(U_2)$, is calculated across the five states of nature, according to Equation 12.4.

In this model of uncertainty, the tree of possible futures branches only once, in the first period; after that point there are five separate, unbranching trunks (although they are tied together for the first 70 years). That is, the future is deterministic once climate sensitivity has been picked, even though no one knows, for quite a while, which of the possible futures is occurring. In the second period and thereafter, each state of nature has a single value of climate sensitivity, hence no risk, no role for risk aversion and no need for

Table 12.1. Climate sensitivity parameters for five states of nature

State Label	S_1	S_2	S_3	S_4	S_5
Length of Interval (percent)	50	40	5	3	2
Climate Sensitivity at Midpoint	2.43	3.67	6.05	8.20	16.15

calculation of certainty equivalent values. Second-period utility in each state reduces to:

$$(12.6) \qquad U_2 = \left[(1 - \beta)c_2^\rho + \beta U_3{}^\rho \right]^{1/\rho}$$

This is equivalent to the present value, over all remaining time periods, of the much simpler utility function (12.2), with $\rho = 1 - \eta$.

So in our model, the full Epstein–Zin calculation, with its risk-averse evaluation of five possible futures, is needed only once, in the initial period. This simplifies Epstein–Zin utility to an extent that makes it feasible to introduce it into DICE. The modified model, EZ–DICE, chooses the single investment plan and climate policy that applies to all states until 2075, and the five separate investment plans and climate policies, one for each state, after 2075.

These choices are made to maximize Epstein–Zin utility across all five states in the initial period, i.e., U_1 as defined in Equation 12.5 – which, thanks to recursion, includes the evaluation of all future consequences in all five states.

Model Calibration

For climate sensitivity, we use the Roe and Baker (2007) distribution, calibrated to match the results of Murphy et al. (2004).[7] We partition the probability distribution into five unequal intervals, as shown in Table 12.1, using the climate sensitivity at the midpoint of each interval as the value for that state of nature, and the length of the interval as the probability of that state. For example, the 25th percentile climate sensitivity value, 2.43, is assumed to occur in state S_1 with 50 percent probability; the 99th percentile value, 16.15, occurs in state S_5 with 2 percent probability. In this distribution, the median value of climate sensitivity is 3.00, and the mean is 3.55. States S_3, S_4 and S_5, all of them above the 90th percentile, are chosen to allow examination of the role of dangerously high climate sensitivity.

For the Epstein–Zin parameters, there is not yet a consensus on the correct values for modeling financial markets. Two major studies, however, have estimated the IES at 1.5 and the coefficient of relative risk aversion at 9.5 to 10 (Bansal and Yaron 2004; Vissing-Jørgensen and Attanasio 2003).

Table 12.2. Results using DICE utility function

Label	Description	δ	η	Climate Sensitivity	SCC, 2015 (2010 $/tCO_2$)	Abatement, 2075	Implicit Risk-Free Rate of Return $(\delta + \eta g)$
D1	DICE Defaults	.0150	2.0	3.00	$12.70	.333	.041
D2	Higher Climate Sensitivity	.0150	2.0	3.55	$14.95	.368	.041
D3	Lower Discount Rate	.0031	1.3	3.00	$48.03	.647	.020
D4	Lower Discount Rate, Higher Climate Sensitivity	.0031	1.3	3.55	$58.76	.721	.020
D5	5 States, Expected Value of DICE Utility	.0150	2.0 (5 values)		$13.95	.346	.041

It is not clear that financial market parameters are applicable to the different risks encountered in a climate model, but there is no obvious source for more appropriate parameters. It may be of some interest, moreover, to learn what the financial market parameters would imply for optimal responses to climate risks. On this basis, we assume $\psi = 1.5$ and $\gamma = 10$.

There is one more parameter in the utility function Equation 12.3, influencing the rate of time preference – the discount factor, β, based on the rate of pure time preference, δ. This can be calibrated to the risk-free rate of return: in the absence of risk, Equation 12.1 should apply, with r representing the risk-free rate and $\eta = 1/\psi$. The other element of Equation 12.1 is the growth rate of per capita consumption, g. In DICE scenarios, g typically declines over time; in the default scenario, g averages 1.3 percent per year for the first 150 years – a reasonable value, and the same as the average value of g in the Stern Review modeling (Stern 2006). Here we are ignoring the variance in g, which might be significant in reality, and would imply a lower discount rate, as noted above.

We assume a long-run average risk-free rate of return of 2.0 percent. This is higher than some empirical estimates, which are often closer to 1.0 percent.[8] Under our assumptions, Equation 12.1 implies that $\delta = .0113$ – well above the Stern Review rate of .001, although lower than the rates often assumed in DICE and other conventional models.

Results

Our principal results consist of five runs using the DICE utility function (Equation 12.2), shown in Table 12.2, and five runs using the Epstein–Zin

Table 12.3. Results using Epstein-Zin utility function

Label	Description	δ	ψ	γ	SCC 2015 (2010 \$/ t CO_2)	Abatement, 2075	Implicit Risk-Free Rate of Return $(\delta + g/\psi)$
E1	Epstein–Zin Defaults	.0113	1.5	10	\$51.35	.673	.020
E2	IES = 2.0	.0113	2.0	10	\$64.06	.734	.018
E3	Zero Risk Aversion	.0113	1.5	0	\$51.14	.658	.010
E4	High Risk Aversion	.0113	1.5	20	\$51.87	.690	.020
E5	Calibrated to Risk-Free Rate = 1%	.0013	1.5	10	\$163.59	.995	.010

Figure 12.1. Rate of abatement in five states of nature, run E1

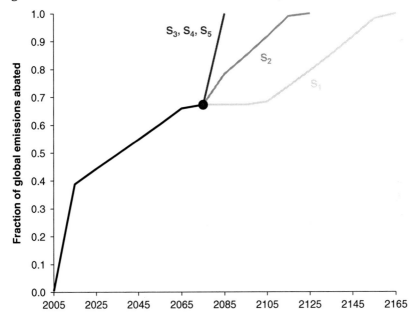

utility function (Equation 12.3), shown in Table 12.3. We compare model runs on the basis of two principal statistics: the social cost of carbon (SCC), or marginal damages per ton of CO_2, for emissions in 2015; and the fraction of global emissions abated by 2075, the final year of decision making under uncertainty. To facilitate comparison to finance literature, we include the risk-free rate of return implied by the parameters in each run.[9]

Running DICE with its default values for all parameters and inputs (run D1, Table 12.2) yields a SCC of about \$13, with one-third of emissions abated by 2075, broadly consistent with other DICE analyses.[10] Switching from the median to the mean value of climate sensitivity (D2) causes a slight increase in both the SCC and the rate of abatement.

Lowering the discount rate, to match the 2 percent risk-free rate assumed in our Epstein–Zin analysis, has a large effect on the results: it roughly doubles the rate of abatement and quadruples the SCC (compare D3 and D4 to D1 and D2, respectively).[11] In a final calculation using DICE utility (D5), we use DICE default parameters, but adopt our five-state model of uncertainty about climate sensitivity. Maximizing the expected value of DICE utility, from Equation 12.2, across the five states, yields results comparable to DICE defaults with median or mean climate sensitivity (i.e., D5 results fall between D1 and D2). Thus the introduction of the five-state model per se does not cause a major change in results.

In contrast, using the same five-state model of uncertainty but maximizing Epstein–Zin utility (run E1, Table 12.3) yields a SCC more than four times as high as the DICE default, with two-thirds of emissions abated by 2075. Consistent with other applications of Epstein–Zin utility to climate models, we find that the optimal policy involves much higher carbon prices and more rapid abatement when maximizing Epstein–Zin utility.

The additional runs are sensitivity analyses, to explore the properties of this solution. Changes in the IES make a noticeable difference (E2). As expected, a larger IES implies that greater weight is given to future outcomes, raising the SCC and the pace of abatement.

On the other hand, fairly large changes in risk aversion have very small effects on the results (E3 and E4). Switching from $\gamma = 10$ to either 0 or 20 changes the SCC by 1 percent or less, and changes the extent of abatement in 2075 by less than 2 percentage points. The effect is in the expected direction – greater risk aversion increases the SCC and the rate of abatement – but it appears much less significant than the effect of the IES, consistent with the findings of Crost and Traeger (2010). In fact, our initial numerical experiments with the model showed that the choice of 2075 for the resolution of uncertainty maximizes the (always small) effect of risk aversion on the outcomes.

Interpretation of Results

A possible explanation of the insensitivity to risk aversion is suggested by Figure 12.1, showing the rate of abatement over time in the Epstein–Zin default run (E1). EZ–DICE calculates a single rate of abatement for all five states until 2075, when the true value of climate sensitivity is discovered; thereafter, it calculates optimal abatement paths separately for each state. After the paths separate, state S_1, with the lowest climate sensitivity, takes 90 additional years to reach

Table 12.4. Temperature and climate damages in 2075, five states of nature, run E1

State	S_1	S_2	S_3	S_4	S_5
Climate Sensitivity	2.43	3.67	6.05	8.20	16.15
Temperature Increase in 2075 (°C above 1900)	1.59	2.07	2.62	2.90	3.37
Climate Damages in 2075 (percent of output)	0.7	1.2	1.9	2.3	3.1

100 percent abatement. State S_2 needs 50 years to reach the same goal. States S_3, S_4 and S_5, however, all jump to 100 percent abatement in a single decade.

DICE, both in its original form and in our modification, offers the option of any rate of abatement, up to 100 percent, at any time. Over time, the unit costs of abatement decline while the damages from unabated climate change increase, making it increasingly attractive to abate. In EZ-DICE, the potential future damages from climate change are so great in the high climate-sensitivity states, S_3, S_4 and S_5, that the optimal solution is to jump to 100 percent abatement as soon as the uncertainty is resolved. In effect, DICE will always avoid the worst extremes of possible future damages, by instead opting for immediate 100 percent abatement.

The only difference, therefore, between the perceived damages in states S_3, S_4 and S_5, despite their very different climate sensitivity values, results from the modest impacts that occur before 2075. In run E1, the temperature increase in 2075, relative to the level in 1900, differs by less than 2°C between S_1 and S_5, and less than 1°C between S_3 and S_5 (Table 12.4). Using the DICE damage function, these temperatures imply climate losses in 2075 of only 0.7 percent of world output in S_1, ranging up to 3.1 percent in S_5. (For discussion of the DICE damage function and the importance of alternative damage estimates, see Ackerman and Stanton 2012.)

Even in S_5, with a climate sensitivity that is disastrously high (implying disastrously rapid warming) by many standards, DICE projects losses of just over 3 percent of output by the end of the long period of uncertainty – comparable to a moderate-sized business cycle downturn (Table 12.4). The much greater potential damages after 2075 are avoided by the 100 percent abatement option. Numerical experiments, not shown here, reveal that an immediate jump to 100 percent abatement (from the point reached by E1 in 2075) occurs whenever climate sensitivity exceeds 5.25, which is the 89th percentile value in the probability distribution. Anything above 5.25 looks about the same to DICE; that is, the model is unable to distinguish differences within the upper 11 percent of the probability distribution. The problems of tail risk, associated with extreme values from the right-hand tail of the distribution, cannot be analyzed in a model that does not "see" those values.

If risk aversion is almost immaterial in EZ–DICE, then similar results should be attainable in a simpler, risk-free environment. In the absence of risk, our Epstein–Zin calibration amounts to using the assumed risk-free rate of 2 percent as the consumption discount rate. Confirming this interpretation, our Epstein–Zin results (E1, Table 12.3) are quite similar to the DICE results with a 2 percent risk-free rate (D3 and D4, Table 12.2).

From this perspective, the principal contribution of Epstein–Zin utility in a model that truncates extreme risk, such as DICE, is its rationale for discounting at the risk-free rate, which is lower than discount rates adopted in many climate analyses (see arguments by Howarth 2003 along similar lines). If we were to assume a risk-free rate of 1 percent, consistent with some readings of the historical record, then the results would be more extreme, as shown in run E5: worldwide emissions would be all but eliminated by 2075. This would make for a less interesting analysis of the Epstein–Zin methodology, since the response in the early decades is so strongly precautionary that it leaves little scope for variation among the five states or response to parameter changes. Yet it might be the logical result of a strict application of findings from financial markets.

Conclusions

We have successfully introduced Epstein–Zin utility into the DICE model, and confirmed the findings of similar analyses with simpler climate models: with Epstein–Zin utility, the SCC is higher and the optimal pace of emission reduction is much faster than with the conventional DICE utility function; the results are sensitive to the intertemporal elasticity of substitution but remarkably insensitive to the level of risk aversion.

The latter finding, though, poses an unresolved puzzle. The threat of unchecked climate change is often described in terms of catastrophic risks of low but growing probability; how can an economic analysis of this phenomenon find that the level of risk aversion is unimportant? The apparent minimization of catastrophic risk in DICE is a logical consequence of the model's strong and optimistic assumptions about mitigation. The only climate risk that arises in DICE, the threat of escalating temperature increases, can be prevented with certainty, at limited cost, in a comparatively short period of time. If this were true of all climate risks, then the available, precautionary responses to the worst risks would clearly pass a cost–benefit test; rational policy makers would accept and act on this analysis, and the climate problem would be solved.

The optimistic assumptions made by DICE are not unique to that model, but are shared by many economic analyses. Many climate modelers have developed scenarios for rapid abatement, often leading to phasing out virtually all carbon emission by the end of this century. Ackerman and Stanton (2012b) demonstrate that under plausible hypotheses about future uncertainties, the SCC is at or above the marginal cost of several rapid abatement scenarios. If such abatement scenarios could reliably eliminate all catastrophic climate risks, then DICE's optimism would be well-founded, complete mitigation would pass a cost–benefit test and the level of risk aversion would indeed be of secondary importance. In such a world, catastrophic future outcomes would be avoided by immediate mitigation, as seen in Figure 12.1, above, for states S_3, S_4 and S_5 – with roughly the same response at many levels of risk aversion.

Unfortunately, we may not live in such a world. Climate science has emphasized the potential for "tipping points" at which the earth's climate may make a relatively abrupt, and perhaps irreversible, transition to a different state; once the tipping point has been identified with certainty, it may be too late to avoid it (Lenton et al. 2008). A deeper explanation of the unimportance of risk aversion in this paper's results is that the most important risks may be overlooked by models such as DICE. If catastrophic risks cannot be prevented with certainty, if rival policy responses differ widely in costs as well as probabilities of success or if there are long delays between the initiation of policy responses and the reduction in risk, then there is a need for a different analysis in which risk and risk aversion play a central role. Incorporating such approaches to risk into an integrated assessment model is a challenge for future modeling efforts.

The issues raised here in the context of DICE may also be relevant to more complex integrated assessment models of climate change. While other models may offer greater detail and precision than DICE in modeling climate and economic dynamics, they face similar dilemmas to those identified here if they rely on the expected utility framework. Use of CRRA utility functions leads to the contradictory treatment of risk discussed above, which the Epstein–Zin framework seeks to address. Epstein–Zin utility combined with the simplified model of learning under uncertainty used in this paper may be of even greater importance in complex models with more state variables, where more sophisticated models of learning would introduce an infeasible computational burden.

New approaches to modeling risk need to be approached carefully; any treatment of truly catastrophic risk has the potential to overwhelm ordinary economic analysis. Weitzman's "dismal theorem" (2009) demonstrates that if knowledge of the climate system is necessarily incomplete, and the disutility of worst-case outcomes (such as extinction of the human race) is unbounded, then the marginal benefit of emission reduction is literally infinite. This implies the implausible conclusion that willingness to pay for emission reduction should approach 100 percent of income. The problem is not unique to the dismal theorem; in a pattern that has been dubbed the "tyranny of catastrophic risk," any unbounded risk, no matter how small its (non-zero) probability of occurrence, will lead to the same implausible result (Buchholz and Schymura 2012). Since limitless willingness to pay for risk avoidance seems implausible, there must be a limit to the disutility of even the worst risks.

In the end, we are left with an agenda for further research, falling somewhere in the gap between the optimistic, risk-minimizing assumptions of DICE and similar models on the one hand, and the risk-obsessed framework of the dismal theorem and the tyranny of catastrophic risk on the other hand. There is a need to develop subtler analyses of catastrophic climate risks that cannot or will not be quickly prevented with certainty, applying realistic measures of societal risk aversion to calibrate appropriate responses.

Chapter 13

FAT TAILS, EXPONENTS, EXTREME UNCERTAINTY: SIMULATING CATASTROPHE IN DICE

Frank Ackerman, Elizabeth A. Stanton and Ramón Bueno

The problem of low-probability, catastrophic risk is increasingly central to discussion of climate science and policy. But the integrated assessment models (IAMs) of climate economics rarely incorporate this possibility. What modifications are needed to analyze catastrophic economic risks in an IAM? We explore this question using DICE, a well-known IAM. We examine the implications of a fat-tailed probability distribution for the climate sensitivity parameter, a focus of recent work by Martin Weitzman, and the shape of the damage function, one of the issues raised by the Stern Review. Forecasts of disastrous economic outcomes in DICE can result from the interaction of these two innovations, but not from either one alone.

Introduction

Economic assessment of climate change and climate policy depends on information that is not currently available, and may not become available until it is too late to do anything about it. Two central uncertainties, in particular, pose challenges to quantitative economic analysis. First, how bad will the climate get – that is, how much will temperatures rise as a result of increasing atmospheric concentrations of greenhouse gases? Second, how bad will the worsening climate be for the economy – that is, how much economic damage will be caused by increased temperatures and associated physical impacts of climate change?[1] Such questions remain unanswered and perhaps intrinsically unanswerable except in retrospect, despite the increasingly detailed understanding of climate processes that is emerging from scientific research.

Yet with bad enough answers to these questions, climate change might lead to disastrous results for the global economy.

Conventional economic analysis does not appear to be stymied by the problems of irreducible uncertainty and catastrophic risks. Integrated assessment models (IAMs) often adopt deterministic estimates or "best guesses" about a number of crucial unknowns. This procedure eliminates uncertainty from the model, at the cost of making the results dependent on the particular estimates that are employed. (On the theory and limitations of IAMs in general, see Ackerman et al. 2009b; Stanton et al. 2009). Using their chosen resolutions of key uncertainties, IAMs have often found that the optimal policy response is to do relatively little about climate change in the near term. The catastrophic risks that are increasingly discussed in climate science and policy analyses almost never translate into catastrophic economic outcomes in IAMs.

This paper explores what it would take to make DICE, one of the best-known IAMs, forecast an economic catastrophe. William Nordhaus, the creator of DICE, reports that his model does not appear to display extreme responses to uncertainties about key input parameters, and concludes that: " [...] models such as [DICE] have limited utility in looking at the potential for catastrophic events"(Nordhaus 2008, 147).

"Catastrophe" can be interpreted in two ways, either as an abrupt discontinuity or as an unexpected, very bad outcome. As Nordhaus suggests, in the absence of hard scientific information about discontinuities, it is difficult to incorporate them into a deterministic model like DICE. (The probabilistic logic of the PAGE model is better suited to this task, as discussed below.) The other interpretation of catastrophe – things turning out really badly – is easier to model; the upbeat conclusion of the DICE default scenarios is not the only message that this model can convey. We offer a new way of looking at DICE, in which disastrous economic outcomes are natural results of plausible values for key uncertain parameters.

Two recent contributions to the economics of climate change have produced a richer understanding of the role of uncertainty. Martin Weitzman's theoretical analysis of "fat-tailed" probability distributions examines the uncertainty about the temperature increase that will result from rising greenhouse gas emissions (Weitzman 2007a, 2009). The Stern Review (Stern 2006), among its other important points, explores the uncertainty about the shape of the damage function, which relates economic impacts to temperature.

Each of these theoretical contributions highlights the role of a specific parameter used in IAMs. Weitzman's analysis addresses uncertainty about the climate sensitivity parameter, i.e., the long-term temperature change that will result from a doubling of atmospheric CO_2 concentrations.

The Stern Review illustrates the importance of the "damage function exponent": global economic damages from climate change are often assumed to depend on the square of temperature, but could just as easily be tied to the cube or other power of temperature (measured as degrees above a preindustrial or twentieth-century baseline).

How much would DICE outputs and recommendations be changed by variation in the climate sensitivity parameter and damage function exponent? DICE normally forecasts steady economic growth, even under the impacts of business-as-usual climate change. It finds that the optimal policy is a modest carbon tax, starting at $7.40 per ton of CO_2 today and rising only to $25 in 2050 and $55 in 2100 (Nordhaus 2008, 14–16). That policy slows the growth of carbon emissions, but does not cause a reduction: while business-as-usual emissions grow by 166 percent during this century, emissions under the optimal tax regime grow by 52 percent (calculated from Nordhaus 2008, 100).

Our results suggest that changing either the climate sensitivity parameter or the damage function exponent alone has only a limited effect on DICE's upbeat projections. Simultaneous changes in both parameters, however, can lead to a forecast of severe losses under business as usual, and an optimal policy of very rapid reduction in emissions. Thus the optimistic projections and modest optimal policies often attributed to models such as DICE may be artifacts of parameter choices, rather than robust forecasts about an uncertain future.

Catastrophic Risk and Damages in DICE

Like many IAMs, DICE is a deterministic model, using best guesses or expected values over a hypothesized probability distribution in order to address uncertainties about future costs and benefits (Stanton et al. 2009). In particular, DICE makes the common assumptions that the value of the climate sensitivity parameter is 3 (the best estimate according to IPCC 2007d), and that global damages depend on the square of temperature increases.

DICE is one step ahead of a number of other IAMs in addressing uncertainty: it assumes that an abrupt loss of a significant share of world output could occur, with a probability that is low but rises with increasing temperatures (Nordhaus 2008). The magnitude of the catastrophe was initially derived from a survey of expert opinion in the early 1990s, and has since been revised upward as climate projections have become more ominous. The initial survey itself elicited a wide distribution of estimates, with a noticeable minority of forecasts of an enormous potential catastrophe (Roughgarden and Schneider 1999).

DICE, however, sidesteps uncertainty by calculating the expected value of low-probability, high-cost catastrophic damages. In DICE-2007, the expected value of a climate catastrophe is 1.2 percent of world output at 2.5°C of warming, and 4.7 percent at 6°C (Nordhaus 2007a, 24). The expected value is then included in the calculation of damages that will predictably result from a given temperature increase. Thus DICE addresses catastrophic risk in theory, only to turn it into a deterministic guess in practice; we describe it as a guess because there is very little empirical information available about the values of either the probability or the magnitude of the damages in question.

Letting climate damages as a fraction of world output be d, and temperature increase since a base year be T, it has become common to assume a simple power law, such as:

(13.1) $D = aT^N$

DICE uses a slight variant, which is quite similar to Equation 13.1 at low temperatures:

(13.2) $D = aT^N / (1 + aT^N)$

The use of Equation 13.2 prevents climate damages from exceeding the value of world output; this would be a matter of common sense if damages could only reduce current income, as DICE assumes. If, more realistically, climate damages may also include the destruction of capital assets, then damages could exceed 100 percent of a year's output.

Nordhaus estimates that for a 2.5°C temperature increase from 1900, annual climate damages, including the expected value of a possible catastrophe, amount to just 1.77 percent of world output.[2] This represents net damages, combining benefits in some areas with costs in other areas: a relatively large monetary value is placed on subjective enjoyment of warmer temperatures, offsetting some but not all of the predicted damages in other areas. (The subjective enjoyment of warming played an even bigger role in the previous version of DICE, as discussed in Ackerman and Finlayson 2006; the same calculation is used in DICE-2007, but the new version does not allow global net benefits from warming.) On the assumption that $N=2$ in Equation 13.2, the Nordhaus estimate for damages at 2.5°C implies that $a = 0.002838$, which is the value used in DICE-2007.

Fat Tails and Unbounded Risks

Martin Weitzman (2007a, 2009) has argued that the economic analysis of climate change is dominated by the problem of intrinsically limited information about potentially unbounded risks. Let the value of climate damages be $D(x)$, where x is the climate sensitivity parameter, and let $p(x)$ be the probability distribution of x. As x increases, $D(x)$ also increases, with no obvious upper limit. The expected value of climate damages is:

$$(13.3) \qquad E[D(x)] = \int D(x)p(x)dx$$

If there is a sufficiently large body of empirical evidence about x, then the best estimate of $p(x)$ might be a normal distribution or other "thin-tailed" distribution – that is, a distribution which is known to have low probabilities of extreme values. On the other hand, in a complex, changing system, old information may become obsolete as fast as new information is gathered; as a result, there may be an upper limit on how much can be known about $p(x)$. Informally, if we never have more than 100 valid, current observations, we can never learn much about the 99th percentile of $p(x)$. With a small number of observations, Weitzman argues that the best available estimate of $p(x)$ may be a Student's t or other fat-tailed distribution, with relatively high probabilities of extreme values.

There are plausible damage functions, such as $D(x) = be^{cx}$ (with $c>0$), for which the integral in Equation 13.3 converges if $p(x)$ is a normal distribution, but diverges, or tends toward infinity, if $p(x)$ is a Student's t distribution. Weitzman's "dismal theorem" formalizes and generalizes this notion, proving that in cases of limited information about unlimited risks, the expected value of damages is infinite – due to the irreducible probabilities of worst-case outcomes (Weitzman 2009). In practice, the infinite expected value of damages should be detectable by a Monte Carlo analysis with a very large number of runs: the calculated average value of damages should become ever larger as the number of runs increases, reflecting the weight of the occasional draws of parameters farther and farther out on the fat tail of the distribution. The damages associated with those extreme parameter values should grow large more rapidly than they become rare, driving the average steadily upward as the number of runs increases.

In terms of climate policy, cost–benefit analysis implies that the expected value of damages in Equation 13.3, per ton of carbon, is the amount that should be spent, at the margin, to reduce emissions. If that value is infinite, detailed cost–benefit calculation becomes pointless, and nothing is as important as reduction in emissions.

The Shape of the Damage Function

The Stern Review (Stern 2006) challenged conventional approaches to climate economics modeling in several respects. Stern's low discount rate, similar to the rate used by Cline (1992, 2004), greatly increases the importance of future climate damages (among many others, see Ackerman 2009; Nordhaus 2007c). Of comparable importance is Stern's treatment of uncertainty, which also causes a marked increase in the present value of future damages.

The PAGE model, used in the Stern Review, incorporates an estimate of catastrophic risk, with the magnitude of potential catastrophe based on the work of Nordhaus. As with DICE, the catastrophe becomes possible at a temperature threshold, and becomes more likely as temperatures rise above the threshold. In PAGE, however, the catastrophe is modeled through a Monte Carlo analysis, not a certainty equivalent cost estimate; catastrophic costs are calculated separately from ordinary damages, not subsumed into an aggregate damage function (Hope 2006a).

PAGE is far from the last word in climate economics modeling. Questions have been raised about whether its default input data lead to serious underestimates of climate damages (Ackerman et al. 2009b; Baer 2007). On the other hand, the PAGE damage estimates are higher than those produced by many other models; sensitivity analyses have shown that the Monte Carlo approach sharply increases the PAGE estimates, since the few runs with extreme parameter values have a big effect on average outcomes (Dietz et al. 2007).

PAGE makes the damage function exponent, N in Equation 13.1 a Monte Carlo parameter using a triangular distribution with minimum 1.0, mode 1.3 and maximum 3.0; this raises the damage estimates compared to a fixed exponent of 2. Even though the mean value of N is only 1.7, the few runs with values closer to 3 have a large effect on the average.

A sensitivity analysis on Stern's results found that fixing the exponent at 3 would increase Stern's estimate of global damages by 23 percent of world output (Dietz et al. 2007). Since there is virtually no empirical evidence on the likely damages from large temperature changes, estimates of the shape of the damage function remain highly uncertain. Seen in this light, the sensitivity of Stern's estimates to changes in the damage function exponent underscores the substantial, currently inescapable uncertainty in the economic analysis of climate change.

Our Experiment

To test the importance of these ideas we modified DICE-2007, allowing us to treat the damage function exponent and the climate sensitivity parameter as random variables in a Monte Carlo analysis. This provides one important perspective on the significance of uncertainty in DICE.

We are not the first to perform Monte Carlo analysis on DICE; Nordhaus himself presents a small-scale example (Nordhaus 2008, Chapter 7). For eight key parameters, he makes judgments about their standard deviations, and assumes that they are normally distributed about his estimates of the most likely values. He draws 100 sets of the eight parameters, and runs DICE once for each set. The small number of iterations and the use of normal distributions imply that this analysis has little to say about the risks of extreme events.

The eight parameters affect changes in the economy as well as the climate. The unexpected result of the analysis – in the 100 runs of DICE, greater climate changes are associated with higher, not lower, incomes – simply means that Nordhaus's parameter distributions include more uncertainty about economic growth than about climate dynamics. Faster growth in some DICE runs means more output and more emissions, causing more climate change; the DICE damage function is not damaging enough to reverse the connection between higher incomes and faster climate change.

A Monte Carlo analysis of a model such as DICE is not the only way to represent uncertainty; indeed, under many assumptions about uncertainty, other methods might be more appropriate. A dynamic model of decision making under uncertainty might calculate the optimal policy response, under the assumption of continuing uncertainty throughout the time frame of the model. In each time period, decisions would be made to maximize the expected value of welfare (which is the objective function of DICE and many other integrated assessment models). This, however, would require a different, nondeterministic model structure, within which a more complex optimization process could take place.

Our Monte Carlo analysis, in contrast, amounts to an assumption of a different, stylized picture of uncertainty: the true values of key parameters are unknown at present, but will be revealed with certainty in the relatively near future. This is the implicit assumption in many Monte Carlo analyses on a deterministic model – including, among countless others, Nordhaus's own Monte Carlo analysis, as described above. For an explicit assumption of this stylization of uncertainty, see Weitzman's well-known analysis presenting the theoretical basis for declining discount rates (Weitzman 1998).

Compared to dynamic optimization in a probabilistic model, our approach provides less subtlety in its treatment of uncertainty, but greater simplicity and transparency. It can be thought of as providing a sensitivity analysis on a familiar model, rather than introducing an unfamiliar new analytical framework. In this spirit, we began by developing probability distributions for the two key parameters in our analysis.

Climate sensitivity

In his discussion of uncertainty in the climate sensitivity parameter, Weitzman cites several IPCC estimates as well as his own extrapolations.[3] According to

Figure 13.1. Lognormal distribution for climate sensitivity

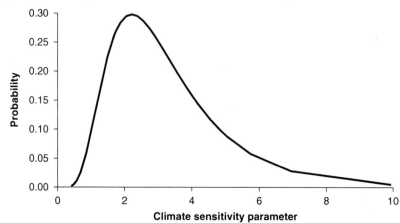

Figure 13.2. Cumulative distribution function fitted to climate sensitivity estimates

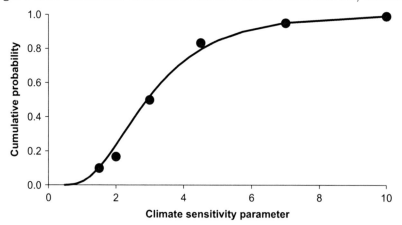

the 2007 IPCC assessment (as cited in Weitzman 2009), the central estimate for climate sensitivity is 3; the value is likely to be between 2 and 4.5, and very likely to be above 1.5. In IPCC terminology, "likely" means a two-thirds probability, while "very likely" means a 90 percent probability. So the IPCC estimates imply that the 10th percentile value for climate sensitivity is 1.5; the 17th percentile is 2; the 50th percentile is 3; and the 83rd percentile is 4.5. Weitzman adds his own estimates that the corresponding 95th percentile value is 7, and the 99th percentile is 10.

A lognormal probability distribution provides a very good fit to these estimates.[1] The cumulative distribution, with the IPCC and Weitzman data

Figure 13.3. Damage function exponents: DICE and variants

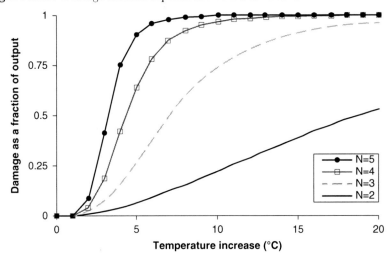

points included as large dots, is shown in Figure 13.1, and the corresponding probability distribution is shown in Figure 13.2. The underlying normal distribution of the log of the variable has a mean of 1.071 and a standard deviation of 0.527. The lognormal distribution itself has a mean of 3.352 and a standard deviation of 1.896. We use this lognormal distribution for the climate sensitivity parameter in our Monte Carlo analysis.[5]

The damage function exponent

As noted above, DICE uses Equation 13.2 to model damages, with $N = 2$ and $a = 0.002838$. We are not aware of any empirical support for relationships such as Equations 13.1 or 13.2, even at historical temperatures – let alone for "out of sample" forecasting of damages at temperatures beyond the historical range, which is what really matters. In particular, there is no clear explanation for the crucial assumption that $N = 2$.[6] The exponent N measures the speed with which damages increase as temperatures rise. Figure 13.3 graphs Equation 13.2, the DICE damage function, holding a constant, for $N = 2, 3, 4$ and 5. Damages rise at a leisurely pace for $N = 2$, with less than half of world output destroyed by climate change until $T = 19$ °C, which is far beyond the temperature range that has been considered in even the most catastrophic climate scenarios. In contrast, as N rises, half of world output is lost to climate change at temperatures of about 7°C for $N = 3$; 4.5°C for $N = 4$; or 3.5°C for $N = 5$. If Equation 13.2 is used with the Nordhaus value of a, then N in the range of 3 to 5 implies a sense of urgency about preventing temperature increases of a few degrees, whereas $N = 2$ does not.

As N approaches infinity, Equation 13.2 approaches a vertical line. This would be the appropriate shape for the damage function under the hypothesis that there is a threshold for an abrupt world-ending (or at least economy-ending) discontinuity, while damages below that threshold are so small that they can be ignored by comparison.

Thus choosing a larger N ("closer to infinity") means moving closer to the view that complete catastrophe sets in at some finite temperature threshold. Choosing a smaller N means emphasizing the gradual rise of damages rather than the risk of discontinuous, catastrophic change.

In our Monte Carlo analysis we used Equation 13.2, allowing N to vary from a minimum of 1 to a maximum of 5, assuming a triangular distribution with the most likely (modal) value at $N = 2$. On the low end, it does not seem plausible to consider $N < 1$; at the other extreme, Figure 13.3 suggests that the damage curve for $N = 5$ is close enough to vertical to reflect a substantial risk of catastrophe.

Research methods

We made a minor software modification, to allow DICE to run in a Monte Carlo mode, reading in new parameter values, running the model, saving selected output and repeating. We used @RISK,[7] a commercially distributed Monte Carlo software package, to generate random values for the climate sensitivity parameter and the damage function exponent, drawn from the probability distributions described above.

Our only changes to DICE itself, other than the Monte Carlo analysis on the two parameters, were the removal of the ceiling on temperature increases and the floor under the capital stock; the latter effectively implies a floor under per capita consumption. These ad hoc features of DICE artificially prevent forecasts of extreme outcomes, although neither is a binding constraint in the DICE default business-as-usual or optimal policy forecasts. In all other respects, we used the 2007 version of the DICE software and default data sets.

We performed a series of Monte Carlo analyses of DICE ranging from 1,000 to 500,000 runs. For each run we drew a climate sensitivity parameter from the lognormal distribution shown in Figure 13.2, and a damage function exponent from the triangular distribution described above. The huge number of iterations was motivated by curiosity about the effects of the tails of the distributions, particularly for the climate sensitivity parameter.

The burden of calculation for this analysis was potentially overwhelming; if carried out in a straightforward manner, it would have required running DICE 500,000 times. After running Monte Carlo analyses with tens of thousands of iterations, we switched to a discrete approximation, analogous to the "finite element method" used in engineering to obtain numerical solutions to complex systems of equations. This approximation made it possible to push the effective number of iterations even higher. Specifically, we rounded each randomly drawn value for the climate sensitivity parameter to the nearest integer, and rounded each damage exponent to the nearest multiple of 0.25. DICE is continuous in both parameters throughout the range we explored, so very little information is lost by this procedure.[8] As a result, we could associate each parameter pair with a point on a two-dimensional grid: since the largest climate sensitivity in any of our samples was 35, and damage exponents ranged from 1 to 5 in steps of 0.25, every parameter pair was approximated by one of the 35*17 = 595 grid points. Hence only 595 runs of DICE were sufficient to approximate the outcomes for each parameter pair, even for our largest samples.

To arrive at the results presented below, we drew random samples of up to 500,000 instances for each parameter, and then, for each parameter pair, used the model results at the closest of the grid points. The expected values of model results presented below are the averages of those grid-point approximations. For the smaller samples, where we also ran individual calculations for each parameter pair, we confirmed that the discrete approximation produces results that are very close to the exact values.

Results

Measures of economic catastrophe

DICE is designed to maximize welfare, or utility, which, in the 2007 version of the model, is a linear function of the inverse of per capita consumption.[9] The present value of utility in the business-as-usual scenario is an interesting but limited measure of economic impacts of climate change. It is hard to interpret because it is not expressed in any natural or familiar units: how much of a welfare loss represents a catastrophe, as opposed to a minor downturn? Moreover, the present value of utility over six centuries is being maximized; the result is shaped by the discount rate, determining the relative weights of future versus present welfare. (For this analysis we made no changes to the DICE discount rate.[10]) In light of these problems, we also used two other, more intuitive measures of economic performance.

One measure is the minimum level of per capita consumption reached at any time during the 600 years of the business-as-usual scenario. The DICE default projection is that despite climate damages, per capita incomes are monotonically increasing. (PAGE, the Stern Review's model, also projects continuous growth throughout its multi-century forecasts.) Climate damages and climate policies have some effect on the rate of economic growth, but for small perturbations of the DICE defaults, the growth rate always remains positive. In such cases, the minimum per capita consumption for the DICE business-as-usual scenario is the value in the initial year, a worldwide average of about $6,600.[11] On the other hand, if climate damages become severe enough, growth rates will turn negative, and eventually incomes and consumption in later years will drop below the initial levels. The lower the scenario minimum per capita consumption falls, the worse the economic impact of climate change has become.

Our second measure is the time required to reach complete abatement of carbon emissions in the optimal (welfare-maximizing) policy scenario. DICE assumes that any degree of abatement, up to and including 100 percent reduction in carbon emissions, is available in any year. At any moment in time, costs rise steeply as the percentage reduction in emissions approaches 100 percent; over time the cost of any level of emission reduction gradually declines. It would be possible to eliminate all carbon emissions in the first time period, at an assumed cost of about 5.2 percent of world output. However, using DICE default values, the optimal reduction path does not reach 100 percent abatement until 200 years have passed. In scenarios with greater climate damages, it becomes desirable to phase out emissions more quickly. The more serious the economic consequences of climate change become, the shorter the time required for complete abatement on the optimal path.

Monte Carlo analysis summary results

Our results for the whole sample showed a reasonable match to the DICE defaults, and remarkably little variation with sample size, as shown in Table 13.1. The first two columns of results – the sample averages for the present value of total utility and for the minimum per capita consumption – are for the business-as-usual scenario. The last column, the sample average for the decades to reach complete abatement, is for the corresponding optimal policy scenario.

In other experiments (not shown here), we fixed the damage function exponent at 2, and then at 5, allowing only the climate sensitivity parameter to vary. In both cases, the results likewise showed no significant changes with sample size.

Mapping the grid

To understand this surprising pattern of results, it may be helpful to examine the grid of outcomes used in our calculations. For our three outcome

Table 13.1. Monte Carlo analysis results

Sample Size	PV of Scenario Total Utility	Minimum per Capita Consumption	Decades to Complete Abatement
1,000	139,700	$6,590	17.9
10,000	140,300	$6,610	18.0
50,000	140,700	$6,610	18.0
100,000	140,600	$6,610	18.0
200,000	140,500	$6,610	18.0
500,000	140,500	$6,610	18.0
DICE defaults	149,800	$6,620	20

Climate sensitivity drawn from lognormal distribution (Figure 2 above).
Damage function exponent drawn from triangular distribution: min=1, mode=2, max=5.

measures, Figures 13.4, 13.5 and 13.6 present three-dimensional graphs, with the outcome on the vertical axis, and the climate sensitivity parameter and damage function exponent on the horizontal axes.[12] In each graph, outcomes become precipitously worse when moving toward the lower front corner, i.e., increasing both parameters. In contrast, the upper back corner, representing low values of both parameters, shows consistently better outcomes. The DICE defaults are represented by the circular dot in each graph, relatively close to the upper back corner.

The graphs present only a portion of our parameter grid; they are truncated at a climate sensitivity parameter of 20 because almost nothing qualitatively different occurs beyond that point. That is, by the time climate sensitivity reaches 20, the results have become about as bad as they are going to get. This represents a point quite far down the tail of the probability distribution; the probability of exceeding 20 is 0.00013, or about 1 in 8,000.

Figure 13.4 presents the graph of utility in the business-as-usual scenario (measured in arbitrary units of utility, with an arbitrary constant added for convenience in graphing). The DICE default values (the large dot) are located well within a region in parameter space where the present value of utility is high and relatively invariant. As both parameters increase, utility eventually plunges downward.

Figure 13.5 presents a similar graph of the minimum level of per capita consumption that occurs in the business-as-usual scenario. The large, nearly flat area toward the upper back of the graph represents cases in which climate damages never drive per capita incomes below the initial value. The DICE defaults are again well within the high plateau of happy outcomes, while the terrain slopes rapidly downward as both parameters rise toward the lower front corner. The lowest points shown here represent drastic, potentially unsustainable losses of income and consumption due to climate damages.

A somewhat different picture is presented in Figure 13.6, showing the number of decades required to reach 100 percent abatement in the optimal policy scenario. By this measure, there is no plateau of constant outcomes; the optimal path to decarbonization is a leisurely, multi-century stroll at low values of both parameters, but becomes a more and more rapid dash as the parameters rise toward the front of the graph. At the DICE defaults (again, the circular dot on the graph), 100 percent abatement does not occur for 200 years; at the highest parameter values shown here, it occurs in the model's first decade.

In light of these graphs, the explanation of our nearly invariant Monte Carlo results, in Table 13.1, is that those results are probability-weighted averages across the entire parameter space. The good outcomes in the low-parameter region of the map have high probability and dominate the averages. The averages conceal the fact that outcomes become much worse as both parameters increase. The DICE treatment of climate and economic processes does not allow outcomes to worsen rapidly enough to cause the Weitzman effect, i.e., an infinite expected value of loss. In DICE, the risk of both parameters increasing at once is not infinitely bad for economic welfare – just very bad.

If we were confident in the probability distributions used in our Monte Carlo analysis, then the more moderate, average result would be the answer that matters, and the much worse results in one corner of parameter space would be just an improbable oddity. In fact, as explained in the next section, we do not have high confidence in these probability distributions, particularly the one for the damage function exponent. Therefore, the finding that huge losses are implied by some combinations of parameters can be interpreted as a sensitivity analysis, highlighting the conditions under which DICE predicts economic catastrophe.

Credible worst cases

While Figures 13.4, 13.5 and 13.6 help to visualize the parameter space of the DICE model, they do not display our assumptions about the probability distributions for the two parameters. The graphs' upper limit of 20 for climate sensitivity is reached or exceeded, as mentioned earlier, with a probability of about 1 in 8,000. Thus one could argue that the figures implicitly make the unfair suggestion that very unlikely values should be given equal credence with much more likely ones.

Our probability distributions for the two parameters have differing foundations. The climate sensitivity parameter is the subject of significant

Figure 13.4. Present value of utility, business-as-usual scenario

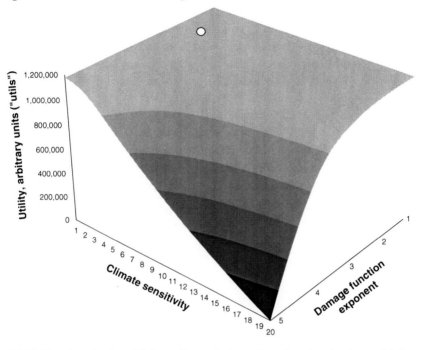

All DICE utility estimates have been shifted upward by a constant amount, to avoid negative values for ease of display.

empirical research; while there is limited information available, leading to a fat-tailed distribution, this is not a case of arbitrary or fact-free assignment of probabilities. Unfortunately, "arbitrary" and "fact-free" are reasonable characterizations of the distribution we used for the damage function exponent – and our work is not at all unique on this point. There is essentially no relevant empirical research, and it is not clear whether there ever could be any, except after the fact. Our assumed distribution was selected purely for comparability with guesses made by other analysts.

Our final look at the data focuses on what might be considered credible worst cases for climate sensitivity, and considers the implication of different damage function exponents. Recall that the 50th percentile for climate sensitivity is 3, and the 99th percentile is 10. The climate changes of the twenty-first century are an experiment with immense stakes, which will only happen once; in the absence of better information, it is surely worth considering what risks up to the 99th percentile would look like. To that end, Figures 13.7, 13.8 and 13.9 show how our three measures of economic outcomes change as climate sensitivity rises from 3 to 10, at damage function exponents of 2, 3, 4 and 5.

Figure 13.5. Minimum per capita income, business-as-usual scenario

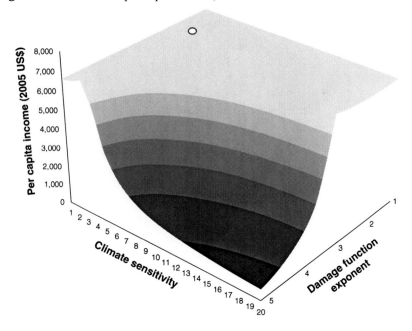

Figure 13.6. Decades to reach 100 percent abatement in optimal scenario

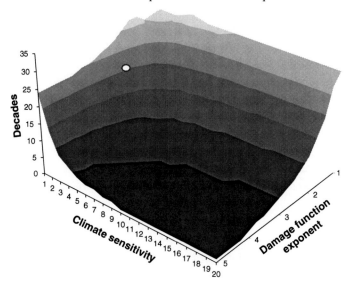

Figure 13.7. Present value of scenario total utility, business-as-usual scenario

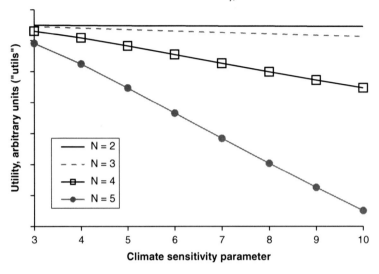

Figure 13.8. Minimum per capita consumption, business-as-usual scenario

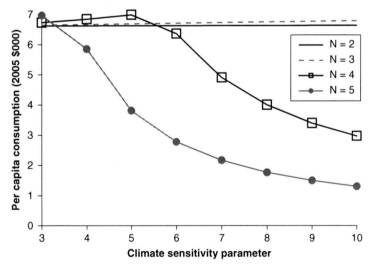

Figure 13.7 graphs the relationship between climate sensitivity and the present value of total scenario utility, in the business-as-usual scenario. (Again, the units are arbitrary.) At a damage function exponent of 2 or 3, utility is nearly invariant across this range. At an exponent of 4, and even more so at 5, utility is strongly related to climate sensitivity. In short, growing climate sensitivity, implying worsening climate outcomes, hardly matters to DICE, with the

Figure 13.9. Decades to 100 percent abatement in optimal scenario

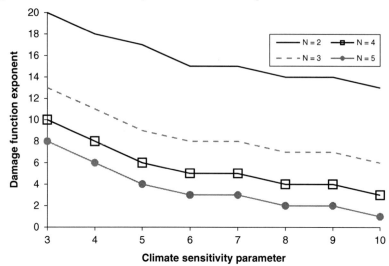

default exponent of 2; it is barely beginning to matter at 3. DICE confirms, on the other hand, that climate sensitivity and climate outcomes are of great importance when an exponent of 4 or 5 is used.

Figure 13.8 tells essentially the same story, in terms of the business-as-usual scenario minimum per capita consumption. At a damage function exponent of 2 or 3, climate damages never drive per capita consumption below the initial value, so long as climate sensitivity stays below 10. On the other hand, minimum per capita consumption begins falling midway through this range of climate sensitivity with an exponent of 4, and throughout the range with an exponent of 5.

Again, a credible range of worst-case values for climate sensitivity yields a dramatic worsening of economic outcomes at higher exponents, while leaving the baseline conditions more or less unchanged at exponents of 2 or 3.

The story is different in terms of the optimal time to reach complete abatement, as shown in Figure 13.9. Increases in climate sensitivity accelerate the abatement process, regardless of the damage function exponent; indeed, the lines on the graph move in lockstep, with the greatest acceleration of abatement occurring between climate sensitivity values of 3 and 6. The difference in urgency expressed by the different exponents can be read in the values (of the vertical coordinates) shown in Figure 9. At the DICE default exponent of 2, the optimal path to complete abatement takes two centuries at a climate sensitivity of 3, and still needs more than one century at climate sensitivity of 10. At an exponent of 4 or 5, complete abatement occurs in a century or less at climate sensitivity of 3, and in 30 years or less at climate sensitivity of 10. Again, the sense of urgency about reducing carbon emissions in the next few decades is endorsed by DICE with an exponent of 4 or 5, at climate sensitivity values well below the 99th percentile.

Conclusions

The DICE model, with two parameter changes, projects that immediate action to address the climate crisis is the optimal policy. If the climate sensitivity parameter turns out to be well above 3, and the damage function exponent is 4 or 5, then business-as-usual utility and minimum consumption levels collapse, and the optimal policy involves very rapid elimination of carbon emissions. At an exponent of 2 or even 3, in contrast, dangerously higher climate sensitivity inspires DICE to offer only a modest acceleration of its leisurely default path to decarbonization, but barely perturbs total utility or minimum per capita consumption. In short, a damage function exponent of 4 or 5, at a high climate sensitivity, leads DICE to project catastrophic economic outcomes; a lower exponent generally will not, regardless of climate sensitivity.

Our study found that uncertainty about climate sensitivity alone does not have much effect on DICE projections. If either the damage function exponent remains at or near the default value of 2, or climate sensitivity remains at or near the default value of 3, then DICE projects relatively little economic harm. With plausible changes in both parameters, however, DICE forecasts disastrous economic decline and calls for rapid mitigation.

The bad news is that the optimal policy recommended by a standard IAM such as DICE is completely dependent on the choice of key, uncertain parameters. The good news is that there is no reason to believe that sound economics, or even the choice of established, orthodox models, creates any grounds for belittling the urgency of the climate crisis.

Chapter 14

CLIMATE DAMAGES IN THE FUND MODEL: A DISAGGREGATED ANALYSIS

Frank Ackerman and Charles Munitz

We examine the treatment of climate damages in the FUND model. By inserting software switches to turn individual features on and off, we obtain FUND's estimates for 15 categories of damages, and for components of the agricultural category. FUND, as used by the US government to estimate the social cost of carbon, projects a net benefit of climate change in agriculture, offset by a slightly larger estimate of all other damages. Within agriculture there is a large benefit from CO_2 fertilization, a moderate cost from the effect of temperature on yields and a much smaller impact of the rate of change.

In FUND's agricultural modeling, the temperature-yield equation comes close to dividing by zero for high-probability values of a Monte Carlo parameter. The range of variation of the optimal temperature exceeds physically plausible limits, with 95 percent confidence intervals extending to 17°C above and below current temperatures. Moreover, FUND's agricultural estimates are calibrated to research published in 1996 or earlier. Use of estimates from such models is arguably inappropriate for setting public policy. But as long as such models are being used in the policymaking process, an update to reflect newer research and correct modeling errors is needed before FUND's damage estimates can be relied on.

Introduction

The FUND model of climate economics, developed by Richard Tol and David Anthoff, is widely used, both in research and in the development of policy proposals. It was one of three models used by the US government's Interagency Working Group on the Social Cost of Carbon (2010). The Working Group's "central estimate"[1] of the social cost of carbon (SCC), i.e., the monetary value of the incremental damages from greenhouse gas emissions, was $21 per ton of CO_2. FUND differs from the other two models used by the Interagency Working Group, DICE and PAGE, in at least two important respects. First, it produces the lowest central estimate of the SCC, $6, compared with $30 in PAGE and $28 in DICE. (Here and throughout, SCC estimates are in 2007 dollars per ton of CO_2.) Second, FUND is far more complex than the other models, with, among other features, 15 major categories and additional subcategories of climate damages, each based on a separate analysis and estimated for each of 16 regions of the world. Many of the constants defining these damages, as well as those used in other aspects of FUND, are modeled as Monte Carlo parameters, often with means and standard deviations specified separately for each region. As a consequence of this level of detail and complexity, it seems likely that many economists and policy analysts who use FUND results are unaware of the contribution of individual features of FUND to the final outcomes.

Serious questions have been raised about the use of integrated assessment models (IAMs) of climate economics, such as FUND, in the development of public policy. IAMs apply an economic framework that is ill suited to evaluation of intergenerational tradeoffs, and frequently ignore or minimize problems of catastrophic risk, which are central to the climate debate (Ackerman et al. 2009a; Schneider 1997). Welfare optimization models, a category that includes FUND and DICE, reopen fundamental questions, such as the optimal amount of warming to allow, offering economic judgments that may clash with well-established policy goals (Stanton et al. 2009; Stern 2008). In general, the reliance on detailed calculation of costs and benefits, including monetization of "priceless" externalities, creates numerous problems for environmental policymaking (Ackerman and Heinzerling 2004).

Despite such questions, IAMs, including FUND, remain important in the climate policy process, particularly in the United States. It is therefore important to understand the inner workings of the models that play a role in policy debates. This paper presents a disaggregation of the FUND model, followed by a more detailed examination of agricultural damages. It then raises two issues about the modeling of agricultural damages in FUND, reviews recent literature relevant to agricultural damage and recommends changes in FUND.

Methods

The analysis described here begins with the Working Group's modified version of FUND.[2] Software switches were then installed, making it possible to turn off individual damage components while keeping other features of the model unchanged. FUND was then rerun with various categories turned off. Turning off a damage category X produces what might be called the "all-but-X" estimate of the SCC; the impact of X can be defined as the Working Group estimate minus the all-but-X estimate.

This can be done in either of two modes. In the Monte Carlo mode, used in the Working Group analysis and most FUND-based research, the Monte Carlo variables are all allowed to vary, and the mean outcome (typically, over 10,000 iterations) is the reported result. Alternatively, in the best-guess mode, each Monte Carlo variable is fixed at its modal value (FUND, in effect, uses "best-guess" as a synonym for modal values).[3] The contrast between Monte Carlo and best-guess results offers one readily available measure of the impact of uncertainty as modeled in FUND.

Damage calculations play two distinct roles in FUND. First, for market impact categories (i.e., excluding externality valuations), each year's damages are subtracted from the next year's output, reducing the resources available for consumption. Second, for all damage categories, the present value of the future stream of damages is the basis for the calculation of the SCC. In that calculation, the model is run twice with nearly identical patterns of emissions, differing only in an added pulse of emissions in a specific year. The SCC for that year is the present value of the difference between future damages in the two runs, per ton of carbon in the emissions pulse. The Working Group performed this calculation for several years; only the 2010 results are discussed in this paper.

Results

Comparing FUND and DICE

An initial experiment with FUND demonstrates that the gap between the FUND and DICE "central estimates" of the SCC can be entirely explained by the difference in their treatment of climate damages.[4] In place of FUND's disaggregated analysis, DICE uses a single equation to model damages:

(14.1)   output net of damages = gross output/ $(1 + 0.002838T^2)$

Gross output is the output that would have been produced in the absence of climate change, and T is the change in temperature in °C since 1900 (Nordhaus 2008).

When damages are calculated by substituting Equation 14.1 from DICE into the Working Group version of FUND, keeping everything else unchanged, the result is an SCC of \$31 per ton, about 10 percent greater than the DICE value. That is, if the two models agreed on DICE's climate damages, they would roughly agree in their estimates of the SCC.

Figure 14.1. Fund SCC: Major components

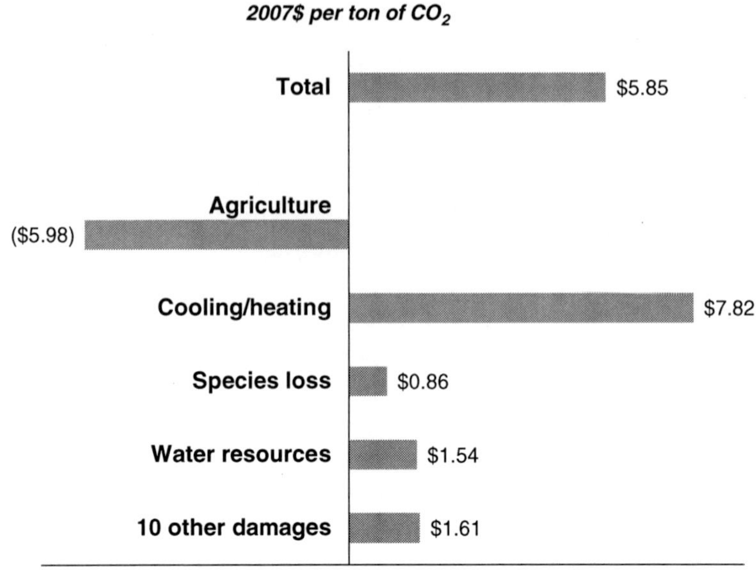

2007$ per ton of CO_2

Disaggregating FUND damages

FUND presents separate calculations for 15 major impact categories (of which several, including health and agriculture, include separate calculations for multiple subcategories). Two of the major categories are closely related to each other, namely the increased costs for space cooling and decreased costs for space heating, as consequences of rising average temperatures. They are combined into a single cooling/heating category in the following presentation. The cooling/heating category is always a net cost of warming, since FUND's estimate of air conditioning costs increases with temperature more rapidly than its estimate of heating costs decreases.

The agriculture and cooling/heating categories are the only large components of the FUND SCC estimate; the other 12 are quite small. Figure 14.1 shows the impacts of the most important categories, when running FUND in the Monte Carlo mode used by the Interagency Working Group.

FUND's $6 SCC estimate is the sum of a $6 net benefit in agriculture, a $8 net cost in cooling and heating and a total of $4 of net costs in the other 12 damage categories combined. The largest of the other 12 are water resources and species loss; the remaining 10 categories, including sea-level rise, storm damages, wetland losses, human health and migration impacts, amount to a combined total of less than $2 per ton of CO_2. One of the 10 smaller categories, forestry impacts, is a very small net benefit; the others are all small net costs.

Note that the impact of cooling and heating is greater than the SCC as a whole. Thus under the Working Group assumptions, FUND estimates that all impacts of climate change, excluding the increased costs of air conditioning, would amount to a net benefit to the world.

Many or all of the categories of impacts would benefit from a review and updating. Indeed, a 2009 memorandum to US EPA evaluating the FUND model, coauthored by FUND developer Richard Tol, observed that "the model relies on literature that frequently is a decade old or more," and suggested hundreds of additional sources that could be consulted in an update.[5]

Best-guess values versus effects of uncertainty

FUND also offers the option of calculation in "best-guess" mode, fixing all the Monte Carlo parameters at their modal values. Running the Working Group analysis in best-guess mode produces a SCC estimate of $11, compared with $6 in the Monte Carlo analysis. One readily available measure of the effect of uncertainty in FUND is the difference between the Monte Carlo estimates and the best-guess estimates. Using that definition of

Figure 14.2. Fund SCC components: Best-guess vs. uncertainty

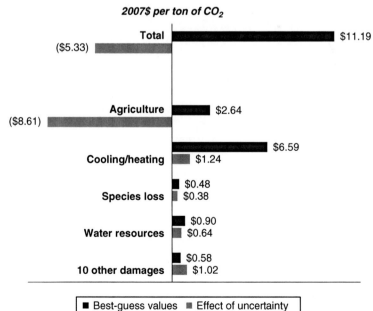

2007$ per ton of CO$_2$

Total $11.19
($5.33)

Agriculture $2.64
($8.61)

$6.59
Cooling/heating $1.24

$0.48
Species loss $0.38

$0.90
Water resources $0.64

$0.58
10 other damages $1.02

■ Best-guess values ▩ Effect of uncertainty

the effect of uncertainty, the estimates shown in Figure 14.2 can be broken down as follows:

The sum of the two bars for each category in Figure 14.2 is the value shown for that category in Figure 14.1. The effect of uncertainty is positive (increases the SCC) in all cases except agriculture. Uncertainty is only a small part of the impact of cooling and heating, and about half of the impact for the 12 smaller categories. In agriculture, however, the best-guess impact is a small positive amount, or net cost, while the effect of uncertainty is a larger negative, or net benefit.

Agricultural impacts

In view of the dominant role of agricultural impacts, as seen in Figures 14.1 and 14.2, it is worth taking a closer look at this category. FUND models agricultural impacts as the sum of three effects:

- The CO_2 fertilization effect assumes that agricultural production is proportional to the logarithm of CO_2 concentrations. This is always a net benefit of climate change (i.e., reduction in the SCC).
- The optimum temperature effect assumes that agricultural production is a quadratic function of temperature, reaching a maximum at a temperature with a most likely value somewhat above current levels. The sign of this effect can vary.
- The adjustment rate effect assumes that agricultural production is decreased by adjustment costs, which are proportional to the rate of change in temperature; this is always a small net cost (increase in the SCC).

Using the same methodology, these effects can be turned off one at a time to determine their effects on the SCC. The results corresponding to Figure 14.1 are shown in Figure 14.3, with the Working Group SCC and the total agricultural impact repeated from Figure 14.1, for ease of comparison. The negative (beneficial) impact in agriculture is entirely due to CO_2 fertilization, which is estimated to provide a net benefit of more than $14 per ton of CO_2 emissions.

The best-guess values and the effects of uncertainty can be compared for the three agricultural subcategories,[6] as was done for the broader categories in Figure 14.2. The results are presented in Figure 14.4. For CO_2 fertilization, both the best-guess value and the effect of uncertainty are net benefits (reductions in the SCC); this large category drives the overall estimate of net benefits in agriculture. For the optimum temperature impact, the

Figure 14.3. Agricultural impacts: Contribution to SCC

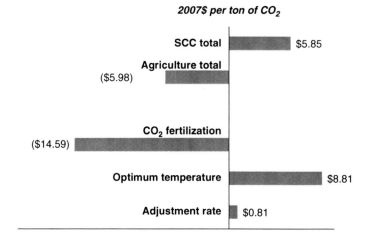

Figure 14.4. Agricultural impacts: Best-guess vs. uncertainty

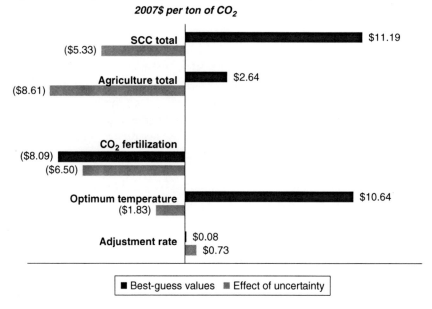

best-guess value and the effect of uncertainty have opposite signs – unlike the other agricultural subcategories, or the other impact categories shown in Figure 14.2. The best-guess optimum temperature impact is a large net cost (increase in the SCC), while uncertainty about this impact reduces the SCC. The much smaller adjustment rate impact is essentially entirely a result of uncertainty.

Modeling Agriculture Impacts: Two Issues

Further examination of FUND's agricultural calculations reveals two issues that need attention; both involve the optimum temperature impact.

Risk of division by zero

The manner in which the optimum temperature effect is modeled in FUND 3.5 could cause division by zero for a plausible value of a Monte Carlo parameter. The equation for the optimum temperature impact, modeled as a percentage change in agricultural output, is (in slightly simplified notation):

$$(14.2) \qquad Impact = \frac{-2A\,T^{opt}}{10.24 - 6.4T^{opt}}\,T + \frac{A}{10.24 - 64T^{opt}}\,T^2$$

This is calculated for each time period and region. T is the average change in temperature, a global variable, and T^{opt} is the optimum temperature for agriculture. Both A and T^{opt} are Monte Carlo parameters, specified separately for each region.

In Equation 14.2, the denominators of both fractions would be zero if $T^{opt} = 1.6$. This is not a problem in FUND's best-guess mode; the regional values of T^{opt} are never equal to 1.6. The closest is 1.51, and most are much farther away. In Monte Carlo mode, however, T^{opt} is a normally distributed variable; the critical value of 1.6 is within 0.25 standard deviations of the mean for every region. This implies that it will be reasonably common to draw a value very close to 1.6, making the denominator very small and the impact very big. In such cases, the magnitude of the impact will depend primarily on how close to 1.6 the value of T^{opt} turns out to be. Ironically, this problem could become more severe as the number of Monte Carlo iterations rises, since the likelihood of coming dangerously close to the critical value steadily increases. (In the Working Group analysis, there are 10,000 iterations, each involving selection of 16 values of T^{opt}, one for each region.)

The problem is generic to formulations such as Equation 14.2. If X is a non-negative random variable with a probability density function f that is positive at zero (i.e., $f(0) > 0$), then $Y = 1/X$ has a "fat tailed" probability of arbitrarily large values: for sufficiently large r, the probability $p(Y > r) = p(X < 1/r) \approx (1/r)f(0)$. In formal mathematical terms, Y is regularly varying with tail index 1; that is, the tail of Y is decreasing at a polynomial rate of degree -1. Whether the mean of Y exists depends on the distribution of X, but in any case, the expected value $E(Y^a)$ is infinite for $a > 1$. In particular, the variance of Y is infinite.

The same problem arises, of course, for the function $Y = 1/(X - c)$, if there is a positive probability of the value $X = c$. Consider a numerical example, where X has a standard normal distribution (mean 0, standard deviation 1), and $c = 0.25$. Using Excel, we drew repeated values of X, and calculated $Y = 1/(X - 0.25)$. The standard deviation of Y, for sample sizes up to 40,000, is shown in Figure 14.5. The standard deviation of Y quickly becomes orders of magnitude greater than the standard deviation of X, and continues to grow. We discontinued our numerical simulation when, after about 42,000 iterations, the Excel random number generator drew a value of $X = 0.24999902$, leading to Y greater than 1,000,000 in absolute value, and increasing the standard deviation of Y by another order of magnitude. That is exactly the problem: the larger the sample, the greater the danger of drawing values of X so close to c that Y becomes meaninglessly large (in absolute value).

Both coefficients in Equation 14.2 have structures comparable to Y in this example (after linear transformation of variables): the denominator is a normally distributed random variable, minus a constant that is within 0.25 standard deviation of the mean of the random variable. Thus the variance of each coefficient will increase without limit as the number of Monte Carlo iterations increases, and Equation 14.2 will provide an increasingly unreliable estimate of agricultural impacts.

Two simple ways of removing the problem would imply similar changes in the estimate of the SCC. (These changes are introduced solely to explore the sensitivity of FUND outputs to the structure of Equation 14.2, not as recommendations for a corrected model structure; the authors of FUND have, quite reasonably, responded that this simple tinkering with one equation is not an appropriate way to revise the model.[7]) First, FUND can be run

Figure 14.5. Increasing variance of $Y = 1/(X - .25)$

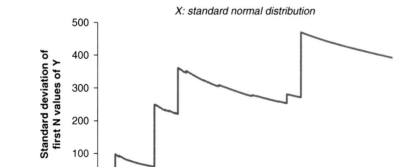

with T^{opt} fixed at its best-guess value for each region; that is, Equation 14.2 is unchanged, but T^{opt} is no longer a Monte Carlo parameter.[8] Everything else about the model, including the definition of A in Equation 14.2 as a Monte Carlo parameter, is also unchanged. This change has no effect on the best-guess value, but increases the Working Group's central estimate of the SCC by more than $10, from $5.85 to $16.21.

Alternatively, Equation 14.2 can be modified to use the global average value of T^{opt}, roughly 1.28, in the denominator of both fractions. The denominator becomes equal to 2.056, so the equation becomes:

$$(14.3) \qquad Impact = \frac{-2AT^{opt}}{2.056}T + \frac{A}{2.056}T^2$$

In this variant, both A and T^{opt} are still Monte Carlo parameters, but T^{opt} no longer appears in the denominator. This change alone increases the best-guess value of the SCC only slightly, from $11.19 (as shown in Figure 14.2) to $11.68. The Monte Carlo estimate, corresponding to the Working Group's $5.85, becomes $17.98, or an increase of $12. Thus two different ways of eliminating the problem in the optimum temperature equation, making no other changes, would raise the FUND estimate of the SCC by $10–$12. This result suggests that the FUND estimate of the SCC is significantly affected by the Monte Carlo iterations in which T^{opt} is dangerously close to the critical value of 1.6.

A fix for the optimum temperature equation bug is planned for the next version of FUND.[9] The anomaly is unfortunately present, however, in the versions that have been used in the past, including version 3.5, which was used for the Working Group's calculation of the SCC. In FUND versions 2.8 and 3.3, the earlier versions for which documentation is available online, the optimum temperature impact is defined by an equation with the same structure as 14.2, but with the denominators of the two fractions equal to $(1-2T^{opt})$. Thus the critical value that would cause a zero denominator was $T^{opt} = 0.5$ in FUND version 3.3 and earlier.

Implausible temperature ranges

In addition to the potential problem of near-zero denominators, the optimum temperature equation employs an extremely wide range of variation in its Monte Carlo analysis. Table 14.1 presents data, from the FUND 3.5 data tables, on optimal temperature increases for the model's 16 regions of the world: the means and standard deviations of the normal distributions used in the Monte Carlo analysis, and a calculation of the 95 percent confidence intervals (the mean plus or minus 1.96 standard deviations). The means are smaller than the standard deviations in every case, much smaller in most cases; if this is the best information available about optimum temperatures, one could argue that they may not be significantly different from zero. (The same could be said, for the same reason, of the agricultural adjustment rate effect parameter; but as seen in Figures 14.3 and 14.4, the adjustment rate effect is close to zero in any case.)

The width of the confidence intervals in Table 14.1 appears to exceed physically plausible temperature ranges for agriculture. FUND asserts 95 percent confidence that the optimal temperature for agriculture in South America, for instance, is between 17 °C below and almost 18 °C above 1990 levels; the intervals for Canada, and for Australia and New Zealand, are almost equally extreme. For the United States, the corresponding range is from –7 °C to + 9 °C. The upper end of the 95 percent confidence interval is more than 5 °C above 1990 temperatures everywhere. In five regions, it is more than 10 °C above 1990; at that global average temperature, many parts of the world would be too hot for human beings to survive (Sherwood and Huber 2010). The lower end of the confidence interval is more than 5°C below 1990 temperatures – that is, at or below the temperature of the last ice age – in eight regions.

Monte Carlo analysis across these intervals – including the even higher "optimum temperatures" that will be chosen for each region in 250 of the 10,000 iterations would seem to be exploring hypotheses about the state of the world that could safely be ruled out in advance. In each Monte Carlo iteration that selects a very high optimum temperature, FUND calculates a double benefit from climate change: both the fertilization from increasing CO_2 concentrations, and the increasing (but still suboptimal) temperature, are estimated to have separate, positive effects on agriculture. Since FUND has a lower bound on agricultural damages but no upper bound on agricultural benefits, Monte Carlo analysis across an excessively wide range of possibilities increases the reported average agricultural benefits.

Implications: The Need for Updated Agricultural Estimates

Since the FUND model remains important in the ongoing discussion of climate policy, there is a need to update and improve its damage estimates. In the area of agricultural impacts, the technical description for FUND 3.5, written in 2010, states that the model's estimates are calibrated to research results published in 1992–96. There has been a substantial advance in the understanding of agriculture and climate change since 1996, which might lead to different estimates.

Table 14.1. Optimal temperature for agriculture in FUND 3.5

| | (°C above 1990) | | | |
| | | | 95% Confidence Interval | |
	Mean (μ)	Standard Deviation (σ)	$\mu - 2\sigma$	$\mu + 2\sigma$
USA	1.09	4.14	-7.19	9.37
CAN	2.92	7.64	-12.36	18.20
WEU	0.79	3.29	-5.79	7.37
JPK	0.98	6.61	-12.24	14.20
ANZ	2.00	8.00	-14.00	18.00
EEU	1.31	2.73	-4.15	6.77
FSU	1.46	2.44	-3.42	6.34
MDE	1.32	2.03	-2.74	5.38
CAM	1.05	3.60	-6.15	8.25
SAM	0.35	8.82	-17.29	17.99
SAS	1.13	2.41	-3.69	5.95
SEA	0.70	5.12	-9.54	10.94
CHI	1.43	2.49	-3.55	6.41
NAF	1.20	2.74	-4.28	6.68
SSA	1.22	2.76	-4.30	6.74
SIS	1.51	2.92	-4.33	7.35

Early studies of carbon fertilization, usually done in greenhouses, suggested that it would lead to very large gains in agricultural yields. Recently, however, more realistic outdoor experiments have suggested that the benefits will be much smaller, perhaps half the size of the earlier estimates (Leakey et al. 2009; Long et al. 2006). A recent economic analysis of agriculture and climate change concluded that an increase in atmospheric concentration to 550 ppm of CO_2 would, on average, increase agricultural yields by 9 percent (Cline 2007).

When a simple carbon fertilization relationship is assumed to apply to all future CO_2 concentrations, there is a risk of out-of-sample forecasting: as concentrations rise, in high-emission climate scenarios, do yields keep rising forever? An unbounded logarithmic relationship between CO_2 concentrations and yields, as assumed in FUND, means that each doubling of CO_2 concentrations produces the same increase in agricultural output. Yet there is very little empirical information available about yields at higher concentrations.

A more cautious modeling approach might assume moderate yield gains, along the lines of Cline (2007), for the initial increases in CO_2 concentration, but little or no further gains thereafter. This would reduce the large net benefits which FUND currently estimates from CO_2 fertilization, particularly in high emission, business-as-usual scenarios.

The optimum temperature effect, as modeled in FUND, makes agricultural output a quadratic function of temperature (see Equation 14.2); even with the simplest fixes for the division-by-zero problem, as proposed in the last section, the relationship is still quadratic. This implies perfect symmetry between the impacts of higher- and lower-than-ideal temperatures: with a quadratic relationship, the projected yield is necessarily the same at 1° above and 1° below the optimum. Again, recent research suggests a different pattern.

In a detailed empirical study of the effects of temperature on US corn, soybeans and cotton yields, Schlenker and Roberts (2009) found very slow, small increases in yields on the way up to an optimum temperature (which was 29°C for corn, 30°C for soybeans and 32°C for cotton), followed by rapid declines in yields above the optimum. For corn, replacing 24 hours of the growing season at 29°C with 24 hours at 40°C causes a predicted yield decline of about 7 percent.

Their results do not at all resemble a quadratic relationship; a closer approximation would be a horizontal line (constant yield) up to the optimum temperature, followed by a steep drop-off in yield at higher temperatures. This would require a different functional form for the optimum temperature effect, in place of Equation 14.2. Schlenker and Roberts find no evidence of successful adaptation, such as development of heat-resistant crop varieties, in parts of the United States which have long been above the optimum temperatures for much of the growing season.

Corn, soybeans and cotton are three of the world's highest-value crops, and the United States produces a significant fraction of global supply, including 41 percent of corn and 38 percent of soybeans (Schlenker and Roberts 2009). Thus this is not just a case study, but a description of a large part of world agricultural production. Use of the Schlenker and Roberts curves, in place of FUND's current quadratic relationship between yield and temperature, would have a major effect on the estimates of agricultural impacts of climate change: it would reduce the large estimated gains from warming, particularly in the Monte Carlo iterations where FUND currently picks very high optimum temperatures.

Conclusions

One conclusion from this discussion is that, as we noted at the outset, questions could be raised about the use of models such as FUND in setting public policy. Yet as long as such models remain in use, model results matter. The estimate of the SCC adopted by US government agencies, for use in calculations such as cost–benefit analyses of proposed regulations, is based on the results of three models of climate economics – of which FUND is the most complex and least understood. Models that play such a prominent role need to be transparent, widely understood and up to date and consistent with the latest empirical research.

This chapter has introduced a software innovation that increases the transparency of the FUND model: switches that allow individual damage categories to be turned on and off, in order to understand their relative contributions to the final results. FUND's $6 SCC estimate, lower than some other models, is the sum of an estimated net benefit in agriculture, a net cost in heating and cooling and very small net costs in all other areas.

All of the damage categories in FUND should be examined and updated; some widely discussed climate impacts, such as sea-level rise and extreme weather events, are estimated to add almost nothing to the SCC in FUND. While this could be a surprising and important result about the magnitude of the empirical evidence, it could also be an indication that FUND's impact estimates are in need of revision.[10]

In the area of agriculture, FUND currently relies on research from 1996 or earlier to estimate a large net benefit from CO_2 fertilization, an optimum temperature effect on yields and a small effect from the rate of temperature change. The first two, which account for virtually the entire agricultural estimate, are both in need of revision.

Newer research suggests smaller benefits from CO_2 fertilization, and says nothing about whether these benefits continue at very high concentrations. A flaw in FUND's optimum temperature equation needs to be fixed, to prevent the risk of division by zero; and the quadratic shape of that equation is inconsistent with recent research on temperature and yields.

Since model results matter, so do the damage calculations used inside the models. The two quick fixes to the division-by-zero problem described above would raise the FUND estimate of the SCC from $6 to $16–$18, a substantial change that highlights the importance of this problem. This is not to say that either of those quick fixes would produce the right estimate of the SCC. Nonetheless, the problems identified here require attention. Much more careful work, including examination of damage categories beyond agriculture, should be done to produce a thorough revision of FUND.

We have demonstrated that problems in model specification and methodology, and failure to update the empirical evidence used in the model, can have relatively large effects on the results. The fact remains that model estimates are being treated as establishing a precise SCC value that can be used in policy analysis. Therefore it is essential to revisit those estimates, and the assumptions and inputs behind them, starting now, and continuing on a regular basis.

Chapter 15

CLIMATE POLICY AND DEVELOPMENT: AN ECONOMIC ANALYSIS

Frank Ackerman, Elizabeth A. Stanton and Ramón Bueno

We use the Climate and Regional Economics of Development (CRED) model to explore the interconnections between climate and development policy. CRED scenarios, based on high and low projections of climate damages, and high and low discount rates, are used to analyze the effects of varying levels of assistance to the poorest regions of the world. We find that climate and development choices are nearly independent of each other if the climate threat is seen as either very mild or very serious. The optimal climate policy is to do very little in the former case, and a lot in the latter case, regardless of development. In the latter case, however, assistance may be required for the poorest regions to respond to serious climate threats in the globally "optimal" manner. Under intermediate assumptions about the severity of climate risks, development policy plays a greater role. In one scenario, which falls within the range of current debate, a high level of development assistance makes the difference between success and failure in long-term stabilization of the global climate.

Introduction: An Economic Analysis of Climate Policy and Development

Climate change is the ultimate global public good (or public bad): the severity of the problem depends on total world emissions, so anyone's greenhouse gas emissions affect everyone. The impacts, however, are unevenly distributed, often falling most heavily on the hottest and poorest countries. The capacity to deal with the problem may be even more unequally distributed, since significant investments in mitigation and adaptation will be required.

The tradeoff between investment in climate protection and investment in economic growth will be evaluated differently by countries at different income levels. At higher incomes, additional economic growth is less urgent, and climate investments will often be more acceptable (although in practice, high-income countries differ greatly in their willingness to make such investments, for reasons beyond the scope of this chapter). At lower incomes, it is more urgent to raise average standards of living, so countries may be less willing to sacrifice immediate growth for long-run climate goals. This argument rests on the declining marginal utility of income, a thoroughly orthodox (and intuitively plausible) principle of economic theory.

The interaction between climate policy and development has been widely discussed (see, e.g., Ackerman et al. 2012), leading to innovative proposals for international equity in climate policy (Kartha et al. 2009). Yet economic analysis of climate change has often overlooked questions of equity and development – either through overly aggregated analysis of the world as a whole, or through the use of modeling techniques that ignore differences in marginal utility between rich and poor (Stanton et al. 2009; Stanton 2011c). Such analyses identify "optimal" climate policies in isolation from the inescapable pressures of inequality and the need for development.

In this chapter we use the Climate and Regional Economics of Development (CRED) model to explore the interconnections between climate and development policy. We identify some circumstances under which climate and development policy display virtually no interaction, and other circumstances under which development choices are decisive for climate outcomes.

Broadly speaking, we find that climate and development choices are nearly independent of each other if the climate threat is seen as either very mild or very serious. The optimal climate policy is to do very little in the former case, and a lot in the latter case, regardless of development – although in the latter, arguably realistic, case, international equity concerns may still affect the political feasibility of the optimal policy (Kartha et al. 2009). Under intermediate assumptions about the severity of climate risks, development policy plays a greater role. In one of our scenarios, which falls within the range of current debate, a high level of development assistance makes the difference between success and failure in long-term stabilization of the global climate.

The CRED Model

CRED is an integrated assessment model (IAM), created by the Stockholm Environment Institute (Ackerman et al. 2011, 2013). Like many IAMs, it calculates the policy choices that maximize a utility function, and spells out the long-run climate and economic implications of those choices. One crucial technical choice in CRED is that utility is based on the logarithm of the level of consumption.[1]

The utility function embodies the principle of declining marginal utility,[2] and is the key to CRED's approach to equity and development. All else being equal, the same absolute increase in consumption is more valuable – it adds more to global utility – if it occurs in a lower-income region. Specifically, logarithmic utility implies that equal *percentage* changes in consumption, at any income level, create equal changes in utility. The 16 regions used in CRED v1.4 are shown in Table 15.1, with their per capita consumption levels in 2010 (at market exchange rates, not purchasing power parity[3]). These data imply that $1 of additional consumption in India creates the same amount of utility as $7 in Eastern Europe or $38 in the United States.

The central economic decision modeled in an IAM is the three-way choice between current consumption, conventional investment and investment in emission reduction. Conventional investment stimulates economic growth, leading to greater future consumption; mitigation of emissions limits future climate damages, also allowing greater future consumption; there is a tradeoff between current consumption and both routes to future consumption. The sequence of decisions that maximizes utility depends on the discount rate, and on many other climate and economic parameters.

In view of the inequality among regions of the world, another dimension of choice could be considered: where should investment occur? Global utility might be increased if investment from rich countries went to poor countries instead of staying at home. Is investment 38 times as productive, in monetary terms, in the United States as in India? If not, then it could be more productive, in terms of utility, to invest in India.

CRED is designed to explore this spatial dimension of decision making, by allowing resource transfers, or capital exports, from one region to another. (No return flows of income on exported capital are modeled; the transfers can be thought of either as foreign aid grants, or as foreign direct investment with 100 percent local reinvestment of earnings.) With no constraints on the extent of transfers, the optimal scenario simultaneously achieves robust global economic growth and rapid emission reduction. This creates higher worldwide utility, greater equality and better climate outcomes than any other scenario – at the expense of a steep drop in the standard of living in high-income regions, down to global middle-income levels. Thus the scenario with unconstrained transfers, while analytically informative, is irrelevant to practical policy debates.

In order to focus on more realistic choices, two constraints are imposed on inter-regional resource flows in CRED. First, consumption per capita in every region must grow by at least 0.5 percent per year – indirectly requiring significant domestic investment. Second, there is a user-specified upper limit on the fraction of a region's output that can be transferred to other regions.

Table 15.1. CRED Regions

	2010	
	Per Capita Consumption (thousand US$)	Population (millions)
High-Income	**32.8**	**990**
USA	38.0	318
Japan	33.4	127
Western Europe	31.4	409
Other High-Income	25.1	136
Middle-Income	**6.9**	**1,252**
Other Europe	9.1	177
Brazil	8.9	195
Mexico	7.4	111
Eastern Europe	7.0	223
Middle East	5.6	215
Other Latin America/Caribbean	5.5	281
South Africa	5.4	50
Low-Income	**1.6**	**4,685**
China	2.7	1361
Southeast Asia/Pacific	2.2	616
Other Africa	1.1	981
India	1.0	1,214
Other Developing Asia	0.9	513

Definitions

Western Europe	EU-15, Iceland, Norway, Switzerland
Other High Income	Australia, Canada, New Zealand, Singapore, South Korea, Taiwan
Other Europe	EU except EU-15, Turkey
Eastern Europe	Russia, Ukraine, Belarus, Moldova, Albania, non-EU ex-Yugoslavia
Middle East	Excludes North Africa, includes Iran
Southeast Asia/Pacific	Myanmar, Thailand, Malaysia, Cambodia, Laos, Vietnam, Indonesia, Philippines, island nations
Other Africa	Includes North Africa
Other Developing Asia	Pakistan, Bangladesh, Nepal, Bhutan, Afghanistan, Mongolia, North Korea, Asian ex-USSR

With a limit of 3 percent, for example, CRED makes an unconstrained global calculation of the optimal use of the first 3 percent of a region's output, and then calculates the optimal domestic allocation of the remaining 97 percent to consumption, conventional investment and mitigation. High-income regions are normally exporters of capital, and low-income regions are importers. Middle-income regions can either be importers or exporters of capital, depending on the scenario.

CRED contains a number of other innovations, including an updated climate module calibrated to recent research results, and abatement cost curves derived from the McKinsey database of projections for 2030. Steady technological change is assumed after 2030, expanding abatement opportunities to allow 100 percent mitigation of emissions in 2100 and thereafter. The expansion from 9 to 16 regions in the latest revision of CRED allows a more detailed and flexible analysis of global inequality and its interaction with climate change (Ackerman et al. 2011).

Climate Modeling Assumptions

CRED results can be contrasted under high and low choices for two key assumptions: the discount rate and the extent of climate damages. For the discount rate, we compare a 0.1 percent rate of pure time preference[1], the rate used in the Stern Review (Stern 2006) with a 1.5 percent rate, which is used in DICE and some other climate economics models (Nordhaus 2008). Climate benefits accrue over the long run following investment in mitigation, so their present value is strongly affected by the discount rate. In contrast, development occurs more rapidly; in CRED, resource transfers typically lead to a new long-term global distribution of income within a few decades. As a result, development benefits are much less sensitive to the discount rate. Therefore a lower discount rate gives greater weight to climate protection, while a higher discount rate gives greater weight to development.

For damages, we use two functions expressing the fraction of output lost to climate damages as a function of temperature increases (see Figure 15.1). The low estimate is the DICE damage function, in which damages are less than 2 percent of output at 2.5°C and rise only gradually thereafter, reaching 50 percent of output around 19°C. The high estimate, which we have dubbed the "HW" damage function, combines Michael Hanemann's reestimate of damages at 2.5°C (amounting to 2.4 times the DICE estimate) with Martin Weitzman's suggestion that risks of catastrophic climate losses can be represented by assuming 50 percent loss of output at 6°C, and 99 percent loss at 12°C (see Ackerman and Stanton 2012a).[5]

Figure 15.1.

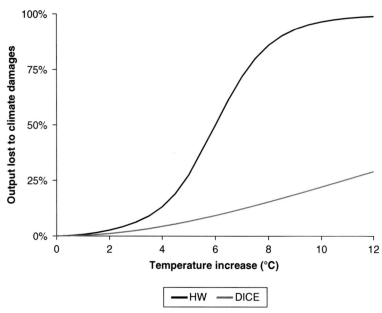

Varying these two factors independently leads to four scenarios, for high and low discount rates, at DICE and HW damages. Within each scenario, we compare results with resource transfer limits of 0, 3 percent, 6 percent and 10 percent of output. (Experiments with higher limits yielded greater equality and more rapid development, with climate results essentially indistinguishable from the 10 percent case.)

Development Results

Economic growth in low-income regions is strongly dependent on the level of resource transfers between regions, but little affected by discount rates and damage assumptions. Using per capita consumption in 2100 as a measure of development, the results are shown in Table 15.2. (CRED projects little change in the relative incomes of high, middle and low-income regions after 2100; all continue to grow at similar rates.) Each figure in Table 15.2 is the average of the values under all four scenarios. Consumption is generally higher with the DICE damage function, which implies smaller climate losses, but the differences are not large; in all but one case, the estimates under the four scenarios differed by 15 percent or less.

As the transfer limit rises, the level of per capita consumption in 2100 declines in both middle-income and high-income regions; in these cases, the

Table 15.2. Consumption per capita by region, 2010 and 2100

		(thousands of 2010 US$)			
	2010	2100			
Transfer Limit		0	3%	6%	10%
Low-Income Regions	1.6	6.1	7.3	8.1	9.2
Middle-Income Regions	6.9	25.3	24.3	23.3	21.8
High-Income Regions	32.8	114.5	108.7	101.1	91.2

Values for 2100 are averages across four sets of climate assumptions (see text).

middle-income and high-income regions are all contributing the maximum amount to the development of low-income regions. (The sole exception is one 10 percent limit result in which South Africa, the least affluent middle-income region, is a capital exporter, but sends less than 10 percent of its output to low-income regions.)

In fact, the optimal solution under some assumptions includes redistribution among the low-income regions. As shown in Table 15.1, China and Southeast Asia are much less poor than Africa and South and Central Asia. When resource transfers are limited to 3 percent of output, CRED calls for transfers from China and Southeast Asia (as well as all high- and middle-income regions) to the lowest-income regions. At 6 percent, as increased resources become available from high- and middle-income regions, Southeast Asia becomes a recipient of capital from abroad, while China still exports capital to lower-income regions. At the 10 percent limit, with even greater resources available, China also receives an inflow of capital from abroad. These results occur under all four scenarios, depending solely on the transfer limit.

Although the transfer limits explored here may seem extreme – the 10 percent limit is at least an order of magnitude beyond the magnitude of existing foreign aid programs – the resulting equalization of living standards is comparatively modest. As seen in Table 15.2, the ratio of high-income to low-income regions' consumption per capita drops only from 20:1 today to 10:1 in 2100 with 10 percent transfers. The difference between zero and 10 percent transfers, for the low-income regions, determines whether they end the century near the top or the bottom of the current range of middle-income regions (see Table 15.1). For high-income regions, it is the difference between ending the century at 2.4 or 3.0 times greater than current US consumption per capita.

Climate Results

With DICE damages and a high discount rate – the assumptions that minimize the importance of climate impacts – CRED projects that the climate will never

Figure 15.2. Temperature increase: DICE damages high discount

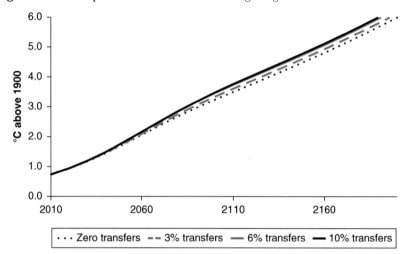

be stabilized, and temperatures will rise steadily throughout the next 200 years (see Figure 15.2).[6] Emissions from both low- and middle-income regions rise steadily as well.

In high income regions, emissions drop in the later years of this century and are close to zero in the next century; in these regions, the lower marginal utility of increases in consumption make it worthwhile to trade some consumption growth for climate mitigation. Even with substantial resource transfers, however, low and middle-income regions never make that choice, so global emissions and temperatures are never brought under control. The climate results are virtually identical under widely different limits on resource transfers.

At the opposite extreme, the assumptions of HW damages and a low discount rate maximize climate impacts. Global temperatures peak at 1.7–1.8°C in 2100 and then gradually decline (see Figure 15.3; note the change in the vertical axis scale).[7] The tradeoff between consumption growth and climate mitigation is now tilted strongly toward mitigation; emissions drop to zero by 2100 (the time when complete abatement first becomes possible) in every region, in almost every case.[8] The climate results are again virtually insensitive to changes in resource transfers. More diverse results appear in the intermediate cases. With HW damages and a high discount rate, the temperature stabilizes in the next century. In this case, the peak temperature is higher and occurs later than in the HW damages/low discount case (see Figure 15.4). The peak temperature of 2.9°C occurs in 2160 with no transfers, compared to 2.6°C in 2120 with 10 percent transfers.

Figure 15.3. Temperature increase: HW damages, low discount

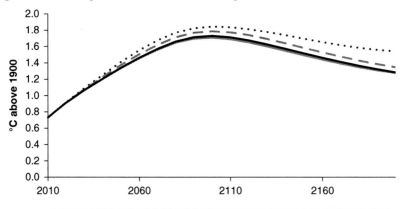

Figure 15.4. Temperature increase: HW damages, high discount

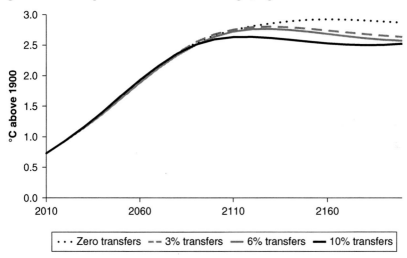

These differences are largely attributable to the pattern of low-income region emissions. High- and middle-income region emissions decline to roughly zero by 2100 and remain there, with little variation by transfer level. Low-income region emissions, in contrast, never quite go to zero, but are reduced below their 2010 level (see Figure 15.5). Greater resource transfers lead to lower cumulative emissions in low-income regions, accounting for the improved climate outcomes with higher transfers.

Figure 15.5. Low-income emissions: HW damages, high discount

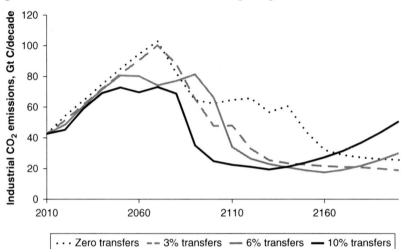

Figure 15.6. Temperature increase: DICE damages, low discount

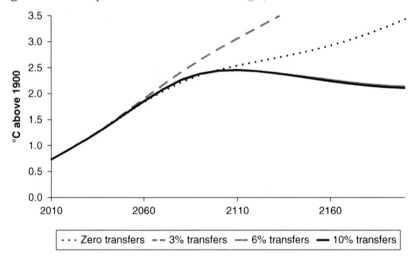

The effect of resource transfers is more dramatic in the final case, with DICE damages and a low discount rate (see Figure 15.6). Temperatures are never controlled in the zero and 3 percent cases, rising throughout the 200-year period. In fact, the increase is noticeably faster with 3 percent transfers than with none. With 6 percent or 10 percent transfers, however, the temperature reaches a peak of just under 2.5°C in 2110, and then drifts slightly downward.

Figure 15.7. Low-income emissions: DICE damages, low discount

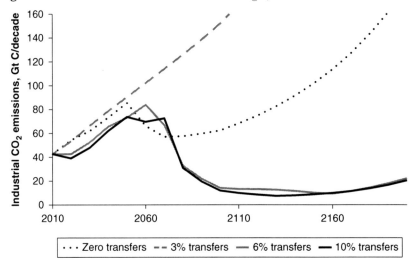

The differences are again attributable to low-income region emissions. Both high- and middle-income regions reach zero emissions by 2100, and stay there, with little differences by transfer level. Low-income emissions, however, differ sharply by transfer level (see Figure 15.7). At both zero and 3 percent, emissions rise without limit, driving the similar pattern in temperatures. The additional resources provided to low-income regions with a 3 percent transfer limit are enough to spur more rapid economic growth and emissions, but not to make it worthwhile to curtail emissions.

A threshold occurs between 3 percent and 6 percent transfers: at the higher levels of transfers, low-income regions experience enough income growth to make mitigation attractive to them later in this century. Emissions do not quite reach zero, but remain at one-quarter to one-half of 2010 levels despite rapid economic growth. Additional transfers beyond the threshold lead to greater equality between rich and poor regions, but have almost no effect on emissions and climate outcomes, as shown by the nearly identical results at 6 percent and 10 percent.

Discussion

Our results suggest that the relationship between climate and development policy is not simple or immutable, but rather is contingent on assumptions about the nature and severity of climate risks. At either extreme, the much-discussed link between the two policy domains appears to be attenuated. If the climate problem is assumed to be mild enough that it's not worth doing much about it, then similar policies of near inaction are appropriate with or without equity and development assistance. This is a perfectly logical deduction, but from an implausible premise.

If, perhaps more plausibly, potential climate damages are assumed to be large enough and the discount rate low enough that the climate threat looms large in present value terms, then the optimal policy is to do a lot about it – again with or without progress on equity and development. In this case, the problem is not with the premise, but with the conclusion. The difficulty arises from the somewhat obscure technical meaning of "optimal policy."

In a model such as CRED, an optimal policy is one that maximizes global utility – a measure of the present value of human welfare, for generations to come. If policy makers in every region act to maximize global utility, and if they all use the same assumptions about climate risks and discount rates, then they will presumably converge on the optimal policy identified by the model. In practice, this convergence could fail to occur for several reasons.

Policy could be narrowly focused on national rather than international outcomes, undermining hopes for cooperation in addressing the thoroughly global climate externality. The elaborate processes of international climate negotiations and related debates over the fairness of alternate solutions are aimed at overcoming this obstacle.

Policy differences could also arise from differing assumptions about climate risks or discount rates. The lowest-income countries, where economic growth and poverty reduction are most urgent, may find it difficult to make decisions focused on the long run, based on the very low discount rates that are often advocated for climate analysis. Resource transfers from higher income countries may be essential in allowing low-income countries to accept the need for very future-oriented investments – that is, development aid may be essential if climate solutions require everyone to act on the basis of very low discount rates.

Modeling differing national assumptions about climate parameters and discount rates is a challenging analytical task, requiring a computational apparatus far beyond the level of CRED (or most IAMs). It may be instructive, nonetheless, to look at our results for the intermediate scenarios. Under both intermediate cases, we find that the level of development assistance has a significant effect on climate outcomes.

Development is an incremental process, in which a little more is always possible, and is always better than a little less. In contrast, climate policy is subject to thresholds: either we have sufficient collective will and resources to bring emissions down far enough and fast enough stabilize the climate, or we do not. Under intermediate scenario, there is a strongly nonlinear, threshold relationship between resource transfers and climate results: transfers of up to

3 percent of output do nothing for the climate; 6 percent achieves complete climate stabilization; and 10 percent does no more than 6 percent.

The point is not that this set of results should be taken as literal predictions, or 6 percent transfers be taken as a precise requirement. CRED is a simplified model of climate–economy interactions, designed to illuminate underlying relationships rather than to provide detailed plans. Rather, the qualitative message of these quantitative results is worth considering: interactions between climate and development may be crucial at intermediate levels of severity of climate threats, and there may be thresholds requiring significant levels of development assistance to bring the world together in cooperating on climate solutions.

Appendix

SUPPLEMENTARY DATA FOR CHAPTER 3

This appendix, in combination with the section titled, "A review of current practices," in chapter 3, reviews assumptions regarding GDP, population and per capita GDP in a broad range of integrated assessment models.

Forecasting GDP Growth

WEO 2010 projects that Organization for Economic Co-operation and Development (OECD)[1] countries' real economic output (that is, GDP after adjusting for inflation) in PPP terms will grow 1.8 percent per year from 2008 to 2020 and 1.9 percent per year from 2020 to 2035. In non-OECD countries, the projections are 5.6 percent from 2008 to 2020 and 3.8 percent from 2020 to 2035. The pace of projected growth in non-OECD countries, however, is dominated by two exceptional cases: China (8.8 percent and 3.9 percent in the two periods, respectively); and India (7.0 percent and 6.6 percent). Together, China and India make up 45 percent of the 2005 population in non-OECD countries, and 37 percent of world population. Economic growth in the remaining non-OECD countries is expected to take place at a slower pace, as shown in Table A.1.[2]

Projecting the official IEA growth rates forward (as described in the main text), with the assumption that real GDP growth slows down as per capita incomes rise, results in global GDP (in 2005 PPP dollars) reaching $537 trillion in 2105, up from $56 trillion in 2005. For simplicity the extended WEO 2010 GDP growth projections are referred to as "standard" growth throughout this article (see Figure A.1).

The models with the fastest GDP growth in the EMF comparison show a slightly quicker pace of growth in India and China, and one IPCC scenario (A1T) shows much faster global GDP growth, but, with these exceptions, most of the other scenarios represented in Table A.1 assume slower growth than the standard projections. Models may assume even slower growth than IEA for a variety of reasons. Some scenarios, such the SRES B2 and A2, explicitly use

Table A.1. WEO 2010 projections for annual real GDP (PPP) growth

	2008–2020	2020–2035
OECD	1.8	1.9
Non-OECD	5.6	3.8
Eastern Europe/Eurasia	3.0	3.1
Russia	3.3	3.1
Other	2.6	3.1
Asia/Pacific	7.2	4.2
China	8.8	3.9
India	7.0	5.6
Other	3.7	3.4
Middle East/North Africa	4.5	3.8
Sub-Saharan Africa	4.7	2.8
Latin America/Caribbean	3.1	2.7
Brazil	3.1	3.1
Other	3.1	2.4

Source: IEA (2010b) and author's calculation based on IEA (2010b) data (see text for methodology).

Figure A.1. World GDP by income group in 2005 and 2105, standard growth

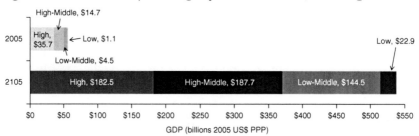

Source: Author's calculation based on World Bank data for 2005 (World DataBank, (http://databank.worldbank.org/ddp/home.do?Step=3&id=4. Accessed 28 June 2013.) and IEA (2010b) growth rates (see text for methodology), limited to countries used in the dataset for this article.

slow economic growth assumptions as part of a suite of scenarios designed to represent a range of possible futures. Overall, most climate economics models assume that economic growth in developing countries (excluding China and India) will proceed at a pace similar to or slower than that used in the standard, extended WEO 2010 projections.

Forecasting Population Growth

The IEA's WEO publications and the PIK model comparison rely on the medium variant of the UNDESA long-range projections of population growth by country; until their most recent installment in 2010, these projections had been changed only gradually over time.[3] In the EMF model comparison and SRES scenarios, population growth varies by model, with levels reaching from 8.7 to 10.6 billion in 2100 in the former – still broadly in the range of the UNDESA medium variant projections – and 7.0 to 15.1 billion in the latter (see Table A.1). The SRES scenarios are designed to represent a broad spectrum of possible socioeconomic futures and therefore include projections of slow, medium and rapid population growth.[4]

In the UNDESA's latest, 2010 revision of *World Population Prospects*, the medium variant projects a global population in 2100 that is only slightly larger than that of the 2008 revision, but there have been important changes in the expected distribution of population increases across countries.[5] In the new projections, high- and low-income countries have slightly faster population growth than previously expected, high-middle-income countries experience slower growth – including a 200 million person decrease in China's 2100 population – and low-middle-income countries experience much faster growth. UNDESA's revised 2010 median variant population projections are used throughout this article.

NOTES

Publication History

1 Charles Munitz encourages interested readers to contact him at charles@munitz.net for more information about this article.

Chapter 1. Climate Economics in Four Easy Pieces

1 Nordhaus (2008, 15). His Figure 5.6 (p. 102) suggests that "optimal" emissions in 2055 would be about one-third higher than in 2005.
2 In 2005, there were 511,000 fires in structures (US Census Bureau 2008, Table 346) and 124 million housing units in the US (US Census Bureau 2008, Table 953).
3 Based on US average death rates by age, as of 2004 (US Census Bureau 2008, Table 101).
4 LIMRA International, an insurance industry research group, reports that in families with dependent children, "Twenty-eight percent of wives and 15 percent of husbands have no life insurance at all. Ten percent of families with children under 18 have no life insurance protection." From "Facts about Life 2007," http://www.limra.com/pressroom/pressmaterials/07USFAQ.pdf.
5 For example, see the recent studies of the costs of reduction by McKinsey & Company (2009), an international consulting firm: Enkvist et al. (2007) and Creyts et al. (2007).

Chapter 2. Carbon Markets Are Not Enough

1 A major exception to this pattern occurs in countries where some of the poorest people cannot afford fossil fuels and instead rely on traditional biomass fuels.
2 Price elasticity is the percentage change in demand that results from a 1 percent change in price.
3 Price elasticities are, strictly speaking, negative numbers. This discussion follows the common convention of referring to values farther from zero as "larger" elasticities: an elasticity of -1 is "larger" than an elasticity of -0.5.
4 See also Reiss and White (2005), who estimate a long-run price elasticity for California households of -0.39 and point out that previous high-quality studies have generally yielded estimates of between -0.15 and -0.35.
5 The EIA (2007) notes that transportation will account for two-thirds of the growth in world oil use through 2030; OPEC data (2007) implies that transport will absorb 62 percent of the growth in oil use.

6 Another study in the United States similarly found that the short-run price elasticity in 2001–2006 was between –0.034 and –0.077 (Hughes et al.2006).
7 The classic references to technological lock-in include those by David (1985) and Arthur (1994).

Chapter 3. Modeling Pessimism: Does Climate Stabilization Require a Failure of Development?

1 See Stanton and Ackerman (2009) and Stanton, Ackerman and Kartha (2009) for a more detailed explanation of these models.
2 McKinsey and Company (2009) follows the *World Energy Outlook* 2007 (International Energy Agency 2007).
3 All money values in this chapter are expressed in real PPP 2005 US dollars. The purchasing power parity (PPP) conversion factor adjusts per capita GDP to reflect international differences in domestic prices for the same goods, which are usually lower in poorer countries. For a more detailed definition, see the World Bank Development Education Program glossary: http://www.worldbank.org/depweb/english/beyond/global/glossary.html. Accessed 28 June 2013.
4 This classification differs slightly from the one used by the World Bank (http://data.worldbank.org/about/country-classifications/country-and-lending-groups. Accessed 28 June 2013.), which is based on incomes for an earlier year and a different upper bound for the low-income group. A small number of countries have been removed from the data set due to missing data for GDP, population or emissions, resulting in a slightly lower 2005 world total than reported by the World Bank. The data set used here includes 176 countries.
5 The World Bank, World DataBank, http://databank.worldbank.org/ddp/home.do?Step=3&id=4#. Accessed 28 June 2013.
6 Energy Modeling Forum (2009). EMF model inputs are reported in 2005 US$ market exchange rates (MER) terms. These values are converted to PPP terms using the ratio of 2005 global GDP (PPP 2005, US$) to 2005 global GDP (MER 2005, US$), 1.24. Increasing 2105 GDP (MER) estimates by this amount very likely overestimate GDP (PPP) – the ratio of PPP to MER GDP would tend to decrease with income convergence.
7 Edenhofer et al. (2010b).
8 Nakicenovic et al. (2000). Converted from 1990 to 2005 dollars using the US Consumer Price Index, http://www.bls. gov/cpi/. Accessed 28 June 2013.
9 Calculated as 2005 total greenhouse gas emissions, including non-CO_2 gases (World Resources Institute's Climate Analysis Indicators Tool. CAIT 8.0. http://cait.wri.org/. Accessed 28 June 2013.), divided by 2005 PPP GDP (World DataBank, http://databank.worldbank. org/ddp/home.do?Step=3&id=4. Accessed 28 June 2013.).
10 Historical CO_2 emissions intensities were calculated using World Bank GDP data (from the World DataBank, http://databank.worldbank.org/ddp/home.do?Step=3&id=4. Accessed 28 June 2013.) and CAIT emissions data (World Resources Institute's Climate Analysis Indicators Tool. CAIT 8.0. http://cait.wri.org/. Accessed 28 June 2013.). The historical data set is slightly smaller than the set of countries with World Bank GDP data for 2005. There is some, but not complete, overlap between OECD and high-income countries per the World Bank data; among high-income countries, emissions

intensities grew with incomes in Barbados, Greece, Israel, New Zealand, Oman, Portugal and Qatar. Among OECD countries, emissions intensities grew with incomes in Chile, Greece, Israel, New Zealand, Portugal and Turkey.

11 CAIT 8.0. http://cait.wri.org/. Accessed 28 June 2013.

12 See Lindmark (2004).

13 Estimates in Bowen and Ranger (2009) range from 1,908 to 2,684 Gt CO_2-e. See also Allen et al. (2009); Gohar and Lowe (2009); Lowe et al. (2011); Meinshausen et al. (2009).

14 EMF, PIK and SRES emissions are reported in CO_2 (excluding non-CO_2 gases). These values have been converted to CO_2e by adding a cumulative 1,100 Gt CO_2e in non-CO_2 greenhouse gas emissions during the twenty-first century following the methodology used in the CRED model (Ackerman, Stanton and Bueno 2011). EMF model comparison: 5,100 to 9,100 Gt CO_2-e; PIK model comparison: 5,000 to 7,000Gt; and SRES emissions scenarios: 4,700 to 9,100Gt.

15 See Chapter 9 in Sathaye et al. (2011).

16 Historical CO_2 emissions intensities calculated using World Bank GDP data (from the World DataBank, http://databank. worldbank.org/) and CAIT emissions data (World Resources Institute 2010).

17 For more on the Environmental Kuznets Curve, see Grossman and Krueger (1995).

18 See CAIT (World Resources Institute 2010).

19 For a discussion of low-carbon policies for the agriculture sector as it relates to economic development see Norse (2012).

20 World Bank GDP data (from World DataBank, http://databank.worldbank.org/ddp/home.do?Step=3&id=4. Accessed 28 June 2013.).

Chapter 4. The Tragedy of Maldistribution: Climate, Sustainability and Equity

1 See also Wikinson and Pickett (2006, 2007); Gerdtham and Johannesson (2003); Kawachi and Kennedy (1999).

2 See Champernowne and Cowell (1999) for a detailed explanation of these measures.

3 For an examination of pre-industrial inequality, see Milanovic et al. (2011).

4 UNU-WIDER (2008). For an additional source of, similarly incomplete, income distribution data see the United Nations University World Institute for Development Economics Research's World Income Inequality Database.

5 The treatment of income redistribution in theoretical welfare economics is outside of the scope of this chapter; on this topic see Thurow (1971).

6 For a defense of cost–benefit analysis see Sunstein (2002, 2005).

Chapter 5. Climate Impacts on Agriculture: A Challenge to Complacency?

1 World Bank data on agricultural value added as a share of GDP in 2008, http://data.worldbank.org. Accessed 28 June 2013.

2 In economic terms, the fact that food is a necessity means that it has a very low price elasticity of demand, implying that it has a very large consumer surplus. If contributions to wellbeing are measured by consumer surplus rather than shares of GDP, as economic theory suggests, then agriculture looms much larger in importance.

238   CLIMATE CHANGE AND GLOBAL EQUITY

3 For the damage estimates used in DICE, including a projection of virtually no net
   global losses in agriculture from the first few degrees of warming, see Nordhaus and
   Boyer (2000); this earlier analysis is still a principal source for damages estimates in
   the latest version of DICE (Nordhaus 2007a, 2008). On the dated and problematical
   treatment of agricultural impacts in FUND, see Ackerman and Munitz (2012); the
   2010 release of FUND relies on agricultural research published in 1996 and earlier.
4 Using historical data from 1961–90, PESETA modeled yields at nine locations, as linear
   functions of annual and monthly average temperatures (as well as precipitation). In three
   locations, there was a negative coefficient on a summer month's temperature as well
   as positive coefficients on springtime and/or annual average temperatures – perhaps a
   rough approximation of the threshold model discussed below (Iglesias et al. 2011).
5 A third photosynthetic pathway exists in some plants subject to extreme water stress,
   such as cacti and succulents; it is not important in agriculture.
6 This article has been criticized by Tubiello et al. (2007); the original authors respond in
   Ainsworth et al. (2008).
7 That is, the equation for yields has both temperature (with a positive coefficient) and
   temperature squared (with a negative coefficient) on the right-hand side.
8 Degree-days are the product of the number of days and the number of degrees above a
   threshold. Relative to a 32°C threshold, one day at 35°C and three days at 33°C would
   each represent three degree-days.
9 End-of-century (2081–2100) precipitation under A1B relative to 1981–2000.
10 Lu (2009) notes that there is significant uncertainty regarding future Sahel drying,
   because it is influenced by sea-surface temperature changes over all the world's oceans,
   and by the radiative effects of greenhouse gas on increased land warming, which can
   lead to monsoon-like conditions.
11 We studied a five-state region: California, Nevada, Utah, Arizona and New Mexico.
   California accounts for most of the population, agriculture and water use of the region.
12 The Colorado River basin includes most of the four inland states in our study region,
   but only a small part of California. Nonetheless, California is legally entitled to, and
   uses, a significant quantity of Colorado River water. Other rivers are also important to
   water supply in California, but much less so in the inland states.

Chapter 6. Did the Stern Review Underestimate US and Global Climate Change?

1 For a summary of these critiques, see Ackerman (2008c).
2 A2 is the IPCC scenario with the second highest emissions. At the 83rd percentile it
   predicts a global average temperature increase of 5.4°C in 2100. Its mean prediction is
   3.4°C in 2100.

Chapter 7. Can Climate Change Save Lives? A Comment on "Economy-Wide Estimates of the Implications of Climate Change: Human Health"

1 See their statement on p.582 that they are "using the projected per capita income
   growth of the 8 GTAP-EF regions for the countries within those regions." The regions

include the US and EU at one extreme of income, and China, India and the "Rest of World" (other non-oil-exporting developing countries) at the other extreme.

2 We are not addressing the estimates of temperature impacts on vector-borne diseases and diarrhea, also presented in Bosello et al. These raise separate analytical issues, and, except in Africa, the impacts of other diseases are generally small in comparison to cardiovascular and respiratory disease.

3 Tol (2002a) also cites EuroWinter (1997) as a source for this relationship, but that appears to be a misreading: the Eurowinter study focuses solely on the pattern of impacts of cold weather in different parts of Europe, with no comment on or comparison to heat-related deaths or illnesses.

4 As of August 2, 2006, the Louisiana Department of Health and Hospitals reported 1,464 deaths in Louisiana, and 346 deaths in other states, due to Hurricane Katrina. http://www.dhh.louisiana. gov. Accessed 22 September 2006.

5 Heidi Cullen, "Heat Wave Death Toll Numbers Trickling In," http://www.weather. com/blog/weather/8_10348.html. Accessed September 2006.

6 We have rounded off all mortality figures to the nearest 10,000 in order to avoid spurious precision and to focus on the overall magnitudes of these projections.

7 Tol (1997) made a similar assumption, again without citation or justification.

8 Since the population that will be over 65 in 2050 was born in 1985 or earlier, its size is dependent only on death rates between now and 2050. That is, it is not dependent on demographic forecasts of future birth rates.

9 We used demographic projections from the UN-DESA's World Population Prospects database. For India, Martens's deaths per 100,000 in China were applied. Since Martens finds generally lower rates in tropical countries, this is likely to be an overestimate for India. For China's mortality in the under-65 group – absent from Martens's results – we inferred an estimate of 1 death per 100,000 population, which appears roughly consistent with his other data. As noted above, the over-65 population is much more important for mortality estimates, and is easier to predict.

10 Bosello et al. use an urbanization scenario taken from Tol (1997), which assumes that the urban share of population will grow to 95 percent by 2200, but does not describe the size of the urban population in 2050. In general terms, the slower the assumed rate of urbanization, the fewer the heat-related deaths in the total population (since such deaths are assumed by Bosello et al. to occur only in urban areas).

Chapter 8. Inside the Integrated Assessment Models: Four Issues in Climate Economics

1 See the Goodess et al. (2003) model classification system, in which AIM and ISGM are both physical impact IAMs.

2 Examples include E3MG and several simulation models.

3 Two climate economics modeling projects published as special issues of the *Energy Journal* were indispensible in preparing this review. The first was organized by the Stanford Energy Modeling Forum (Weyant and Hill 1999) and the second by the Innovation Modeling Comparison Project (Edenhofer et al. 2006b; Grubb et al. 2006; Köhler et al. 2006). For definitions of IAMs and accounts of their development over time, see Goodess et al. (2003), Courtois (2004), Risbey et al. (1996) and Rotmans and Dowlatabadi (1998).

4 A sixth category, macroeconomic models, could be added to this list, although the only example of a pure macroeconomic model being used for climate analysis may be the Oxford Global Macroeconomic and Energy Model (Cooper et al. 1999). Publically available documentation for this model is scarce and somewhat cryptic, perhaps because it was developed by a private consulting firm. Macroeconomic models analyze unemployment, financial markets, international capital flows and monetary policy (or at least some subset of these) (Weyant and Hill 1999). Three general equilibrium or cost minimization models with macroeconomic features are included in this literature review: G-CUBED/MSG3, MIND and MESSAGE-MACRO.

5 In these models, consumption's returns to welfare are always positive but diminish as we grow wealthier. Formally, the first derivative of welfare is always positive and the second is always negative. A popular, though not universal, choice defines individual welfare, arbitrarily, as the logarithm of per capita consumption or income.

6 For a critique of IAMs that focuses on the shortcomings of welfare optimization models, see Courtois (2004).

7 See also DeCanio (2003a).

8 On transparency of value-laden assumptions in IAMs see Schneider (1997), Morgan and Dowlatabadi (1996), Risbey et al. (1996), DeCanio (2003a), Rotmans and Dowlatabadi (1998) and Parson (1996). On transparency of IAMs code and software, see Ha-Duong (2001). For a discussion of how overly complex models can falsely convey model accuracy, see Rotmans and Dowlatabadi (1998).

9 Several discussions of how best to assess IAMs exist in the literature, including Morgan and Dowlatabadi (1996), Risbey et al. (1996) and Rotmans and Dowlatabadi (1998).

10 Numerous reviews of IAMs critique their oversimplification of the physical climate model, the lack of clear standards in interdisciplinary work and the degree to which they lag behind current scientific findings. See Courtois (2004), Hall and Behl (2006), Parson (1996), Risbey et al. (1996) and Rotmans and Dowlatabadi (1998).

11 Morgan and Dowlatabadi (1996) stress the importance of portraying uncertainty in their "hallmarks of good IAMs." For other reviews and general discussions of uncertainty in IAMs, see Scott et al. (1999), Morgan et al. (1999), Warren et al. (2006), Rotmans and Dowlatabadi (1998) and Heal and Kristrom (2002).

12 In more recent work, Weitzman has suggested that climate science implies even greater risks at the 95th–99th percentile (Weitzman 2009). Of course, his argument does not depend on an exact estimate of these risks; the point is that accuracy is unattainable and the risks do not have an obvious upper bound, yet effective policy responses must be informed by those low-probability extreme events.

13 Latin Hypercube sampling, a technical procedure widely used in Monte Carlo analyses, ensures that the selected sets of parameters are equally likely to come from all regions of the relevant parameter space.

14 If the uncertain parameters were all truly independent of each other, such combinations of multiple worst-case values would be extraordinarily unlikely. The danger is that the uncertain parameters, about which our knowledge is limited, may not be independent.

15 For discussions of the problems arising from long time scales in IAMs, see Parson (1996) and Morgan et al. (1999).

16 For a review of damages functions in DICE, RICE, FUND, MERGE and PAGE, see Warren et al. (2006).

17 DICE-2007 actually uses a slightly more complicated equation which is equivalent to our equation (1), with the exponent b= 2, for small damages.
18 See Ackerman et al. (2008) for a more detailed critique of the DICE-2007 damage function.
19 Risbey et al. (1996) refer to this practice as the "whole-sale uncritical adoption of archetype models."
20 Diminishing marginal utility of income is the ubiquitous assumption in neoclassical economics that each new dollar of income brings a little less satisfaction than the last dollar.
21 The terminology of descriptive and prescriptive approaches was introduced and explained in Arrow et al. (1996).
22 If the elasticity of the marginal utility of consumption is a constant, as in Equation (7), and per capita consumption is c, then utility = $c^{(1-\eta)}/(1-\eta)$, except when $\eta = 1$, when utility = ln c. See the Stern Review (Stern 2006), technical annex to Chapter 2 on discounting or other standard works on the subject.
23 The MIND model (Edenhofer et al. 2006a), which combines cost minimization with welfare maximization, uses a pure rate of time preference of 1 percent and a total discount rate of 5 percent.
24 Many models make the implicit assumption that resource availability is infinite and do not explicitly consider resource limitations or resource use efficiency.
25 For examples of how this procedure is discussed in climate economics literature, see Kypreos (2005, 2723), Peck and Teisberg (1998, 3–4) and Yang and Nordhaus (2006, 731–738).
26 The marginal product of capital is the increase in output resulting from the last unit of capital added to the economy. It tends to be higher when capital is scarce, that is, in poorer regions.
27 For an example of the Negishi weights methodology, see Yang and Nordhaus (2006) or Manne and Richels (2004).
28 Earlier versions of PAGE2002, in fact, applied equity weights that boost the relative importance of outcomes in developing countries; the Stern Review modeling effort dropped the equity weights in favor of a more explicit discussion of regional inequality (Chris Hope, personal communication 2008).

Chapter 9. Limitations of Integrated Assessment Models of Climate Change

1 The Lieberman–McCain, Feinstein, Kerry–Snowe and Sanders–Boxer bills specify reductions of 50–80 percent below 1990 emissions levels by 2050. US emissions are now 15 percent above their 1990 levels. A recent MIT assessment of the congressional cap-and-trade proposals estimated net welfare losses ranging up to about 2 percent of GDP by 2050 (Paltsev et al. 2007).
2 Examples of articles dealing with the kinds of issues treated by Hall and Behl (2006) include Kennedy et al. (2008), Hoegh-Guldberg et al. (2007) and Buffett and Archer (2004).
3 One implication of the aggregation method is that if all members of society have equal weight in the social welfare function and all experience diminishing marginal utility to the same degree, the social welfare at any point in time could be increased by redistribution

of income from the wealthy to the poor, provided the effects of this redistribution on incentives to produce and save are ignored. An alternate approach – weighting individuals' contribution to social welfare function by their wealth – has obvious drawbacks from an ethical point of view. The same kinds of problems regarding aggregation across individuals and nations plague estimates of the costs of mitigating climate change – the distribution of the costs has a major impact on both the ethical evaluation of proposed policies and their political feasibility.

4 Or consider the case of equities. Equities have high returns when consumption is high, so the covariance between the equity discount rate and the marginal utility of consumption is negative (because the marginal utility of consumption is lower when consumption is high). Hence the equity discount rate is higher than the risk-free rate because of the negative sign on the covariance term in Eq. 9.6.

5 An expository derivation is given in Mehra (2003).

6 See Ackerman and Heinzerling (2004), especially Chapter 4, 75–81.

7 Some zero-cost adaptations to climate change may also exist. However, the IPCC's *Fourth Assessment Report* notes that "[m]ost studies of specific adaptation plans and actions argue that there are likely to be both limits and barriers to adaptation as a response to climate change. The US National Assessment (2001), for example, maintains that adaptation will not necessarily make the aggregate impacts of climate change negligible or beneficial, nor can it be assumed that all available adaptation measures will actually be taken" (2007b, 733).

8 Ironically, given the subsequent focus on cost–benefit analysis, one of the precursors of current IAMs appeared in a book titled, *Buying Greenhouse Insurance: The Economic Costs of CO_2 Emissions Limits* (Manne and Richels 1992).

9 The "tolerable windows approach" is one promising development in this direction. This methodology "concentrates on a few key attributes (e.g., acceptable impacts and costs) and provides an envelope for future action. Which course should be taken within the envelope?" (Toth et al. 2003, 54–55). A special issue of *Climatic Change* (2003, nos. 1–2; see Toth 2003) contains a number of papers embodying this approach.

Chapter 10. Negishi Welfare Weights in Integrated Assessment Models: The Mathematics of Global Inequality

1 This chapter follows the convention in economics of using the terms "wellbeing," "welfare" and "utility" interchangeably.

2 In these models, consumption's returns to welfare are always positive but diminish as we grow wealthier. Formally, the first derivative of welfare is always positive and the second is always negative. A popular, though not universal, choice defines individual welfare, arbitrarily, as the logarithm of per capita consumption or income.

3 There are several varieties of climate economics models: welfare optimization, general equilibrium, partial equilibrium, simulation and cost minimization models (see Stanton et al. 2009). Only the regionally disaggregated subset of welfare optimization IAMs have a built-in imperative for income equalization across regions and, therefore, only regionally disaggregated welfare optimization IAMs employ Negishi welfare weights to counteract income redistribution.

4 See also Arrow et al. (1996) and Stern (2006, Ch.2).

5 Equalizing the marginal product of capital across regions has an identical impact on regional per capita income as equalizing the marginal utility of income across regions, as suggested by a simple example with a Cobb-Douglas production function:

(10.i) $Y = zK^{-\alpha} L^{1-\alpha}$

(10.ii) $\delta Y / \delta K = \alpha Y / K = \alpha z (L / K)^{1-\alpha}$

(10.iii) $\delta U / \delta Y = (Y / L)^{\wedge}(1-\eta)/((1-\eta)) = [z(L/K)^{\wedge}(-\alpha)]^{\wedge}(1-\eta)/((1-\eta))$

Here Y is gross income, which is a function of capital (K) and labor (L). Equation 10.ii is the shadow price or marginal product of capital. In Equation 10.iii, the marginal utility (U) of income has an elasticity with respect to per capita consumption of η. Both the marginal product of capital and the marginal utility of income depend directly on (L/K). Assuming that the total factor productivity (z), the elasticity of capital (α) and the elasticity of marginal utility with respect to per capita consumption (η) are all constant, equalizing either the marginal product of capital or the marginal utility of income would require the addition of a set of weights (by region and time period) that would have the effect of equalizing the labor–capital ratio.

6 Negishi's social welfare function is defined over individual production and consumption choices, not public goods or public choices, and hence is not comparable to Arrow's (1950) better-known discussion of the impossibility of a useful social welfare function.

7 Pareto optimality requires a solution in which no one can be made better off without making someone else worse off. This concept is explained in greater detail below.

8 See also Nordhaus and Yang (1996, 746).

9 See Chapter 6 of the Stern Review for a discussion of equity weighting.

10 Versions of these ideas were published independently by Willam Stanley Jevons, Carl Menger, Leon Walras and Alfred Marshall, starting in the 1870s. For discussion and analysis of the marginalist revolution in economics see Ackerman (1997) and Cooter and Rappoport (1984).

11 See Chapter 2 in Ackerman and Heinzerling (2004) for a more complete discussion.

12 Note that the criterion of Pareto improvement prohibits any form of redistribution, which must necessarily leave the rich worse off.

13 For an example of a Negishi-weighted model using more explicit assumptions regarding distribution, see DeCanio (2009).

Chapter 11. Climate Risks and Carbon Prices: Revising the Social Cost of Carbon

1 According to the US Environmental Protection Agency, there are 8.8 kg of CO_2 emissions from a gallon of gasoline, implying that 114 gallons of gasoline yield one metric ton of emissions (the standard unit for analysis of emissions); 103 gallons yield one short ton of emissions (see http://www.epa.gov/oms/climate/420f05001.htm, accessed April 22, 2011). Thus a useful rule of thumb is that $1 per ton of CO_2 is equivalent to roughly $0.01 per gallon of gasoline. The estimate in the text of $0.21 per gallon is offered solely for the sake of comparison; there are no existing or proposed federal regulations that would add a carbon charge to the price paid for gasoline.

2 On the implications of low SCC values, see Ackerman and Stanton (2010a).

3   It is new only for US policy; other countries, notably the United Kingdom, are several
    years ahead of the United States in this respect. The US policy process is unfortunately
    parochial, however, so that the introduction of climate economics into American policy
    analysis is presented with almost no reference to other countries' experience.

4   For a description of DICE, see Nordhaus (2008); for PAGE, see Hope (2006a); for
    FUND, see Anthoff and Tol (2009).

5   A lower discount rate increases the importance of events farther in the future, when
    temperatures are higher and catastrophes are more likely. Higher climate sensitivity
    makes higher temperatures and increased risks of catastrophe occur sooner. For these
    reasons, PAGE estimates a larger SCC than DICE at a 2.5 percent discount rate, and
    at 95th percentile climate sensitivity; see Interagency Working Group on Social Cost of
    Carbon (2010), Table 3.

6   IPCC scenario data are from http://sres.ciesin.org/final_data.html, downloaded March
    1, 2011. EMF scenario data are from http://emf.stanford.edu/events/emf_briefing_
    on_climate_policy_scenarios_us_domestic_and_international_policy_architectures,
    downloaded February 15, 2011.

7   Figure 11.1 presents cumulative emissions because CO_2 persists in the atmosphere
    for long periods of time; Figure 11.2 presents current emissions because methane is
    removed from the atmosphere much more quickly.

8   Hanemann compares his calculations to an earlier version of DICE; Hanemann's
    estimate is 4.0 times the DICE-99 estimate, or 2.4 times the DICE-07 estimate, of
    damages at 2.5°C.

9   Nordhaus presents some numerical estimates of damages at 6°C, suggesting they are
    between 8 and 11 percent of output (Nordhaus 2007a); these estimates are not well
    documented, and do not appear to be used in the calibration of DICE.

10 This equation follows Weitzman's method but differs slightly from his numerical
    estimates. He appears to have taken the DICE coefficient in (11.1) to be .00239 rather
    than .002839. Our equations (11.4) and (11.4) were fitted to minimize the sum of
    squared deviations from the Nordhaus and Hanemann damage estimates, respectively,
    at 2.5°C, and the Weitzman point estimates at 6°C and 12°C.

11 A small anomaly is that between 6°C and 12°C the N–W damage function, despite
    its lower low-temperature damages, is slightly higher than H–W; the gap is widest at
    6.9°C, where N–W damages are 1.5 percent above H–W.

12 Since World War II, real returns have averaged 1.4 percent per year on Treasury bills
    and 1.1 percent on government bonds (DeLong and Magin 2009).

13 The EMF scenarios adopted by the Working Group have variable rates of growth
    by region and time period throughout the scenarios. Using Stern's formula, or any
    version of the prescriptive approach, this should call for a time-varying, often declining
    discount rate. We follow the Working Group's practice of using a fixed discount rate,
    for the sake of comparability with their results and minimization of changes to their
    version of the DICE model.

14 Thanks to Steve Newbold for making the Working Group's modified version of DICE
    available for independent analysis. We used the Working Group's DICE code, written
    in MatLab, with no modifications other than those described in this chapter.

15 See Edenhofer et al. (2010a); Kitous et al. (2010); Magne et al. (2010); Leimbach et al.
    (2010); Barker and Scrieciu (2010); and van Vuuren et al. (2010).

16 All dollar figures for abatement costs in this section are in 2005 dollars, roughly comparable to our SCC estimates in 2007 dollars; US consumer prices increased 6 percent from 2005 to 2007.

17 Data downloaded from http://www.iiasa.ac.at/web-apps/tnt/RcpDb, accessed December 2011.

18 DICE uses an estimate of non-CO_2 forcings to capture the climate impacts of all greenhouse gases other than CO_2.

19 These SCC values bear an even closer resemblance to the concept of "machine infinity" in computer science, i.e., the largest number that a computer can represent. Doubling machine infinity cannot increase it (within that computer), but dividing by two decreases it. The same is true for the practical significance of an SCC estimate, which is, for instance, 1.5 times the marginal cost of maximum feasible abatement.

Chapter 12. Epstein–Zin Utility in DICE: Is Risk Aversion Irrelevant to Climate Policy?

1 If g is normally distributed with variance σ^2, and the CRRA utility function (12.2) is assumed to apply, then (12.1) becomes $r = \delta + \eta g - 1/2 \eta^2 \sigma^2$ (see, e.g., Ackerman et al. 2009a).

2 When $\eta = 1$, (12.2) is replaced by $u(c) = \ln c$ – which is the limit of (12.2) as η approaches 1.

3 It is theoretically possible to simultaneously model strong risk aversion with a large η, and strong future orientation with a negative δ – but it is difficult to develop a plausible argument for $\delta < 0$.

4 The symbols α, β and ρ are introduced solely in order to make (12.3) and (12.4) as transparent as possible; as explained in the text, they are simple transformations of, respectively, γ (coefficient of relative risk aversion), δ (rate of pure time preference) and ψ (intertemporal elasticity of substitution).

5 DICE, developed by Nordhaus, is described in Nordhaus (2008).

6 If precise, noise-free measurements were possible – as the simple, deterministic treatment of climate variables in DICE may suggest – then it would be possible to calculate the value of climate sensitivity much sooner. In reality, precision is difficult to achieve: both year-to-year climate variability and the positive feedback nature of the relevant climate dynamics lead to great uncertainty in estimates of climate sensitivity (Roe and Baker 2007).

7 See Roe and Baker (2007), Figure 4B.

8 For example, the real rate of return on US treasury bonds has averaged 1.1 percent since World War II (DeLong and Magin 2009).

9 The risk-free rate is calculated using Equation 12.1, with $g = .013$; in Table 3, we assume $\eta = 1/\psi$. The calculation of the implied equity premium is more complex and requires information beyond the scope of our results.

10 Nordhaus (2008) uses DICE to find a SCC of $30 per tonne of carbon emissions in "today's prices," equivalent to $8 per tonne of CO_2; adjusted to the 2010 prices used in this chapter, this would be $9 or $10 per tonne of CO_2. The year of emissions for the Nordhaus calculation is not specified, but is likely earlier than 2015, which would tend to make the SCC lower than our value.

11 The same reduction in the DICE discount rate can be achieved with many combinations of δ and η – with similar results.

Chapter 13. Fat Tails, Exponents, Extreme Uncertainty: Simulating Catastrophe in DICE

1 Climate damages result not only from increasing temperatures, but also from other physical changes such as rising sea levels, changes in precipitation and increasing frequency of extreme weather events. Since these are all broadly correlated, growing more intense as greenhouse gas concentrations and temperatures rise, we use temperature as an index of the severity of the physical impacts of climate change in general.

2 The supporting documentation for DICE-2007 also offers an estimate that climate damages at 6 °C would amount to a mere 8.23 percent of world output, but this number is barely explained, and the final form of the damage function does not appear to rely on it (Nordhaus 2007a, 24).

3 For use in DICE, the relevant estimate is Weitzman's S1, the direct effect without the longer-term, indirect feedback; Weitzman argues that the ultimate effect S2 is roughly twice as large. The technical case for a long-term climate sensitivity twice as large as the IPCC estimates is discussed, for instance, in Hansen et al. (2008).

4 The curve was fitted to minimize the sum of squared errors at the six point estimates shown in Figure 13.1.

5 For a demonstration, in a very simple climate model, that a lognormal probability distribution for climate sensitivity implies the "Weitzman property" of infinite expected willingness to pay for reduction in climate risk, see Newbold and Daigneault (2009). As that article makes clear, there are a variety of possible distributions, some with much "fatter" tails than the lognormal; the choice of probability distributions can be significant for analysis of extreme values.

6 The documentation for the latest version of DICE contains only a brief, cryptic statement that an unspecified elasticity calculation supported the choice of exponent. For an earlier version of DICE, Nordhaus and Boyer (2000, 89–95) propose different functional forms for individual categories of damages such as health impacts, sea level rise and agricultural losses; some are assumed to be quadratic functions of temperature and others are not. Little is said there to support the specific assumptions for the individual damage categories, and nothing is said to support the assumption that the aggregate damages are a quadratic function of temperature.

7 @RISK v4.5 (2005), Palisade Corporation, Ithaca, NY, http://www.palisade.com. Accessed 28 June 2013.

8 We found that DICE behaves erratically with a climate sensitivity parameter below about 0.6. Therefore we rounded all climate sensitivity estimates between 0 and 1 up to 1. This affects a very small fraction of the samples: the probability that the climate sensitivity parameter is less than 0.5 (so that it would not naturally round to 1) is 0.0004.

9 In the standard IAM formulation, if C is per capita consumption and $\eta > 1$ is the income elasticity of the marginal utility of consumption, then welfare is proportional to $-C^{1-\eta}$. DICE-2007 assumes $\eta = 2$, implying that welfare is proportional to $-C^{-1}$. Since the units of welfare are arbitrary, DICE applies an affine transformation, reporting welfare $= a - bC^{-1}$.

10 A parallel calculation using the Stern Review's discount rate yielded qualitatively similar, although quantitatively different, results. For simplicity of exposition, only the results with the DICE discount rate are presented here.

11 An artifact of our calculations is that, for $N > 2$, damages are lower and incomes are higher than in the DICE base case until the temperature increase reaches 1°C (see Eq. 12.2). So for high exponents, initial damages are lower and initial consumption

is higher than in the DICE defaults. Initial per capita consumption levels range from about $6,600 to $7,000 across our grid of DICE runs.

12 The perspective is the same in all three graphs: the viewer is looking toward the origin (which is hidden behind the graphed surface) from a point high in the positive orthant – i.e., from a high, positive value for all three-axis variables.

Chapter 14. Climate Damages in the FUND Model: A Disaggregated Analysis

1 "Central estimate," the Working Group's terminology, refers to the estimate of the SCC under assumptions made in the Working Group analysis, including a fixed 3 percent discount rate, other specified inputs and a set of five scenarios, the results of which are averaged. Results at the 5 percent and 2.5 percent discount rates, also used by the Working Group, are qualitatively similar, and are omitted from this chapter to simplify the presentation.

2 Thanks to David Anthoff for providing the FUND files, and for assistance in getting FUND running on our computers. He is, of course, not responsible for any statements about FUND made in this chapter.

3 There are 73 Monte Carlo variables in FUND (listed in the FUND 3.5 data tables, available at http://www.fund-model.org/. Accessed 28 June 2013.). Of these, 63 are assumed to have normal distributions –12 unconstrained, and 51 truncated at zero (i.e., restricted to only positive, or only negative values). The remaining variables include 5 with triangular distributions, 3 with exponential distributions and 2 with gamma distributions. For the truncated normal distributions, the mean of the underlying normal is the mode of the truncated distribution. The mode is not defined for the exponential distribution; for these 3 variables, which have small effects in practice, the "best-guess" value may be the mean.

4 PAGE has a more complex treatment of damages than DICE, making it difficult to repeat the same experiment with the PAGE damage function.

5 "Assessment of Current FUND Modeling, by Sector," Memorandum to Stephanie Waldhoff, US Environmental Protection Agency, by Joel Smith, Karen Carney, Charles Rodgers, et al., May 1, 2009. A copy is on file with the authors (confirmed to be in the public domain by personal communication from Stephanie Waldhoff, April 2011).

6 In Figures 14.1 and 14.2, the components of the SCC add up precisely to the total; in Figure 14.3, the subcategories of agricultural impacts do not add up to the total for agriculture. FUND limits each region's total agricultural impacts to being no greater than the contribution of agriculture to the region's GDP. This constraint is not binding in the best-guess run, but it is in some of the Monte Carlo iterations. In the presence of this constraint, the impacts of the individual agricultural effects do not sum to the total agricultural impact. Thus the best-guess estimates for the three agricultural effects sum to the total agricultural best-guess value, but the same is not true of the Monte Carlo estimates. The difference, however, is only about $1.

7 Personal communication, David Anthoff, December 2010.

8 We implemented this change by setting the standard deviation of $T^{\theta\rho\prime}$ to zero for every region in the FUND data file.

9 Personal communication, David Anthoff, December 2010.

10 For a recent review of new developments in climate science and economics that should inform models such as FUND, see Ackerman and Stanton (2011a).

Chapter 15. Climate Policy and Development: An Economic Analysis

1 A region's utility is the log of its average per capita consumption, multiplied by regional population. Global utility is the sum of regional utilities; CRED maximizes the present value of global utility over the 300-year span of its scenarios. This is well within the range of corresponding assumptions in other integrated assessment models – it is a standard assumption, though it will be shown to have nonstandard implications.

2 If utility is u(c) = ln c, then marginal utility u'(c) = 1/c, a declining function of c.

3 CRED uses market exchange rates throughout, in order to facilitate calculation of inter-regional resource flows, discussed below.

4 The rate of pure time preference is the discount rate that would apply if all generations were equally wealthy, or equivalently, the discount rate that applies to utility rather than to monetary values. In CRED the discount rate for monetary values would be the rate of pure time preference plus the rate of growth of per capita consumption (although the only discounting that occurs in CRED is in the utility function).

5 In the DICE damage function, the ratio (output net of climate damages/gross output without damages) can be written as $1 / [1 + (T / 18.8)^2]$, where T is temperature increase since 1900 in °C. In the HW damage function, the same ratio is $1 / [1 + (T / 12.2)^2 + (T / 6.24)^{7.02}]$. The seventh-power term in the HW function is insignificant when T is much less than 6.24, but quickly becomes large as T rises above that level.

6 CRED scenarios are calculated over 300 years; results for the last 100 years are discarded to avoid end effects.

7 The climate module in CRED v1.4 has been recalibrated to reflect recent research demonstrating that temperatures will not fall significantly for centuries in response to the post-peak decline in carbon dioxide emissions (Matthews and Caldeira 2008). The modest declines seen here result from the reduction in non-CO_2 greenhouse gases.

8 The one exception: with no resource transfers from other regions, low-income region emissions do not quite reach zero, but average less than 20 percent of the 2010 level throughout the 22nd century.

Appendix. Supplementary Data for Chapter 3

1 OECD members include most high income countries: Australia, Austria, Belguim, Canada, Chile, Czech Republic, Denmark, Estonia, Finland, France, Germany, Hungary, Iceland, Ireland, Israel, Italy, Japan, Korea, Luxembourg, Mexico, Netherlands, New Zealand, Norway, Poland, Portugal, Slovak Republic, Slovenia, Spain, Sweden, Switzerland, Turkey, United Kingdom and United States. See http://www.oecd.org. Accessed 28 June 2013.

2 Growth rates for Eastern Europe not including Russia, Asia not including China and India and Latin America not including Brazil were calculated as the residual of each region, based on WEO 2010 real GDP (PPP) projections and World Bank 2008 real GDP (PPP 2005 US$), from the *World DataBank*, http://databank.worldbank.org/ddp/home.do?Step=3&id=4. Accessed 28 June 2013.

3 UN-DESA "World Population Prospects: The 2010 Revision," (2011). http://www.un.org/en/development/desa/publications/world-population-prospects-the-2010-revision.html. Accessed 28 June 2013.

4 SRES storylines: http://sedac.ciesin.columbia.edu/ddc/sres/. Accessed 28 June 2013.

5 For a detailed explanation of the UNDESA's new methodology, see UNDESA (2011).

REFERENCES

Abernathy W. J. and K. Wayne. 1974. "Limits of the Learning Curve." *Harvard Business Review* 52, no. 4: 109–119.

Ackerman F. 1997. "Utility and Welfare I: The History of Economic Thought." In F. Ackerman, D. Kiron, N. R. Goodwin, J. M. Harris, K. Gallagher (eds). *Human Well-Being and Economic Goals*. Washington, DC: Island Press.

_____. 2002. "Still Dead after All These Years: Interpreting the Failure of General Equilibrium Theory." *Journal of Economic Methodology* 9, no. 2: 119–39.

_____. 2008a. *Can We Afford the Future? Economics for a Warming World*. London: Zed Books.

_____. 2008b. *Poisoned for Pennies: The Economics of Toxics and Precaution*. Washington, DC: Island Press.

_____. 2008c. "The New Climate Economics: The Stern Review Versus Its Critics." In J. M. Harris and N. R. Goodwin (eds). *Twenty-First Century Macroeconomics: Responding to the Climate Challenge*. Cheltenham, UK: Edward Elgar Publishing, 32–57.

_____. 2009. "Can We Afford the Future?" in *Economics for a Warming World*. London, UK: Zed Books.

Ackerman F., S. J. DeCanio, R. B. Howarth and K. Sheeran. 2009a. "Limitations of Integrated Assessment Models of Climate Change." *Climate Change* 95, nos. 3–4: 297–315.

Ackerman F. and I. Finlayson. 2006. "The Economics of Inaction on Climate Change: A Sensitivity Analysis." *Climate Policy* 6, no. 5: 509–526.

Ackerman F. and L. Heinzerling. 2004. *Priceless: On Knowing the Price of Everything and the Value of Nothing*. New York: New Press.

Ackerman F., R. Kozul-Wright and R. Vos (eds). 2012. *Climate Protection and Development*. London: Bloomsbury Academic.

Ackerman F. and C. Munitz. 2012. "Climate Damages in the FUND Model: A Disaggregated Analysis." *Ecological Economics* 77: 219–24.

Ackerman F. and E. A. Stanton. 2008. "Climate Change and the US Economy: The Costs of Inaction." Medford, MA: Tufts University Global Development and Environment Institute and Stockholm Environment Institute-US Center.

_____. 2010a. "The Social Cost of Carbon." Somerville, MA: Stockholm Environment Institute-US Center. Online: http://sei-us.org/publications/id/194 (accessed on 28 June 2013).

_____. 2010b. *Testimony on EPA's "Coal Combustion Residuals: Proposed Rule."* Somerville, MA: Stockholm Environment Institute-US Center.

_____. 2011a. *Climate Economics: The State of the Art*; Somerville, MA: Stockholm Environment Institute-US Center.

_____. 2011b. *Regulation of Cooling Water Intake Structures at Existing Facilities*. Testimony to the US Environmental Protection Agency, Docket ID EPA-HQ-OW-2008-0667.

_____. 2011c. "The Last Drop: Climate Change and the Southwest Water Crisis." Somerville, MA: Stockholm Environment Institute-US Center. Online: http://sei-us. org/publications/id/371 (accessed on 28 June 2013).

_____. 2012a. *Climate Economics: The State of the Art,* London: Routledge.

_____. 2012b. "Climate Risks and Carbon Prices: Revising the Social Cost of Carbon." *Economics: The Open-Access, Open Assessment E-Journal* 62.

_____. 2013. *Climate Economics: The State of the Art.* London: Routledge.

Ackerman F., E. A. Stanton and R. Bueno. 2008. "Fat Tails, Exponents and Extreme Uncertainty: Simulating Catastrophe in DICE." Working Paper WP-0901, Stockholm Environment Institute, US Center.

_____. 2011. "CRED V.1.3 Technical Report." Somerville, MA: Stockholm Environment Institute-US Center. Online: http://sei-us.org/publications/id/411S (accessed on 28 June 2013).

_____. 2013. "CRED: A New Model of Climate and Development." *Ecological Economics* 85: 167–76.

Ackerman F., E. A. Stanton, C. Hope and S. Alberth. 2009b. "Did the Stern Review Underestimate US and Global Climate Damages?" *Energy Policy* 37: 2717–21.

Agarwal A. and S. Narain 1991. *Global Warming in an Unequal World: A Case of Environmental Colonialism.* New Delhi, India: Centre for Science and the Environment.

Ainsworth E. A., A. D. B. Leakey, D. R. Ort and S. P. Long. 2008. "FACE-ing the Facts: Inconsistencies and Interdependence Among Field, Chamber and Modeling Studies of Elevated CO_2 Impacts on Crop Yield and Food Supply." *New Phytologist* 179, no. 1: 5–9.

Ainsworth E. A. and J. M. McGrath. 2010. "Direct Effects of Rising Atmospheric Carbon Dioxide and Ozone on Crop Yields." *Climate Change and Food Security Advances in Global Change Research* 37, part II: 109–30.

Alberth S. and C. Hope. 2007. "Climate Modelling with Endogenous Technical Change: Stochastic Learning and Optimal Greenhouse Gas Abatement in the PAGE2002 Model." *Energy Policy* 35, no. 3: 1795–1807.

Alesina A. and D. Rodrik. 1994. "Distributive Politics and Economic Growth." *Quarterly Journal of Economics* 109: 465–90.

Allen M. R., D. J. Frame, C. Huntingford, C. D. Jones, J. A. Lowe, M. Meinshausen and N. Meinshausen. 2009. "Warming Caused by Cumulative Carbon Emissions towards the Trillionth Tonne." *Nature* 458: 1163–66.

Amano A. 1997. "On Some Integrated Assessment Modeling Debates." Paper presented at IPCC Asia-Pacific Workshop on Integrated Assessment Models, United Nations University, Tokyo, March: 10–12.

Ananthapadmanabhan G., K. Srinivas and V. Gopal. 2007. *Hiding Behind the Poor.* Bangalore, India: Greenpeace India Society.

Anthoff D. and R. S. J. Tol. 2007. "On International Equity Weights and National Decision Making on Climate Change." Milan, Fondazione Eni Enrico Mattei Working Papers. Online: http://www.bepress.com/feem/paper65 (accessed on 28 June 2013).

_____. 2009. "The Impact of Climate Change on the Balanced Growth Equivalent: An Application of FUND." *Environmental and Resource Economics* 43, no. 3: 351–67.

Arrow K. J. 1950. "A Difficulty in the Concept of Social Welfare." *Journal of Political Economy* 58, no. 4: 328–46

_____. 2002. "Distributed Information and the Role of the State in the Economy." In *Inequality Around the World.* London: Palgrave.

Arrow K., S. Bowles and S. N. Durlauf. 2000. *Meritocracy and Economic Inequality.* Princeton, NJ: Princeton University Press.

Arrow K., W. R. Cline, K. G. Maler, M. Munasinghe, R. Squitieri and J. E. Stiglitz. 1996. "Chapter 4 – Intertemporal Equity, Discounting, and Economic Efficiency." In J. P. Bruce, H. Lee and E. F. Haites (eds). *Climate Change 1995 – Economic and Social Dimensions of Climate Change.* Contribution of Working Group III to the Second Assessment Report of the IPCC. New York: IPCC and Cambridge University Press: 125–44. Online: http://www2.gsb.columbia.edu/faculty/jstiglitz/download/papers/1996_Intertemporal_Equity.pdf (accessed on 28 June 2013).

Arrow K. J. and G. Debreu. 1954. "Existence of an Equilibrium for a Competitive Economy." *Econometrica* 22, no. 3: 265–90.

Arrow K., R. Solow, P. R. Portney, E. E. Leamer, R. Radner and H. Schuman. 1993. "Report of the NOAA Panel on Contingent Valuation." Washington, DC: 58 Federal Register 4601.

Arthur B. 1994. Increasing Returns and Path Dependence in the Economy." Ann Arbor, MI: University of Michigan Press.

Atkinson G., S. Dietz, J. Helgeson, C. Hepburn and H. Sælen. 2009. "Siblings, Not Triplets: Social Preferences for Risk, Inequality and Time in Discounting Climate Change." *Economics E-Journal* 3: 2009–2026.

Auffhammer M., V. Ramanathan and J. R. Vincent. 2011. "Climate Change, the Monsoon, and Rice Yield in India." *Climatic Change* 111, no. 2: 411–24.

Azar C. 1999. "Weight Factors in Cost–Benefit Analysis of Climate Change." *Environmental and Resource Economics* 13, no. 3: 249–68.

Babiker M., A. Gurgel, S. Paltsev and J. Reilly. 2008. "A Forward Looking Version of the MIT Emissions Prediction and Policy Analysis (EPPA) Model." MIT Joint Program on the Science and Policy of Global Change, Report No. 161.

Bacon R. W. and S. Bhattacharya. 2007. "Growth and CO2 Emissions: How Do Different Countries Fare? World Bank Environment Department." Washington, DC: World Bank.

Baer P. 2007. "The Worth of an Ice-Sheet: A Critique of the Treatment of Catastrophic Impacts in the Stern Review." *EcoEquity.* Online: http://www.ecoequity.org (accessed on 28 June 2013).

Baer P., T. Athanasiou and S. Kartha. 2007. *The Right to Development in a Climate Constrained World.* Berlin: Heinrich Böll Foundation.

Baer P., T. Athanasiou, S. Kartha, E. Kemp-Benedict. 2008. *The Greenhouse Development Rights Framework: The Right to Development in a Climate Constrained World.* Berlin: Heinrich Böll Foundation, Christian Aid, EcoEquity and Stockholm Environment Institute.

Baer P. and M. Mastrandrea. 2006. "High Stakes: Designing Emissions Pathways to Reduce the Risk of Dangerous Climate Change." *London: Institute for Public Policy Research.* Online: http://www.ippr.org (accessed on 28 June 2013).

Baer P. and P. Templet. 2001. "GLEAM: A Simple Model for the Analysis of Equity in Policies to Regulate Greenhouse Gas Emissions Through Tradable Permits." In M. Munasinghe, O. Sunkel, C. de Miguel (eds). *The Sustainability of Long-Term Growth: Socioeconomic and Ecological Perspectives.* Cheltenham: Edward Elgar Publishing.

Banerjee A. V. and E. Duflo. 2003. "Inequality and Growth: What Can the Data Say?" *Journal of Economic Growth* 8: 267–99.

Bansal R. and A. Yaron. 2004. "Risks for the Long Run: A Potential Resolution of Asset Pricing Puzzles." *The Journal of Finance* 59: 1481–1509.

Barker T., H. Pan, J. Köhler, R. Warren and S. Winne. 2006. "Decarbonizing the Global Economy with Induced Technological Change: Scenarios to 2100 Using E3MG." *Energy Journal* Special Issue on Endogenous Technological Change and the Economics of Atmospheric Stabilisation: 241–58.

Barker T. and S. Scrieciu. 2010. "Modeling Low Climate Stabilization with E3MG: Towards a 'New Economics' Approach to Simulating Energy-Environment-Economy System Dynamics." *Energy Journal* 31 Special Issue 1: 137–64. Online: http://econpapers.repec. org/article/aenjournl/ 2010se1_5flow_5fstabilization-a06.htm. (accessed on 28 June 2013).

Barnes P. 2006. *Capitalism 3.0: A Guide to Reclaiming the Commons.* San Francisco: Berrett-Koehler Publishers.

Barnett T. P., J. C. Adam and D. P. Lettenmaier. 2005. "Potential Impacts of a Warming Climate on Water Availability in Snow-Dominated Regions." *Nature* 438: 303–309.

Barnett T. P., D. W. Pierce, H. G. Hidalgo, et al. 2008. "Human-Induced Changes in the Hydrology of the Western United States." *Science* 319, no. 5866: 1080–83.

Barro R. J. 2000. "Inequality and Growth in a Panel of Countries." *Journal of Economic Growth* 5: 5–32.

Beckman S. R., J. P. Formby and W. J. Smith. 2004. "Efficiency, Equity and Democracy: Experimental Evidence on Okun's Leaky Bucket." *Research on Economic Inequality* 11: 17–42.

Bella G. 2006. "A Blueprint for Optimal Intertemporal Consumption Under Environmental Constraints: the Modified Green Golden Rule." Online: http://ssrn. com/abstract=936879. (accessed on 28 June 2013).

Bentham J. 1970 (1789). *Introduction to the Principles of Morals.* London: Athlone.

Bernstein M. A. and J. Griffin. 2006. "Regional Differences in the Price-Elasticity of Demand for Energy." Santa Monica, CA: RAND Corporation.

Bernstein P. M., W. D. Montgomery, T. F. Rutherford and G. F. Yang. 1999. "Effects of Restrictions on International Permit Trading: the MS-MRT Model." *Energy Journal,* Special Issue on the Costs of the Kyoto Protocol: A Multi-Model Evaluation: 221–56.

Bhagwati J. 1958. "Immiserizing Growth: A Geometrical Note." *The Review of Economic Studies* 25: 201–205.

_____. 1968. "Distortions and Immiserizing Growth: A Generalization." *The Review of Economic Studies* 35: 481–5.

Biasutti M. and A. H. Sobel. 2009. "Delayed Sahel Rainfall and Global Seasonal Cycle in a Warmer Climate." *Geophysical Research Letters* 36, no. 23.

Bosello F., R. Roson and R. Tol. 2006. "Economy-Wide Estimates of the Implications of Climate Change: Human Health." *Ecological Economics* 58, no. 3: 579–91.

Bosetti V., C. Carraro and M. Galeotti. 2006. "The Dynamics of Carbon and Energy Intensity in a Model of Endogenous Technical Change." *Energy Journal* Special Issue on Endogenous Technological Change and the Economics of Atmospheric Stabilisation: 191–206.

Botzen W. J. W., J. M. Gowdy and J. C. J. M. Van Den Bergh. 2008. "Cumulative CO_2 Emissions: Shifting International Responsibilities for Climate Debt." *Climate Policy* 8: 569–76.

Bourguignon F. and C. Morrisson. 2002. "Inequality Among World Citizens: 1820–1992." *American Economic Review* 92: 727–44.

Bowen A. and N. Ranger. 2009. "Mitigating Climate Change through Reductions in Greenhouse Gas Emissions: The Science and Economics of Future Paths for Global

Annual Emissions." Policy Brief. London, UK: Grantham Research Institute on Climate Change and the Environment, and Centre for Climate Change Economics and Policy.

Boyce J. K. 1994. "Inequality as a Cause of Environmental Degradation." *Ecological Economics* 11: 169–78.

_____. 2002. *Political Economy of the Environment*. Northampton, MA: Edward Elgar.

_____. 2003. "From Natural Resources to Natural Assets." In J. K. Boyce, B. G. Shelley (eds). *Natural Assets: Democratizing Environmental Ownership*. Washington, DC: Island Press.

Boyce J. K., S. Narain and E. A. Stanton. 2007. *Reclaiming Nature: Environmental Justice and Ecological Restoration*. 1st ed. London: Anthem Press.

Boyce J. K. and M. Riddle. 2009. *Cap and Dividend: A State-by-State Analysis*. Amherst, MA: Political Economy Research Institute.

Broome J. 1994. "Discounting the Future." *Philosophy and Public Affairs* 23: 128–56.

Brücker F. 2005. "Vulnerable Populations: Lessons Learnt from the Summer 2003 Heat Waves in Europe." *Eurosurveillance* 10, nos. 7–9: 147.

Buchholz W. and M. Schymura. 2012. "Expected Utility Theory and the Tyranny of Catastrophic Risks." *Ecological Economics* 77: 234–39.

Bueno de Mesquita B. 2002. *Predicting Politics*. 1st ed. Columbus, OH: Ohio State University Press.

Buffett B. and D. Archer. 2004. "Global Inventory of Methane Clathrate: Sensitivity to Changes in the Deep Ocean." *Earth Planetary Science Letters* 227: 185–99.

Byatt I., I. Castles, I. M. Goklany, D. Henderson, N. Lawson, R. McKitrick, J. Morris, A. Peacock, C. Robinson and R. Skidelsky. 2006. "The Stern Review: A Dual Critique—Part II: Economic Aspects." *World Economics* 7, no. 4: 199–229.

Campbell J. Y. 2003. "Consumption-Based Asset Pricing." In G. M. Constantinides, M. Harris and R. Stultz (eds). *Handbook of the Economics of Finance*. Amsterdam: Elsevier: 804–887.

Campbell-Lendrum D. H., C. F. Corvalan and A. Prüss-Ustün. 2003. "How Much Disease Could Climate Change Cause?" In A. J. McMichael, D. H. Campbell-Lendrum, C. F. Corvalan, et al. (eds). *Climate Change and Human Health: Risks and Responses*. Geneva: World Health Organization.

Capoor K. and P. Ambrosi. 2008. "State and Trends of the Carbon Market 2008." Washington, DC: World Bank.

Carraro C., R. Gerlagh and B. van der Zwaan. 2003. "Endogenous Technical Change in Environmental Macroeconomics." *Resource and Energy Economics* 25: 1–10.

Cass D. 1965. "Optimum Growth in an Aggregative Model of Capital Accumulation." *The Review of Economic Studies* 32: 233.

Champernowne D. G. and F. A. Cowell. 1999. *Economic Inequality and Income Distribution*. Cambridge: Cambridge University Press.

Chichilnisky G. 2000. "An Axiomatic Approach to Choice under Uncertainty with Catastrophic Risks." *Resource and Energy Economics* 22: 221–31.

Chichilnisky G. and G. Heal. 1994. "Who Should Abate Carbon Emissions? An International Viewpoint." *Economic Letters* 44: 443–49.

Chichilnisky G., G. Heal and A. Beltratti. 1995. "The Green Golden Rule." *Economics Letters* 49: 175–79.

Christensen N. S. and D. P. Lettenmaier. 2007. "A Multimodel Ensemble Approach to Assessment of Climate Change Impacts on the Hydrology and Water Resources of the Colorado River Basin." *Hydrology and Earth System Sciences Discussions* 11, no. 4: 1417–34.

Chu J. T., J. Xia, C. Y. Xu and V. P. Singh. 2009. "Statistical Downscaling of Daily Mean Temperature, Pan Evaporation and Precipitation for Climate Change Scenarios in Haihe River, China." *Theoretical and Applied Climatology* 99, no. 1–2: 149–61.

Ciscar J. C., A. Iglesias, L. Feyen, et al. 2011. "Physical and Economic Consequences of Climate Change in Europe." *Proceedings of the National Academy of Sciences* 108, no. 7: 2678–83.

Clarke L., J. Edmonds, V. Krey, R. Richels, S. Rose and M. Tavoni. 2009. "International Climate Policy Architectures: Overview of the EMF 22 International Scenarios." *Energy Economics* 31. Online: http://emf.stanford.edu/files/res/2369/EMF22OverviewClarke. pdf (accessed on 28 June 2013).

Clarke L., M. Wise, S. Kim, S. Smith, J. Lurz, J. Edmonds and H. Pitcher. 2007. "Model Documentation for the MiniCAM Climate Change Science Program Stabilization Scenarios: CCSP Product 2.1a." *Report for the US Department of Energy under Contract DE-AC05-76RL01830*, Pacific Northwest National Laboratory, PNNL-16735.

Cline W. R. 1992. "The Economics of Global Warming." Washington, DC: Institute of International Affairs.

———. 2004. "Meeting the Challenge of Global Warming." In B. Lomborg (ed). *Global Crises, Global Solutions*. Cambridge: Cambridge University Press.

———. 2007. "Global Warming and Agriculture: Impact Estimates by Country." Washington, DC: Center for Global Development & Peterson Institute for International Economics. Online: http://www.cgdev.org/content/publications/detail/14090 (accessed on 28 June 2013).

Coase R. H. 1960. "The Problem of Social Cost." *The Journal of Law & Economics* 3: 1–44.

———. 1991. "The Institutional Structure of Production." *Nobel Prize Lecture*. Online: http://www.nobelprize.org/nobel_prizes/economics/laureates/1991/coase-lecture. html (accessed on 1 December 2011).

Cochrane J. H. 2005. *Asset Pricing*, revised edition. Princeton, NJ: Princeton University Press.

Committee on Abrupt Climate Change, National Research Council. 2002. "Abrupt Climate Change: Inevitable Surprises." Washington, DC: National Academies.

Committee on Analysis of Global Change Assessments, National Research Council. 2007. *Analysis of Global Change Assessments: Lessons Learned*. Washington, DC: National Academies.

Cooper A., S. Livermore, V. Rossi, A. Wilson and J. Walker. 1999. "The Economic Implications of Reducing Carbon Emissions: A Cross-Country Quantitative Investigation Using the Oxford Global Macro-Economic and Energy Model." *Energy Journal* Special Issue on the Costs of the Kyoto Protocol: A MultiModel Evaluation: 335–65.

Cooper J. C. B. 2003. "Price Elasticity of Demand for Crude Oil: Estimates for 23 Countries." *OPEC Review* 27: 1–8.

Cooter R. and P. Rappoport. 1984. "Were the Ordinalists Wrong about Welfare Economics?" *Journal of Economic Literature* XXII: 507–30.

Coudouel A., J. S. Hentschel and Q. T. Wodon. 2002. "Poverty Measurement and Analysis." In J. Klugman (ed.). *A Sourcebook for Poverty Reduction Strategies*. Washington, DC: World Bank.

Courtois P. 2004. "The Status of Integrated Assessment in Climatic Policy Making: An Overview of Inconsistencies Underlying Response Functions." *Environmental Science & Policy* 7, no. 1: 69–75.

Crassous R., J. C. Hourcade and O. Sassi. 2006. "Endogenous Structural Change and Climate Targets Modeling Experiments With Imaclim-R." *Energy Journal,* Special Issue on Endogenous Technological Change and the Economics of Atmospheric Stabilisation: 259–76.

Creyts J., A. Derkach, S. Nyquist, K. Ostrowski and J. Stephenson. 2007. *Reducing US Greenhouse Gas Emissions: How Much at What Cost?* New York: McKinsey & Co.: December.

Crost B. and C. Traeger. 2010. "Risk and Aversion in the Integrated Assessment of Climate Change." University of California eScholarship. Online: http://escholarship.org/uc/item/1562s275 (accessed on 28 June 2013).

Curriero F. C., K. S. Heiner, J. M. Samet, S. L. Zeger, L. Strug, J. A. Patz. 2002. "Temperature and Mortality in 11 cities of the Eastern United States." *American Journal of Epidemiology* 155, no. 1: 80–87.

Dasgupta P. 2008. "Discounting Climate Change." *Journal of Risk and Uncertainty* 37: 141–69.

Dasgupta P. and G. M. Heal. 1979. "Economic Theory and Exhaustible Resources." Cambridge: Cambridge University Press.

Dasgupta P., K. G. Mäler, S. Barrett. 1999. "Intergenerational Equity, Social Discount Rates, and Global Warming." In P. R. Portney and J. P. Weyant (eds). *Discounting and Intergenerational Equity.* Washington, DC: Resources for the Future: 51–78.

Dasgupta S., B. Laplante, H. Wang and D. Wheeler. 2002. "Confronting the Environmental Kuznets Curve." *Journal of Economic Perspectives* 16: 147–68.

David P. 1985. "Clio and the Economics of QWERTY." *American Economic Review* 75: 332–37.

De U. S., R. K. Dube, G. S. Prakasa Rao. 2005. "Extreme Weather Events over India in the Last 100 Years." *Journal of the Indian Geophysical Union* 9, no. 3: 173–87.

DeCanio S. J. 2003a. *Economic Models of Climate Change: A Critique.* New York: Palgrave Macmillan.

———. 2003b. "Economic Analysis, Environmental Policy, and Intergenerational Justice in the Reagan Administration: The Case of the Montreal Protocol." *International Environmental Agreements* 3: 299–321.

———. 2009. "The Political Economy of Global Carbon Emissions Reductions." *Ecological Economics* 68, no. 3: 915–24.

DeCanio S. J., C. Dibble and K. Amir-Atefi. 2000. "The Importance of Organizational Structure for the Adoption of Innovations." *Management Science* 46: 1285–99.

———. 2001. "Organizational Structure and the Behavior of Firms: Implications for Integrated Assessment." *Climatic Change* 48: 487–514.

DeCanio S. J. and P. Niemann. 2006. "Equity Effects of Alternative Assignments of Global Environmental Rights." *Ecological Economics* 56: 546–59.

Deininger K. and L. Squire. 1998. "New Ways of Looking at Old Issues: Inequality and Growth." *Journal of Development Economics* 57: 259–87.

DeLong J. B. and K. Magin. 2009. "The US Equity Return Premium: Past, Present, and Future." *Journal of Economic Perspectives* 23, no. 1: 193–208.

Diamond P. A. and J. A. Hausman. 1994. "Contingent Valuation: Is Some Number Better Than No Number?" *Journal of Economic Perspectives* 8: 45–64.

Dietz S., C. Hope, N. Stern and D. Zenghelis. 2007. "Reflections on the Stern Review: A Robust Case for Strong Action to Reduce the Risks of Climate Change." *World Economics* 8, no. 1: 121–68.

Dowlatabadi H. 1998. "Sensitivity of Climate Change Mitigation Estimates to Assumptions About Technical Change." *Energy Economics* 20: 473–93.

Edenhofer O., B. Knopf, T. Barker, L. Baumstark, E. Bellevrat, B. Chateau, P. Criqui, et al. 2010a. "The Economics of Low Stabilization: Model Comparison of Mitigation Strategies and Costs." *Energy Journal* 31 Special Issue 1: 11–48. Online: http://econpapers.repec.org/article/aenjournl/2010se1_5flow_5fstabilization-a02.htm (accessed on 28 June 2013).

Edenhofer O., B. Knopf, M. Leimbach and N. Bauer. 2010b. "ADAM Modeling Comparison Project." *Potsdam Institute for Climate Impact Research*, Potsdam, Germany. Online: http://www.pik-potsdam.de/research/research-domains/sustainable   solutions/research/MitigationScenarios/adamS (accessed on 28 June 2013).

Edenhofer O., K. Lessmann and N. Bauer. 2006a "Mitigation Strategies and Costs of Climate Protection: The Effects of ETC in the Hybrid Model MIND." *Energy Journal* Special Issue on Endogenous Technological Change and the Economics of Atmospheric Stabilisation: 207–22.

Edenhofer O., K. Lessmann, C. Kemfert, M. Grubb and J. Kohler , 2006b. "Induced Technological Change: Exploring Its Implications for the Economics of Atmospheric Stabilization: Synthesis Report From the Innovation Modeling Comparison Project." *Energy Journal* Special Issue on Endogenous Technological Change and the Economics of Atmospheric Stabilisation: 57–108.

Edmonds J., L. Clarke, J. Lurz and M. Wise. 2008. "Stabilizing CO_2 Concentrations with Incomplete International Cooperation." *Climate Policy* 8: 355–76.

Edmonds J., H. Pitcher, and R. Sands. 2004. "Second Generation Model 2004: An Overview." United States Environmental Protection Agency under contracts AGRDW89939464-01 and AGRDW89939645-01. Joint Global Change Research Institute and Pacific Northwest National Laboratory.

EIA. 2007. "International Energy Outlook." Washington, DC: Energy Information Administration, United States Department of Energy (DOE).

Elliott R. N., T. Langer and Nadel. 2006. "Reducing Oil Use through Energy Efficiency: Opportunities beyond Light Cars and Trucks." Washington, DC: American Council for an Energy Efficient Economy.

Energy Modeling Forum. 2009. *EMF Briefing on Climate Policy Scenarios: US Domestic and International Policy Architectures.* Online: http://emf.stanford.edu/events/ emf_briefing_on_climate_policy_scenarios_us_domestic_and_international_policy_architecturesS (accessed on 28 June 2013).

Enkvist P. A., T. Naucler and J. Rosander. 2007. "A Cost Curve for Greenhouse Gas Reduction." *McKinsey Quarterly*, 1: 35–45.

Epstein L. G. and S. E. Zin. 1989. "Substitution, Risk Aversion, and the Temporal Behavior of Consumption and Asset Returns: A Theoretical Framework." *Econometrica* 57, no. 4: 937–69.

———. 1991. "Substitution, Risk Aversion, and the Temporal Behavior of Consumption and Asset Returns: An Empirical Analysis." *Journal of Political Economy* 99, no. 2: 263–86.

Epstein P. and E. Mills. 2005. "Climate Change Futures: Health, Ecological and Economic Dimensions." Center for Health and the Global Environment, Harvard Medical School.

EuroWinter. 1997. "Cold Exposure and Winter Mortality from Ischaemic Heart, Cerebrovascular Disease, Respiratory Disease, and All Causes in Warm and Cold Regions of Europe." *Lancet* 349: 1341–46.

Fankhauser S., R. S. J. Tol, D. Pearce. 1997. "The Aggregation of Climate Change Damages: A Welfare Theoretic Approach." *Environmental and Resource Economics* 10, no. 3: 249–66.

Fearnside P. M. 1998. "The Value of Human Life in Global Warming Impacts." *Mitigation and Adaptation Strategies for Global Change* 3: 83–5.

Finman H. and J. A. Laitner. 2001. "Industry, Energy Efficiency, and Productivity Improvements in Proceedings of the 2001 ACEEE Summer Study on Energy Efficiency in Industry." Washington, DC: American Council for an Energy Efficient Economy.

Folbre N. 1982. "Exploitation Comes Home: A Critique of the Marxian Theory of Family Labour." *Cambridge Journal of Economics* 6: 317–29.

Frederick S., G. Loewenstein and T. O'Donoghue. 2002. "Time Discounting and Time Preference." *Journal of Economic Literature*: 351–401.

Friedman G. 2003. "'A Question of Degree': The Sanctity of Property Rights in American History." *Natural Assets: Democratizing Environmental Ownership*. Washington, DC: Island Press.

Galeotti M., A. Lanza and F. Pauli. 2006. "Reassessing the Environmental Kuznets Curve for CO_2 Emissions: A Robustness Exercise." *Ecological Economics* 57: 152–63.

Gallagher K. S. 2006. "Limits to Leapfrogging in Energy Technologies? Evidence From the Chinese Automobile Industry." *Energy Policy* 34: 383–94.

Gerdtham U. G. and M. Johannesson. 2003. "A Note on the Effect of Unemployment On Mortality." *Journal of Health Economics* 22: 505–18.

Gerlagh R. 2006. "ITC in a Global Growth-Climate Model With CCS: The Value of Induced Technical Change for Climate Stabilization." *Energy Journal* Special Issue on Endogenous Technological Change 1: 223–40.

———. 2007. "Measuring the Value of Induced Technological Change." *Energy Policy* 35: 5287–97.

———. 2008. "A Climate-Change Policy Induced Shift From Innovations in Carbon-Energy Production to Carbon-Energy Savings." *Energy Economics* 30: 425–48.

German Advisory Council on Global Change. 2009. *The WBGU Budget Approach*. Berlin.

Ghini R., W. Bettiol and E. Hamada. 2011. "Diseases in Tropical and Plantation Crops as Affected by Climate Changes: Current Knowledge and Perspectives." *Plant Pathology* 60, no. 1: 122–32.

Gillingham K., R. G. Newell and W. A. Pizer. 2007. "Modeling Endogenous Technological Change for Climate Policy Analysis." Washington DC: Resources for the Future.

Giorgi F. and X. Bi. 2009. "Time of Emergence (TOE) of GHG-Forced Precipitation Change Hot-Spots." *Geophysical Research Letters* 36, no. 6.

Gjerde J., S. Grepperud and S. Kverndokk. 1999. "Optimal Climate Policy Under the Possibility of a Catastrophe." *Resource and Energy Economics* 21: 289–317.

Gleadow R. M., J. R. Evans, S. McCaffery and T. R. Cavagnaro. 2009. "Growth and Nutritive Value of Cassava (Manihot Esculenta Cranz.) Are Reduced When Grown in Elevated CO2." *Plant Biology* 11: 76–82.

Gohar L. K. and J. A. Lowe. 2009. "Summary of the Emissions Mitigation Scenarios: Part 2." *Met Office Hadley Centre*, London. Online: http://www.metoffice.gov.uk/ avoid/files/ resources-researchers/AVOID_WS1_D1_ 03_20090521.pdfS (accessed on 28 June 2013).

Goldemberg J., S. T. Coelho, P. M. Nastari and O. Lucon. 2004. "Ethanol Learning Curve: The Brazilian Experience." *Biomass and Bioenergy* 26: 301–304.

Goodess C. M., C. Hanson, M. Hulme and T. J. Osborn. 2003. "Representing Climate and Extreme Weather Events in Integrated Assessment Models: A Review of Existing Methods and Options for Development." *Integrated Assessment Journal* 4, no. 3: 145–71.

Goodstein E. 2007. *Economics and the Environment*, 5th edition. New York: Wiley: 409–11.

Goulder L. H. and S. H. Schneider. 1999. "Induced Technological Change and the Attractiveness of CO2 Abatement Policies." *Resource and Energy Economics* 21: 211–53.

Government of India. *National Plan on Climate Change*, Prime Minister's Council on Climate change: New Delhi, India, 2008.

Grossman G. M. and A. B. Krueger. 1995. "Economic Growth and the Environment." *Quarterly Journal of Economics* 110: 353–77.

_____. 2008. "The Inverted-U: What Does It Mean?" *Environment and Development Economics* 1: 119–22.

Grubb M., C. Carraro and J. Schellnhuber. 2006. "Technological Change for Atmospheric Stabilization: Introductory Overview to the Innovation Modeling Comparison Project." *Energy Journal* Special Issue on Endogenous Technological Change and the Economics of Atmospheric Stabilisation: 1–16.

Ha-Duong M. 2001. "Transparency and Control in Engineering Integrated Assessment Models." *Integrated Assessment* 2, no. 4: 209–18.

Ha-Duong M. and N. Treich. 2004. "Risk Aversion, Intergenerational Equity and Climate Change." *Environmental and Resource Economics* 28, no. 2: 195–207.

Hales S., S. J. Edwards, R. S. Kovats. 2003. "Impacts on Health of Climate Extremes." In A. J. McMichael, D. H. Campbell-Lendrum, C. F. Corvalan, et al. (eds). *Climate Change and Human Health: Risks and Responses*. Geneva: World Health Organization.

Hall D. C. and R. J. Behl. 2006. "Integrating Economic Analysis and the Science of Climate Instability." *Ecological Economics* 57, no. 3: 442–65.

Hanemann W. M. 1994. "Valuing the Environment through Contingent Valuation." *Journal of Economic Perspectives* 8: 19–43.

_____. 2008. *What is the Economic Cost of Climate Change?* eScholarship. Berkeley, CA: University of California Berkeley.

Hanemann M., L. Dale, S. Vicuña, D. Bickett and C. Dyckman. 2006. "The Economic Cost of Climate Change Impact on California Water: A Scenario Analysis." CEC-500-2006-003. Prepared for the California Energy Commission, Public Interest Energy Research Program. Online: http://www.energy.ca.gov/2006publications/CEC-500-2006-003/CEC-500-2006- (accessed on 28 June 2013).

Hansen J., M. Sato, P. Kharecha, D. Beerling, R. Berner, V. Masson-Delmotte, M. Pagani, M. Raymo, D. L. Royer, J. C. Zachos. 2008. "Target Atmospheric CO2: Where Should Humanity Aim?" *Open Atmospheric Science Journal* 2: 217–31.

Hansen J., M. Sato and R. Ruedy. 2012. "Perception of Climate Change." *Proceedings of the National Academy of Sciences*.

Hardin G. 1968. "The Tragedy of the Commons." *Science* 162: 1243–48.

Heal G. and B. Kristrom. 2002. "Uncertainty and Climate Change." *Environmental and Resource Economics* 22: 3–39.

Hedenus F., C. Azar and K. Lindgren. 2006. "Induced Technological Change in a Limited Foresight Optimization Model." *Energy Journal* Special Issue on Endogenous Technological Change and the Economics of Atmospheric Stabilisation: 109–122.

Heyward M. 2007. "Equity and International Climate Change Negotiations: A Matter of Perspective." *Climate Policy* 7: 518–34.

Hicks J. R. 1940. "The Valuation of the Social Income." *Economica* 10: 105–24.

Hoegh-Guldberg O., P. J. Mumby, A. J. Hooten, R. S. Steneck, P. Greenfield, E. Gomez, C. D. Harvell, P. F. Sale, A. J. Edwards, K. Caldeira, C. M. Knowlton, R. Eakin, R. Iglesias-Prieto, N. Muthiga, R. H. Bradbury, A. Dubi and M. E. Hatziolos. 2007. "Coral Reefs under Rapid Climate Change and Ocean Acidification." *Science* 318: 1737–42.

Hoel M. and T. Sterner. 2007. "Discounting and Relative Prices." *Climatic Change* 84: 265–80.

Holtedahl P. and F. L. Joutz. 2004. "Residential Electricity Demand in Taiwan." *Energy Economics* 26: 201–224.

Hope C. 2005. "Exchange Rates and the Social Cost of Carbon." The Judge Institute of Management Working Paper Series, University of Cambridge WP: May.

_____. 2006a. "The Marginal Impact of CO2 from PAGE2002: An Integrated Assessment Model Incorporating the IPCC's Five Reasons For Concern." *Integrated Assessment Journal* 6, no. 1: 19–56.

_____. 2006b. "The Social Cost of Carbon: What Does It Actually Depend On?" *Climate Policy* 6, no. 5: 565–72.

_____. 2008. "Discount Rates, Equity Weights and the Social Cost of Carbon." *Energy Economics* 30, no. 3: 1011–19.

Howarth R. B. 1996. "Climate Change and Overlapping Generations." *Contemporary Economic Policy* 14: 100–111.

_____. 1998. "An Overlapping Generations Model of Climate-Economy Interactions." *Scandinavian Journal of Economics* 100: 575–91.

_____. 2003. "Discounting and Uncertainty in Climate Change Policy Analysis." *Land Economics* 79, no. 3: 369–81.

_____. 2009. "Discounting, Uncertainty, and Revealed Time Preference." *Land Economics* 85: 24–40.

Howarth R. B. and R. B. Norgaard. 1992. "Environmental Valuation under Sustainable Development." *American Economics Review* 82: 473–77.

Howarth R. B. and R. B. Norgaard. 2007. "CO2 emissions: Getting Bang for the Buck." *Science* 318: 1865–66.

Howitt R., J. Medellín-Azuara and D. MacEwan. 2009. "Estimating the Economic Impacts of Agricultural Yield Related Changes for California." CEC-500-2009-042-F. California Climate Change Center. Online: http://www.energy.ca.gov/2009publications/CEC-500-2009-042/CEC-500-2009-042-F.PDF (accessed on 28 June 2013).

Hughes J. E., C. R. Knittel and D. Sperling. 2006. "Evidence of a Shift in the Short-Run Price Elasticity of Gasoline Demand." NBER Working Paper.

Iglesias A., L. Garrote, S. Quiroga and M. Moneo. 2011. "A Regional Comparison of the Effects of Climate Change on Agricultural Crops in Europe." *Climatic Change* 112, no. 1, 29–46.

Interagency Working Group on Social Cost of Carbon. 2010. "Social Cost of Carbon for Regulatory Impact Analysis Under Executive Order 12866." US Department of Energy, Washington, DC.

Intergovernmental Panel on Climate Change (IPCC). 1996. In J. P. Bruce, H. Lee and E. F. Haites (eds). *Climate Change 1995: Economic and Social Dimensions of Climate Change, Contribution of Working Group III to the Second Assessment Report of the Intergovernmental Panel on Climate Change.* Cambridge: Cambridge University Press.

_____. 2001a. In B. Metz, O. Davidson, R. Swart and J. Pan (eds). *Climate Change 2001: Contribution of Working Group III to the Third Assessment Report of the Intergovernmental Panel on Climate Change.* Cambridge: Cambridge University Press.

_____. 2001b. "Climate Change 2001: Synthesis Report." Cambridge: Cambridge University Press.

_____. 2001c. *Climate Change 2001: The Scientific Basis.* Cambridge: Cambridge University Press.

_____. 2007a. "Summary for Policymakers." In S. Solomon, D. Qin, M. Manning, Z. Chen, M. Marquis, K. B. Averyt, M. Tignor and H. L. Miller (eds). *Climate Change 2007: The Physical Science Basis, Contribution of Working Group I to the Fourth Assessment Report of the Intergovernmental Panel on Climate Change.* Cambridge: Cambridge University Press.

_____. 2007b. *Climate Change 2007: The Physical Science Basis. Contribution of Working Group I to the Fourth Assessment Report of the Intergovernmental Panel on Climate Change.* Cambridge: Cambridge University Press.

_____. 2007c. "Summary for Policymakers." In B. Metz, O. R. Davidson, P. R. Bosch, R. Dave and L. A. Meyer (eds). *Contribution of Working Group III to the Fourth Assessment Report of the Intergovernmental Panel on Climate Change.* Cambridge: Cambridge University Press, 9–12.

_____. 2007d. *Climate Change 2007-IPCC Fourth Assessment Report.* Cambridge: Cambridge University Press.

Interlaboratory Working Group on Energy-Efficient and Clean-Energy Technologies. 2000. "Scenarios for a Clean Energy Future." Oak Ridge, TN: Oak Ridge National Lab and Lawrence Berkeley National Lab. Online: http://www.ornl.gov/sci/eere/cef/ (accessed on 28 June 2013).

International Association for Energy Economics (IAEE). 2006. "Endogenous Technological Change and the Economics of Atmospheric Stabilisation Special Issue." *Energy Journal* 27: 1–276.

International Energy Agency. 2007. "World Energy Outlook 2007." Paris. Online: http://www.worldenergyoutlook.org/2007.aspS (accessed on 28 June 2013).

_____. 2008. "Energy Technology Perspectives 2008: Scenarios & Strategies to 2050." Paris. Online: http://www.iea.org/textbase/nppdf/free/2008/etp2008.pdf (accessed on 28 June 2013).

_____. 2010a. "Energy Technology Perspectives 2010: Scenarios and Strategies to 2050." Paris, July. Online: http://www.iea.org/techno/etp/index.asp (accessed on 28 June 2013).

_____. 2010b. "World Energy Outlook 2010." International Energy Agency. Paris. Online: http://www.worldenergyoutlook.org/2010.aspS (accessed on 28 June 2013).

International Monetary Fund (IMF). 2008. "World Economic Outlook: Housing and the Business Cycle." Washington, DC: International Monetary Fund.

Janssen R. 2001. "On the Use of Multi-Criteria Analysis in Environmental Impact Assessment in The Netherlands." *Journal of Multi-Criteria Decision Analysis* 10: 101–109.

Jensen S. and C. Traeger. 2011. "Growth and Uncertainty in the Integrated Assessment of Climate Change." Berkeley, CA: Ragnar Frisch Centre for Economic Research and University of California-Berkeley. Online: http://www.webmeets. com/files/papers/AERE/2011/141/NCCS.pdf (accessed on 28 June 2013).

John V. O., R. P. Allan and B. J. Soden. 2009. "How Robust Are Observed and Simulated Precipitation Responses to Tropical Ocean Warming?" *Geophysical Research Letters* 36, no. 14.

Jorgenson D. W., R. J. Goettle, B. H. Hurd, L. B. Smith, L. G. Chesnut and D. M. Mills. 2004. "US Market Consequences of Global Climate Change." Arlington, VA: Pew Center on Global Climate Change.

Junginger M., A. Faaij and W. C. Turkenburg. 2005. "Global Experience Curves for Wind Farms." *Energy Policy* 33: 133–50.

Kahneman D. and A. Tversky (eds). 2000. "Choices, Values, and Frames." New York: Russell Sage Foundation.

Kainuma M., Y. Matsuoka and T. Morita. 1999. "Analysis of Post-Kyoto Scenarios: The Asian-Pacific Integrated Model." *Energy Journal* Special Issue on the Costs of the Kyoto Protocol: A Multi-Model Evaluation: 207–220.

Kaldor N. 1939. "Welfare Propositions of Economics and Interpersonal Comparisons of Utility." *The Economic Journal* 49: 549–52.

Kant I. 2005 (1785). *Groundwork for the Metaphysics of Morals (Grundlegung zur Metaphysik der Sitten)*. Thomas K. Abbott (trans.) with revisions and edited by Lara Denis. Orchard Park, NY: Broadview Press.

Kartha S., P. Baer, T. Athanasiou and E. Kemp-Benedict. 2009. "The Greenhouse Development Rights Framework." *Climate and Development* 1, no. 2: 147.

Kaufman N. 2012. "The Bias of Integrated Assessment Models That Ignore Climate Catastrophes." *Climatic Change* 110, no. 3: 575–95.

Kawachi I. and B. P. Kennedy. 1997. "Health and Social Cohesion: Why Care About Income Inequality?" *BMJ* 314: 1037–40.

_____. 1999. "Income Inequality and Health: Pathways and Mechanisms." *Health Services Research* 34: 215–27.

Keller K., Z. Yang, M. Hall and D. F. Bradford. 2003. "Carbon Dioxide Sequestration: When and How Much?" Working Paper 94, Center for Economic Policy Studies, Princeton University.

Kelly D. L. and C. D. Kolstad. 1999. "Integrated Assessment Models for Climate Change Control." In H. Folmer, T. Tietenberg (eds). *International Yearbook of Environmental and Resource Economics* 1999/2000: A Survey of Current Issues. Edward Elgar: 171–97.

Kemfert C. 2001. "Economy–Energy–Climate Interaction: The Model Wiagem." NOTA DI LAVORO 71.2001 Fondazione Eni Enrico Mattei.

Kemfert C. and R. S. J. Tol. 2002. "Equity, International Trade and Climate Policy." *International Environmental Agreements* 2, no. 1: 23–48.

Kennedy M., D. Mrofka and C. von der Borch. 2008. "Snowball Earth Termination by Destabilization of Equatorial Permafrost Methane Clathrate." *Nature* 453: 642–45.

Kitous A., P. Criqui, E. Bellevrat and B. Chateau. 2010. "Transformation Patterns of the Worldwide Energy System: Scenarios for the Century with the POLES Model." *Energy Journal* 31 Special Issue 1: 49–82. Online: http://ideas.repec.org/a/aen/journl/2010se1_low_stabilization-a03.html (accessed on 28 June 2013).

Klinenberg E. 2002. "Heat Wave: A Social Autopsy of Disaster in Chicago." Chicago: University of Chicago Press.

Klinsky S. and H. Dowlatabadi. 2009. "Conceptualizations of Justice in Climate Policy." *Climate Policy* 9: 88–108.

Köhler J., M. Grubb, D. Popp and O. Edenhofer. 2006. "The Transition to Endogenous Technical Change in Climate-Economy Models: A Technical Overview to the Innovation Modeling Comparison Project." *Energy Journal* Special Issue on Endogenous Technological Change and the Economics of Atmospheric Stabilisation: 17–56.

Kok M., B. Metz, J. Verhagen and S. van Rooijen. 2008. "Integrating Development and Climate Policies: National and International Benefits." *Climate Policy* 8: 103–18.

Koopmans T. C. 1965. "On The Concept of Optimal Economic Growth." *Cowles Foundation Paper*. Online: http://cowles. econ.yale.edu/P/cp/p02a/p0238.pdf (accessed on 28 June 2013).

Kopp R. E., A. Golub, N. O. Keohane and C. Onda 2011. "The Influence of the Specification of Climate Change Damages on the Social Cost of Carbon." *Economics*

Discussion Papers, No. 2011–22, Kiel Institute for the World Economy. Online: http://www.economics-ejournal.org/economics/discussionpapers/2011-22 (accessed on 28 June 2013).

Kopp R. E. and B. K. Mignone. 2011. "The US Government's Social Cost of Carbon Estimates after their First Year: Pathways for Improvement." *Economics Discussion Papers*, No. 2011–16, Kiel Institute for the World Economy. Online: http://www.economics-ejournal.org/economics/discussionpapers/2011-16 (accessed on 28 June 2013).

Krause F., S. J. DeCanio, A. Hoerner and P. Baer. 2002. "Cutting Carbon Emissions at a Profit (Part I): Opportunities for the United States." *Contemporary Economic Policy* 20: 339–65.

———. 2003. "Cutting Carbon Emissions at a Profit (Part II): Impacts on US Competitiveness and Jobs." *Contemporary Economic Policy* 21: 90–105.

Kurosawa A. 2004. "Carbon Concentration Target and Technological Choice." *Energy Economics* 26: 675–84.

Kurosawa A., H. Yagita, W. Zhou, K. Tokimatsu and Y. Yanagisawa. 1999. "Analysis of Carbon Emissions Stabilization Targets and Adaptation by Integrated Assessment Model." *Energy Journal*, Kyoto Special Issue: 157–75.

Kuznets S. 1955. "Economic Growth and Income Inequality." *American Economic Review* 45: 1–28.

———. 1957. "Quantitative Aspects of the Economic Growth of Nations: II. Industrial Distribution of National Product and Labor Force." *Economic Development and Cultural Change.* 5: 1–111.

———. 1963. "Quantitative Aspects of the Economic Growth of Nations: VIII. Distribution of Income by Size." *Economic Development and Cultural Change* 11: 1–80.

Kypreos S. 2005. "Modeling Experience Curves in MERGE (Model for Evaluating Regional and Global Effects)." *Energy* 30, no. 14: 2721–37.

———. 2008. "Stabilizing Global Temperature Change below Thresholds: Monte Carlo Analyses with MERGE." *Journal of Computational Management Science* 5, nos. 1–2: 141–70.

Laitner J. A., S. J. DeCanio and I. Peters. 2000. "Incorporating Behavioural, Social, and Organizational Phenomena in the Assessment of Climate Change Mitigation Options." In E. Jochem, J. Sathaye and D. Bouille (eds). *Society, Behaviour, and Climate Change Mitigation*. Dordrecht: Kluwer Academic: 1–64.

Laitner J. A., D. A. Hanson, I. Mintzer and J. A. Leonard. 2006. "Adapting for Uncertainty: A Scenario Analysis of US Technology Energy Futures." *Energy Studies Review* 14: 120–35.

Leakey A. D. B. 2009. "Rising Atmospheric Carbon Dioxide Concentration and the Future of C4 Crops for Food and Fuel." *Proceedings of the Royal Society*: Biological Sciences 276, no. 1666: 2333–43.

Leakey A. D. B., E. A. Ainsworth, C. J. Bernacchi, A. Rogers, S. P. Long and D. R. Ort. 2009. "Elevated CO2 Effects on Plant Carbon, Nitrogen, and Water Relations: Six Important Lessons from FACE." *Journal of Experimental Botany* 60, no. 10: 2859–76.

Leimbach M., N. Bauer, L. Baumstark and O. Edenhofer. 2010. "Mitigation Costs in a Globalized World: Climate Policy Analysis With REMIND-R." *Environmental Modeling and Assessment* 15, no. 3: 155–73.

Lejour A., P. Veenendaal, G. Verweij and N. V. Leeuwen. 2004. "WorldScan: A Model for International Economic Policy Analysis." *CPB Netherlands Bureau for Economic Policy Analysis*, no. 111.

Lenton T. M., H. Held, E. Kriegler, J. W. Hall, W. Lucht, S. Rahmstorf and J. Schellnhuber. 2008. "Tipping Elements in the Earth's Climate System." *Proceedings of that National Academy of Sciences of the USA* 105: 1786–93.

Lindmark M. 2004."Patterns of Historical CO_2 Intensity Transitions Among High and Low-Income Countries." *Explorations in Economic History* 41: 426–47.

Little I. 1955. "A Critique of Welfare Economics." Oxford: Clarendon Press.

Lobell D. B., M. B. Burke, C. Tebaldi, M. D. Mastrandrea, W. P. Falcon and R. L. Naylor R. 2008. "Prioritizing Climate Change Adaptation Needs for Food Security in 2030." *Science* 319, no. 5863: 607–610.

Lobell D. B., M. Bänziger, C. Magorokosho and B. Vivek. 2011. "Nonlinear Heat Effects on African Maize as Evidenced by Historical Yield Trials." *Nature Climate Change* 1, no. 1: 42–45.

Lobell D. B., A. Sibley and J. I. Ortiz-Monasterio. 2012. "Extreme Heat Effects on Wheat Senescence in India." *Nature Climate Change* 2, no. 3: 186–89.

Lomborg B. 2006. "Stern Review: The Dodgy Numbers behind the Latest Warming Scare." *Wall Street Journal.*

———. 2007. *Cool It: The Skeptical Environmentalist's Guide to Global Warming.* New York: Alfred A. Knopf.

Long S. P., E. A. Ainsworth, A. Rogers and D. R. Ort. 2004. "Rising Atmospheric Carbon Dioxide: Plants FACE the Future." *Annual Review of Plant Biology* 55: 591–628.

Long S. P., E. A. Ainsworth, A. D. B. Leakey, J. Nösberger, D. R. Ort. 2006. "Food for Thought: Lower-Than-Expected Crop Yield Stimulation With Rising CO_2 Concentrations." *Science* 312, no. 5782: 1918–21.

Lovins A. B. 2005. "More Profit with Less Carbon." *Scientific American* September: 74–82.

Lowe J. A., L. K. Gohar, C. Huntingford, P. Good, D. Bernie, A. Pardaens, R. Warren and S. C. B. Raper. 2011. "Are the Emission Pledges in the Copenhagen Accord Compatible with a Global Aspiration to Avoid More than 21C of Global Warming?" The Met Office Walker Institute, Tyndall Centre and Grantham Institute, London. Online: http://www.metoffice.gov.uk /avoid/COP15.pdfS (accessed on 28 June 2013).

Lu J. 2009. "The Dynamics of the Indian Ocean Sea Surface Temperature Forcing of Sahel Drought." *Climate Dynamics* 33, no. 4: 445–60.

Ludwig D., W. A. Brock, and S. R. Carpenter. 2005. "Uncertainty in Discount Models and Environmental Accounting." *Ecology and Society* 10: 13.

Luedeling E., E. H. Girvetz, M. A. Semenov and P. H. Brown. 2011. "Climate Change Affects Winter Chill for Temperate Fruit and Nut Trees." *PLoS ONE* 6, no. 5: 20155.

Luo Q. 2011. "Temperature Thresholds and Crop Production: A Review." *Climatic Change* 109, nos. 3–4: 583–98.

Magne B., S. Kypreos and H. Turton. 2010. "Technology Options for Low Stabilization Pathways with MERGE." *Energy Journal* 31 Special Issue 1: 83–108. Online: http://www.pik potsdam.de/research/sustainable-solutions/research/MitigationScenarios/adam/magne (accessed on 28 June 2013).

Mahlstein I., R. W. Portmann, J. S. Daniel, S. Solomon and R. Knutti. 2012. "Perceptible Changes in Regional Precipitation in a Future Climate." *Geophysical Research Letters* 39, no. 5.

Manne A. S. 1999. "Greenhouse Gas Abatement: Toward Pareto-Optimality in Integrated Assessment." In K. J. Arrow, R. W. Cottle, B. C. Eaves, I. Olkin (eds). *Education in a Research University.* Springer, Netherlands.

_____. 2004. "Perspective Paper 1.2." In B. Lomborg (ed). *Global Crises, Global Solutions*. Cambridge: Cambridge University Press: 49–55.

Manne A. S. and R. G. Richels. 1992. "Buying Greenhouse Insurance: The Economic Costs of CO_2 Emissions Limits." Cambridge, MA: MIT.

_____. 2004. "MERGE: An Integrated Assessment Model for Global Climate Change." Online: http://www.standford.edu/group/MERGE/ (accessed on 28 June 2013).

Marmot M. 2005. "Social Determinants of Health Inequalities." *Lancet* 365: 1099–1104.

Martens W. J. M. 1998. "Climate Change, Thermal Stress and Mortality Changes." *Social Science and Medicine* 46, no. 3: 331–44.

Marx K. 1967 *Capital: A Critique of Political Economy*, vol. 1. New York: International Publishers.

Masui T., T. Hanaoka, S. Hikita and M. Kainuma. 2006. "Assessment of CO_2 Reductions and Economic Impacts Considering Energy-Saving Investments." *Energy Journal* Special Issue on Endogenous Technological Change 1: 175–90.

Matthews H. D. and K. Caldeira. 2008. "Stabilizing Climate Requires Near-Zero Emissions." *Geophysical Research Letters* 35, L04705.

McKibbin W. J. and P. J. Wilcoxen. 1999. "The Theoretical and Empirical Structure of the G-Cubed Model." *Economic Modelling* 16: 123–48.

McKinsey & Company. 2009. "Pathways to a Low-Carbon Economy: Version 2 of the Global Greenhouse Gas Abatement Cost Curve." Online: http://www.mckinsey.com/clientservice/ ccsi/pathways_low_carbon_economy.aspS (accessed on 28 June 2013).

McKinsey Global Institute. 2007. "Curbing Global Energy Demand Growth: The Energy Productivity Opportunity." 1–24. Online: http://www.mckinsey.com/mgi/publications/Curbing_Global_ Energy/ index.asp (accessed on 28 June 2013).

Mehra R. 2003. "The Equity Premium: Why Is It a Puzzle?" *Financial Analysis Journal*: 54–69.

Mehra R. and E. C. Prescott. 1985. "The Equity Premium: A Puzzle." *Journal of Monetary Economics* 15, no. 2: 145–61.

_____. 2003. "The Equity Premium in Retrospect." In G. M. Constantinides, M. Harris and R. Stultz (eds). *Handbook of the Economics of Finance*. Amsterdam: Elsevier: 889–938.

Meinshausen M. 2006. "On the Risk of Overshooting 2l C." In H. J. Schellnhuber, W. Cramer, N. Nakicenovic, T. Wigley and G. Yohe (eds). *Avoiding Dangerous Climate Change*. Cambridge: Cambridge University Press.

Meinshausen M., N. Meinshausen, Hare, William, Raper, C. B. Sarah, Frieler, Katja, Knutti, Reto, Frame, J. David, M. R. Allen. 2009. "Greenhouse-Gas Emission Targets for Limiting Global Warming to 2l C." *Nature* 458: 1158–63.

Mendelsohn R. 2004. "Perspective Paper 1.1." In B. Lomborg (ed). *Global Crises, Global Solutions*. Cambridge: Cambridge University Press.

_____. 2006. "A Critique of the Stern Report." *Regulation* 29, no. 4: 42–6.

Mendelsohn R., W. Morrison, M. E. Schlesinger and N. G. Andronova. 2000. "Country-Specific Market Impacts of Climate Change." *Climatic Change* 45: 553–69.

Mendelsohn R., W. D. Nordhaus and D. Shaw. 1994. "The Impact of Global Warming on Agriculture: A Ricardian Analysis." *American Economic Review* 84, no. 4: 753–71.

Mendelsohn R. and L. Williams. 2004. "Comparing Forecasts of the Global Impacts of Climate Change." *Mitigation and Adaptation Strategies for Global Change* 9, no. 4: 315–33.

Milanovic B. 2005. *Worlds Apart: Measuring International and Global Inequality*. Princeton, NJ: Princeton University Press.

_____. 2009. "Global Inequality Recalculated: The Effect of New 2005 PPP Estimates on Global Inequality." *World Bank Policy Research Working Paper*, no. 5061.

Milanovic B., P. H. Lindert, and J. G. Williamson. 2011. "Pre-Industrial Inequality." *Economic Journal* 121: 255–72.

Min S. K., X. Zhang, F. W. Zwiers and G. C. Hegerl. 2011. "Human Contribution to More Intense Precipitation Extremes." *Nature* 470, no. 7334: 378–81.

More T. 1909. *Utopia*. London and New York: Cassel.

Morgan M. G. and H. Dowlatabadi. 1996. "Learning from Integrated Assessment of Climate Change." *Climatic Change* 34: 337–68.

Morgan M. G., M. Kandlikar, J. Risbey and H. Dowlatabadi. 1999. "Why Conventional Tools for Policy Analysis are Often Inadequate for Problems of Global Change." *Climatic Change* 41, no. 3: 271–81.

Morton D. 1999. "The Electrical Century: What Difference Did Semiconductors and Microelectronics Make?" *Proceedings of the IEEE* 87, no. 6: 1049–52.

Munasinghe M. 1999. "Is Environmental Degradation an Inevitable Consequence of Economic Growth: Tunneling Through the Environmental Kuznets Curve." *Ecological Economics* 29: 89–109.

Murphy J. M., D. M. H. Sexton, D. N. Barnett, G. S. Jones, M. J. Webb, M. Collins and David A. 2004. "Quantification of Modelling Uncertainties in a Large Ensemble of Climate Change Simulations." *Nature* 430, no. 7001: 768–72.

Nakicenovic N., J. Alcamo, G. Davis, J. Bert de Vries, S. Fenhann, K. Gaffin, Gregory, et al. 2000. "Special Report on Emissions Scenarios—SRES Final Data." The Hague: Intergovernmental Panel on Climate Change.

Narain S. and M. Riddle. 2007. "Greenhouse Justice: An Entitlement Framework for Managing the Global Atmospheric Commons." In J. K. Boyce and E. A. Stanton (eds). *Reclaiming Nature: Environmental Justice and Ecological Restoration*. London: Anthem Press: 401–14.

Negishi T. 1972. *General Equilibrium Theory and International Trade*. Amsterdam and London: North-Holland Publishing Company.

Newbold S. C. and A. Daigneault. 2009. "Climate Response Uncertainty and the Benefits of Greenhouse Gas Emissions Reductions." *Environmental and Resource Economics*.

Newell R. G. and W. A. Pizer. 2003. "Discounting the Distant Future: How Much Do Uncertain Rates Increase Evaluations?" *Journal of Environmental Economics and Management* 46: 52–71.

Newman P. 1987. *The New Palgrave: A Dictionary of Economics: Four Volume Boxed Set*. London: Palgrave Macmillan.

Nordhaus W. D. 2007a. *Accompanying Notes and Documentation on Development of DICE-2007 Model: Notes on DICE-2007.v8 of September 21, 2007*. New Haven, CT: Yale University.

———. 2007b. *The Challenge of Global Warming: Economic Models and Environmental Policy*. Online: http://nordhaus.econ.yale.edu/DICE2007.htm (accessed on 28 June 2013).

———. 2007c. "A Review of the Stern Review on the Economics of Climate Change." *Journal of Economic Literature* 45, no. 3: 17.

———. 2008. *A Question of Balance: Economic Modeling of Global Warming*. New Haven, CT: Yale University Press.

Nordhaus W. D. and J. Boyer. 2000. "Warming the World: Economic Models of Global Warming." Cambridge, MA: MIT Press.

Nordhaus W. D. and D. Popp. 1997. "What is the Value of Scientific Knowledge? An Application to Global Warming Using the PRICE Model." *Energy Journal* 18, no. 1: 1–45.

Nordhaus W. D. and Z. Yang. 1996. "A Regional Dynamic General-Equilibrium Model of Alternative Climate-Change Strategies." *American Economic Review* 86, no. 4: 741–65.

Norse D. 2012. "Low Carbon Agriculture: Objectives and Policy Pathways." *Environmental Development* 1, no. 1: 25–39.

Olmstead A. L. and P. W. Rhode. 2010. "Adapting North American Wheat Production to Climatic Challenges, 1839–2009." *Proceedings of the National Academy of Sciences* 108, no. 2, 480–85.

OPEC. 2007. "World Oil Outlook 2007." Vienna, Austria: Organization of the Petroleum Exporting Countries.

Ostrom E., J. Burger, C. B. Field, R. B. Norgaard and D. Policansky. 1999. "Revisiting the Commons: Local Lessons, Global Challenges." *Science* 284: 278–82.

Ott H. E., W. Sterk and R. Watanabe. 2008. "The Bali Roadmap: New Horizons for Global Climate Policy." *Climate Policy* 8: 91–5.

Paltsev S., J. M. Reilly, H. D. Jacoby, A. C. Gurgel, G. E. Metcalf, A. P. Sokolov and J. F. Holak. 2007. "Assessment of US Cap-and-Trade Proposals." Online at SSRN: http://ssrn.com/abstract=994225 (accessed on 28 June 2013).

Pant H. M. 2007. "GTEM Draft: Global Trade and Environmental Model." Canberra: Australian Bureau of Agricultural and Resource Economics.

Parson E. A. 1996. "Three Dilemmas in the Integrated Assessment of Climate Change." *Climatic Change*, 34, no. 3: 315–26.

Peck S. C. and T. J. Teisberg. 1995. "Optimal CO_2 Control Policy with Stochastic Losses from Temperature Rise." *Climatic Change* 31: 19–34.

_____. 1998. "CO_2 Concentration Limits, the Costs and Benefits of Control, and the Potential for International Agreement." Fondazione Eni Enrico Mattei Working Paper 6.98. DOI:10.2139/ssrn.122029.

_____. 1999. "CO_2 Emissions Control Agreements: Incentives for Regional Participation." *Energy Journal* 20: 367–90.

Persson T. and G. Tabellini. 1994. "Is Inequality Harmful for Growth?" *American Economic Review* 84: 600–621.

Pesaran H., D. Pettenuzzo and A. Timmermann. 2007. "Learning, Structural Instability, and Present Value Calculations." *Econometric Reviews* 26, nos. 2–4: 253–88.

Pigou A. C. 1952. *The Economics of Welfare*. London: Macmillan.

Popp D. 2006. "Comparison of Climate Policies in the ENTICE-BR Model." *Energy Journal* Special Issue on Endogenous Technological Change 1: 163–74.

Portney P. R. 1994. "The Contingent Valuation Debate: Why Economists Should Care." *Journal of Economic Perspectives* 8: 3–17.

Rabin M. 2000. "Risk Aversion and Expected-Utility Theory: A Calibration Theorem." *Econometrica* 68, no. 5: 1281–92.

Ramsey F. P. 1928. "A Mathematical Theory of Saving." *The Economic Journal* 138, no. 152: 543–59.

Randolph S. M. and W. F. Lott. 1993. "Can the Kuznets Effect Be Relied on to Induce Equalizing Growth?" *World Development* 21: 829–40.

Rao S., I. Keppo and K. Riahi. 2006. "Importance of Technological Change and Spillovers in Long-Term Climate Policy." *Energy Journal* Special Issue on Endogenous Technological Change and the Economics of Atmospheric Stabilisation: 123–39.

Ravallion M., M. Heil and J. Jalan. 2000. "Carbon Emissions and Income Inequality." *Oxford Economic Papers* 52: 651–69.

Rawls J. 1971. *A Theory of Justice*. Cambridge, MA: Harvard University Press.

Redman J. 2008. "World Bank: Climate Profiteer," 10 April. Washington, DC: Institute for Policy Studies.

Reilly J. M., J. Graham and J. Hrubovcak. 2001. "Agriculture: The Potential Consequences of the Potential Consequences of Climate Variability and Change for the United States." *US National Assessment of the Potential Consequences of Climate Variability and Change*, US Global Change Research Program. New York: Cambridge University Press.

Reilly J., S. Paltsev, B. Felzer, X. Wang, D. Kicklighter, J. Melillo, R. Prinn, M. Sarofim, A. Sokolov and C. Wang. 2007. "Global Economic Effects of Changes in Crops, Pasture, and Forests Due to Changing Climate, Carbon Dioxide, and Ozone." *Energy Policy* 35: 5370–83.

Reiss P. C. and M. B. White. 2005. "Household Electricity Demand, Revisited." *Review of Economic Studies* 72: 853–83.

Risbey J., M. Kandlikar and A. Patwardhan. 1996. "Assessing Integrated Assessments". *Climatic Change* 34, no. 3: 369–95.

Robbins L. 1984 [1932]. "Essay on the Nature and Significance of Economic Science." Basingstoke: Palgrave Macmillan.

Roe G. H. and M. B. Baker. 2007. "Why Is Climate Sensitivity so Unpredictable?" *Science* 318: 629–32.

Rotmans J. and H. Dowlatabadi. 1998. "Integrated Assessment Modeling." In S. Rayner and E. L. Malone (eds). *Tools for Policy Analysis* 3. Columbus, OH: Battelle Press.

Roughgarden T., S. H. Schneider. 1999. "Climate Change Policy: Quantifying Uncertainties for Damages and Optimal Carbon Taxes." *Energy Policy* 27, no. 7: 371–434.

Roy J., A. H. Sanstad, J. A. Sathaye and R. Khaddaria. 2006. "Substitution and Price Elasticity Estimates Using Inter-Country Pooled Data in a Translog Cost Model." *Energy Economics* 28: 706–719.

Rutherford T. F. 1999. "Sequential Joint Maximization." In J. Weyant (ed). *Energy and Environmental Policy Modeling*. New York: Springer: 139–56.

Samuelson P. 1954. "The Pure Theory of Public Expenditure." *Review of Economics and Statistics* 36: 387–89.

———. 1956. "Social Indifference Curves." *Quarterly Journal of Economics* 70, no. 1: 1–22.

Sanderson M. G., D. L. Hemming and R. A. Betts. 2011. "Regional Temperature and Precipitation Changes Under High-End (≥4°C) Global Warming." *Philosophical Transactions of the Royal Society A: Mathematical, Physical and Engineering Sciences* 369, no. 1934: 85–98.

Sandsmark M. and H. Vennemo. 2007. "A Portfolio Approach to Climate Investments: CAPM and Endogenous Risk." *Environmental and Resource Economics* 4: 681–95.

Sano F., K. Akimoto, T. Homma and T. Tomoda. 2006. "Analysis of Technological Portfolios for CO_2 Stabilizations and Effects of Technological Changes." *Energy Journal* Special Issue on Endogenous Technological Change and the Economics of Atmospheric Stabilisation: 141–61.

Sathaye J., O. Lucon, A. Rahman, J. Christensen, F. Denton, J. Fujino, G. Heath, et al. 2011. "Renewable Energy in the Context of Sustainable Energy." In Ottmar Edenhofer, Youba Sokona, Kristin Seyboth (coordinating lead authors), Patrick Matschoss, Susanne Kadner, Timm Zwickel, Patrick Eickemeier, Gerrit Hansen, Steffen Schlömer and Christoph von Stechow. *IPCC Special Report on Renewable Energy Sources and Climate Change Mitigation*. Intergovernmental Panel on Climate Change. Cambridge: Cambridge University Press. Online: http://srren.ipcc-wg3.de/report/IPCC_SRREN_Ch09.pdfS (accessed on 28 June 2013).

Schellnhuber H. J., W. Cramer, N. Nakicenovic, T. Wigley and G. Yohe (eds). 2006. *Avoiding Dangerous Climate Change*. Cambridge: Cambridge University Press.

Schlenker W., W. M. Hanemann and A. C. Fisher. 2005. "Will US Agriculture Really Benefit from Global Warming? Accounting for Irrigation in the Hedonic Approach." *American Economic Review* 88, no. 1: 113–25.

———. 2006. "The Impact of Global Warming on US Agriculture: An Econometric Analysis of Optimal Growing Conditions." *Review of Economics and Statistics* 88: 113–25.

Schlenker W. and D. B. Lobell. 2010. "Robust Negative Impacts of Climate Change on African Agriculture." *Environmental Research Letters* 5, no. 1.

Schlenker W. and M. J. Roberts. 2009. "Nonlinear Temperature Effects Indicate Severe Damages to US Crop Yields Under Climate Change." *Proceedings of the National Academy of Sciences of the United States of America* 106, no. 37: 15594–98.

———. 2007. "Water Availability, Degree Days, and the Potential Impact of Climate Change on Irrigated Agriculture in California." *Climatic Change* 81, no. 1: 19–38.

Schneider S. H. 1997. "Integrated Assessment Modeling of Global Climate Change: Transparent Rational Tool for Policy Making or Opaque Screen Hiding Value-Laden Assumptions?" *Environmental Modeling and Assessment* 2, no. 4: 229–49.

Scott M. J., R. D. Sands, J. Edmonds, A. M. Liebetrau and D. W. Engel. 1999. "Uncertainty in Integrated Assessment Models: Modeling With MiniCAM 1.0." *Energy Policy* 27: 855–79.

Scrieciu S. 2011. *MCA4climate: A Practical Framework for Planning Pro-Development Climate Policies*. Paris, France: UNEP.

Sen A. 1987. *On Ethics and Economics*. New York: Blackwell.

———. 2000. "The Discipline of Cost–Benefit Analysis. *Journal of Legal Studies* 29: 931–52.

Sheeran K. A. 2006. "Who Should Abate Carbon Emissions? A Note." *Environmental and Resource Economics* 35: 89–98.

Sherwood S. C. and M. Huber. 2010. "An Adaptability Limit to Climate Change due to Heat Stress." *Proceedings of the National Academy of Sciences of the United States of America* 107, no. 21: 9552–9555.

Shipley A. M. and R. N. Elliott. 2006. "Ripe for the Picking: Have We Exhausted the Low Hanging Fruit in the Industrial Sector?" Washington, DC: American Council for an Energy Efficient Economy, Report No. IE061. Online: http://www.resourcesaver.org/file/toolmanager/ CustomO16C45F69267.pdf (accessed on 28 June 2013).

Solow R. M. 1970. *Growth Theory: An Exposition*. New York: Oxford University Press.

Stanton E. A. 2011a. "Greenhouse Gases and Human Well-Being: China in a Global Perspective." In G. Fan, N. Stern, O. Edenhofer, S. Xu, K. Eklund, F. Ackerman, L. Li and K. Hallding (eds). *The Economics of Climate Change in China: Towards a Low-Carbon Economy*. Oxford: Earthscan.

———. 2011b. *Development without Carbon: Climate and the Global Economy through the 21st Century*. Somerville, MA: Stockholm Environment Institute-US Center.

———. 2011c. "Negishi Welfare Weights in Integrated Assessment Models: The Mathematics of Global Inequality." *Climatic Change* 107, nos. 3–4: 417–32.

Stanton E. A. and F. Ackerman. 2009. "Climate and Development Economics: Balancing Science, Politics, and Equity." *Natural Resources Forum* 33: 262–73.

Stanton E. A. and D. Fitzgerald. 2011. "California Water Supply and Demand: Technical Report." Somerville, MA: Stockholm Environment Institute-US Center. Online: http://sei-us.org/publications/id/369 (accessed on 28 June 2013).

Stanton E. A., F. Ackerman and S. Kartha. 2009. "Inside the Integrated Assessment Models: Four Issues in Climate Economics." *Climate and Development* 1, no. 2: 166–84.

Stern D. 2004. "The Rise and Fall of the Environmental Kuznets Curve." *World Development* 32: 1419–1439.

Stern N. 2006. *The Stern Review: The Economics of Climate Change.* London: HM Treasury. Online: http://www.hm-treasury.gov.uk/stern_review_report.htm (accessed on 28 June 2013).

_____. 2008. "Key Elements of a Global Deal on Climate Change." London: London School of Economics.

Stirling A. 2006. "Analysis, Participation and Power: Justification and Closure in Participatory Multi-Criteria Analysis." *Land Use Policy* 23: 95–107.

Sunstein C. R. 2000. *Cost–Benefit Default Principles* Volume 99. Chicago: Law School, University of Chicago.

_____. 2002. *The Cost–Benefit State: The Future of Regulatory Protection.* Chicago, IL: American Bar Association.

_____. 2005. "Cost–Benefit Analysis and the Environment." *Ethics* 115: 351–85.

Taylor L. 1996. "Income Distribution, Trade and Growth." In M. E. Sharpe, *US Trade Policy and Global Growth.* Armonk, NY.

Thurow LC. 1971. "The Income Distribution as a Pure Public Good." *Quarterly Journal of Economics* 85: 327–36.

Tol R. S. J. 1994. "The Damage Costs of Climate change: A Note on Tangibles and Intangibles, Applied to DICE." *Energy Policy* 22: 436–38.

_____. 1997. "On the Optimal Control of Carbon Dioxide Emissions: An Application of FUND." *Environmental Modeling and Assessment* 2: 151–63.

_____. 1999. "Kyoto, Efficiency, and Cost Effectiveness: Applications of FUND." *Energy Journal* Special Issue on the Costs of the Kyoto Protocol: A Multi-Model Evaluation: 131–56.

_____. 2001. "Equitable Cost–Benefit Analysis of Climate Change Policies." *Ecological Economics* 36, no. 1: 71–85.

_____. 2002a. "Estimates of the Damage Costs of Climate Change: Part I. Benchmark Estimates." *Environmental and Resource Economics* 21: 47–73.

_____. 2002b. "Estimates of the Damage Costs of Climate Change: Part II. Dynamic Estimates." *Environmental and Resource Economics* 21: 135–60: 157.

Tol R. S. J. and G. W. Yohe. 2006. "A Review of the Stern Review." *World Economics* 7, no. 4: 233–50.

Torras M. and J. K. Boyce. 1998. "Income, Inequality, and Pollution: A Reassessment of the Environmental Kuznets Curve." *Ecological Economics* 25, no. 2: 147–60.

Toth F. L. 2003. "Integrated Assessment of Climate Protection Strategies—Guest Editorial." *Climatic Change* 56: 1–5.

Toth F. L., M. Mwandosy (Coordinating Lead Authors), C. Carraro, J. Christensen, J. Edmonds, B. Flannery, C. Gay-Garcia, H. Lee, K. M. Meyer-Abich, E. Nikitina, A. Rahman, R. Richels, Y. Reqiu, A. Villavicencio, Y. Wake, J. Weyant (Lead Authors), J. Byrne, R. Lempert, I. Meyer, A. Underdal (Contributing Authors), J. Pershing and M. Shechter (Review Editors). 2001. "Decision-Making Frameworks." Chapter 10 of *Climate Change 2001: Mitigation, Contribution of Working Group III to the Third Assessment Report of the Intergovernmental Panel on Climate Change.* Cambridge: Cambridge University Press.

Toth F. L., T. Bruckner, H. M. Füssel, M. Leimbach and G. Petschel-Held. 2003. "Integrated Assessment of Long-Term Climate Policies: Part 1—Model Presentation." *Climatic Change* 56: 37–56.

Tsurumi .T and S. Managi. 2010. "Decomposition of the Environmental Kuznets Curve: Scale, Technique, and Composition Effects." *Environmental Economics and Policy Studies* 11: 1–4; 19–36. Online: http://dx.doi.org/10.1007/s10018-009-0159-4 (accessed on 28 June 2013).

Tubiello F. N., J. S. Amthor, K. J. Boote, et al. 2007. "Crop Response to Elevated CO_2 and World Food Supply: A Comment on 'Food for Thought...' by Long et al." *Science* 312: 1918–1921, 2006." *European Journal of Agronomy* 26, no. 3: 215–23.

UK Department of Energy & Climate Change. 2009. *Carbon Valuation in UK Policy Appraisal: A Revised Approach*. London: Climate Change Economics, DECC. Online: http://www.decc.gov.uk/en/content/cms/what_we_do/lc_uk/valuation/valuation (accessed on 28 June 2013).

UN-DESA. 2004. *World Populations Prospects: The 2004 Revision Populations Database*. United Nations Department of Economic and Social Affairs, New York.

UNDP. 2007. "Fighting Climate Change: Human Solidarity in a Divided World." *Human Development Report 2007/2008*. New York: United Nations Development Programme.

Unruh G. C. and J. Carrillo-Hermosilla. 2006. "Globalizing Carbon Lock-In." *Energy Policy* 34: 1185–1197.

UNU-WIDER. 2008. *World Income Inequality Database, Version 2.0c*. Helsinki, Finland.

US Census Bureau. 2008. "Statistical Abstract of the United States." 127th edition. Online: http://www.census.gov/statab (accessed on 1 March 2008).

US National Assessment. 2001. "Climate Change Impacts on the United States: The Potential Consequences of Climate Variability and Change." *Report for the US Global Change Research Program*. Cambridge: Cambridge University Press.

Van Vuuren D. P., M. Isaac, M. G. J. den Elzen, E. Stehfest and J. van Vliet. 2010. "Low Stabilization Scenarios and Implications for Major World Regions from an Integrated Assessment Perspective." *Energy Journal* 31 Special Issue 1: 165–92. Online: http://ideas.repec.org/a/aen/journl/2010se1_low_stabilization-a07.html (accessed on 28 June 2013).

Van Vuuren D. P., J. Lowe, E. Stehfest, L. Gohar, A. F. Hof, C. Hope, R. Warren, M. Meinshausen and G. K. Plattner. 2011a. "How Well Do Integrated Assessment Models Simulate Climate Change?" *Climatic Change* 104, no. 2: 255–85. Online: http://ideas.repec.org/a/spr/climat/v104y2011i2p255-285.html (accessed on 28 June 2013).

Van Vuuren D. P., E. Stehfest, M. G. J. Elzen, T. Kram, J. Vliet, S. Deetman, M. Isaac, et al. 2011b. "RCP2.6: Exploring the Possibility to Keep Global Mean Temperature Increase below 2°C." *Climatic Change* 109, nos. 1–2: 95–116. Online: http://ideas.repec.org/a/spr/climat/v109y2011i1p95-116.html (accessed on 28 June 2013).

Vissing-Jørgensen A. and O. P. Attanasio. 2003. "Stock-Market Participation, Intertemporal Substitution, and Risk Aversion." *American Economic Review* 93: 383–91.

Voitchovsky S. 2009. "Inequality and Economic Growth." In *The Oxford Handbook of Economic Inequality*. Oxford: Oxford University Press.

Wahba M. and Hope C. 2006. "The Marginal Impact of Carbon Dioxide Under Two Scenarios of Future Emissions." *Energy Policy* 34, no. 17: 3305–316.

Waring M. 1990. *If Women Counted: A New Feminist Economics*. New York: HarperCollins.

Warren R., C. Hope, M. Mastrandrea, R. Tol, N. Adger and I. Lorenzoni. 2006. "Spotlighting Impacts Functions in Integrated Assessment." Norwich, UK: Tyndall Centre.

Webster M., M. A. Tatang and G. J. McRae. 1996. "Report #4: Application of the Probabilistic Collocation Method for an Uncertainty Analysis of a Simple Ocean Model."

Massachusetts Institute of Technology, Joint Program on the Science and Policy of Global Change.

Weitzman M. L. 1998. "Why the Far-Distant Future Should Be Discounted at its Lowest Possible Rate." *Journal of Environmental Economics and Management* 36, no. 3: 201–208.

_____. 2007a. "A Review of the Stern Review on the Economics of Climate Change." *Journal of Economic Literature* 45, no. 3: 703–24.

_____. 2007b. "Subjective Expectations and Asset-Return Puzzles." *American Economic Review* 97: 1,102–130.

_____. 2009. "On Modeling and Interpreting the Economics of Catastrophic Climate Change." *Review of Economics and Statistics* 91, no. 1: 1–19.

_____. 2010. "GHG Targets as Insurance Against Catastrophic Climate Damages." Cambridge, MA: National Bureau of Economic Research. Online: http://www.nber.org/papers/w16136 (accessed on 28 June 2013).

Weyant J. P. and J. N. Hill. 1999. "Introduction and Overview." *Energy Journal* Special Issue on the Costs of the Kyoto Protocol: A Multi-Model Evaluation: vii–xliv.

Wilkinson R. G. and K. E. Pickett. 2006. "Income Inequality and Population Health: A Review and Explanation of the Evidence." *Social Science & Medicine* 62: 1768–1784.

_____. 2007. "The Problems of Relative Deprivation: Why Some Societies Do Better than Others." *Social Science & Medicine* 65: 1,965–78.

Winkler H., T. Jayaraman, J. Pan, A. S. de Oliveira, Y. Zhang, G. Sant, J. D. G. Miguez, T. Letete, A. Marquard, S. Raubenheimer. 2011. *Equitable Access to Sustainable Development: Contribution to the Body of Scientific Knowledge*. Beijing, Brasilia, Cape Town, Mumbai: BASIC Expert Group.

Woo J. 2009. "Why Do More Polarized Countries Run More Procyclical Fiscal Policy?" *Review of Economics and Statistics* 91: 850–70.

World Bank. 2011. "World Development Indicators." Online: http://data.worldbank.org/data-catalog/world-development-indicators (accessed on 16 June 2011).

World Commission on Environment and Development. 1987. *Our Common Future*; Oxford: Oxford University Press.

World Resources Institute. 2010. *Climate Analysis Indicators Tool. CAIT 8.0*. Online: http://cait.wri.org/S (accessed on 28 June 2013).

Worrell E., J. A. Laitner, M. Ruth, H. Finman. 2003. "Productivity Benefits of Industrial Energy Efficiency Measures." *Energy Journal* 21: 1081–1098.

Yang Z. and W. D. Nordhaus. 2006. "Magnitude and Direction of Technological Transfers for Mitigating GHG Emissions." *Energy Economics* 28: 730–41.

Lightning Source UK Ltd.
Milton Keynes UK
UKOW03n1428200614

233790UK00002B/23/P